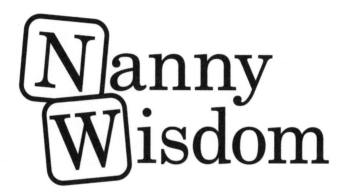

Nanny Wisdom

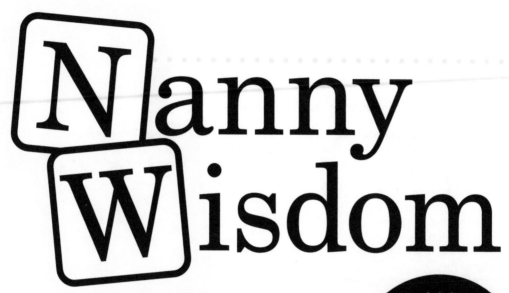

Nanny Wisdom

Our Secrets
for Raising Healthy,
Happy Children
*From Newborns
to Preschoolers*

JUSTINE WALSH

and

KIM NICHOLSON

STEWART, TABORI & CHANG
New York

Published in 2005 by
Stewart, Tabori & Chang
115 West 18th Street
New York, NY 10011
www.abramsbooks.com

Library of Congress Cataloging-in-Publication Data

Walsh, Justine.
Nanny wisdom : our secrets for raising healthy, happy children—from newborns to preschoolers / Justine Walsh and Kim Nicholson.
p. cm.
ISBN 1-58479-473-9
1. Child rearing. 2. Parenting. I. Nicholson, Kim. II. Title.

HQ769.W197 2005
649'.1—dc22
2005016356

Cover photograph © Pamela Hanson
Book Design by Anna Christian
Graphic Production by Kim Tyner

The text of this book was composed in Scala, Quaadrat Sans, and Century Schoolbook.

Printed in the United States of America

10 9 8 7 6 5 4 3 2 1
First Printing

Stewart, Tabori & Chang is a subsidiary of
LA MARTINIÈRE

Contents

Foreword

IT WAS A CRISP MAY MORNING WHEN JUSTINE WALSH ARRIVED ON OUR DOORSTEP. Our son was three months old at the time, and Justine had been referred to us by a friend and came highly recommended. She breezed in, full of confidence, clarity, and fun, with that distinct English accent—Mary Poppins come to life, in our living room. She asked to see our little guy, and it was mutual love at first sight. We hired her soon after, and thus began a long and happy relationship.

Justine's first order of business was to get the baby on a regular sleep schedule. Her approach to this task illustrated how thoroughly professional she was, how well she understood babies, and how her years of experience in many different households with many different children had prepared her. We marveled at the way she combined a loving nature with an unflinching focus on getting the job done. The result was that our son was soon sleeping through the night, and so were we—thank God!

It is a tremendous relief to find that you are not alone in the challenging task of raising children. And nothing is quite as comforting as an experienced English nanny on hand. She not only gives you the gift of her helpful presence; she also serves as a sounding board as you figure out how best to deal with child-raising issues. It is so reassuring to be able to turn to someone who has experienced the battles over sleeping, eating, and proper behavior—not to mention someone familiar with the anguish that parents endure throughout these skirmishes. Justine and her friend, coauthor, and fellow nanny, Kim Nicholson, and the great English nanny tradition they inherited provide that reassurance, in a manner that is simultaneously caring and no-nonsense.

This book is second only to having Justine and Kim and the English nanny tradition actually in your home, helping you every step of the way.

Every parent has questions about the best way to raise a child. How much independence is enough, or too much? How much TV or computer time is permissible, without being damaging? How many candy treats create a sugar freak? And how many playdates cross the line into over-scheduling? This book helps you answer these questions. It's written by nannies who have seen these issues played out numerous times in various incarnations.

One of the best things about the book—and one of the things we appreciate so much—is the English nanny's way of introducing babies to the wonderful world of healthy foods. When our son started on solid foods, he was eating salmon, white fish, green beans, broccoli, corn, and asparagus—to name just a few of the fresh, real foods he learned to love early on. Of course, both Justine and Kim are exceptional and inventive cooks, as you'll find out when you try their recipes.

But by far the greatest gift nannies can provide is an approach to child raising that is structured and safe as well as being fun, affectionate, comforting, exciting, and full of exploration and adventure. These days, when so many parents are juggling hectic schedules and trying to balance parenting and professional life, it is a relief to know that Nanny is there, trustworthy and professional, structuring a reliable routine, insisting on healthy eating, sharing ideas and parenting goals, offering a nurturing approach to learning, and showing respect for the child and the parents. Justine and Kim have set it all down in the pages that follow.

We see the results of Nanny's approach every day in our son, now almost five and becoming more independent every minute (which is exciting to watch but makes us a little nostalgic for the early days). He is an entertaining companion, eager to discuss his ideas on an assortment of subjects, well mannered, polite (mostly), and filled with an adventurous spirit. We take comfort in the fact that he has a strong foundation of self-respect, a love of learning, and a delight in exploring new ideas and challenges. We know this is due in no small part to the gift of care he received from his English nanny, Justine. We are thrilled that everyone will now have access to Nanny's time-tested experience and thoughtful insights.

Richard Gere and Carey Lowell
New York, January 2005

Introduction: The English Nanny

SHE'S MORE BRITISH THAN CRICKET, CRUMPETS, BIG BEN, OR THE BEATLES. She's more admired than the royal family. She brought up the prime ministers and generals and civil servants who built and ran the British Empire, and her influence has reached as far as Britain's language. She's the English nanny, and when it comes to child raising, there's nothing else quite like her.

We should know—we're English nannies. Although one of us is Australian-born, we both claim membership in that very special club, almost a nationality unto itself. We practice English nanny principles and think English nanny thoughts and speak the language of English nannies. We're part and parcel of the English nanny tradition—even though we may not resemble the stereotypes that come to most people's minds when they hear the words *English nanny*.

One of those stereotypes is the stiff, starchy, rules-are-rules matron like the one in the following story:

It is the winter of 1941. London. The Blitz. In the nursery of his upper-class home, a young boy is having his supper under the watchful eye of his nanny. "Nanny!" he calls out as another bomb falls on England's capital. "What's that awful noise?"

"Those are bombs, dear. Elbows off the table. No talking with your mouth full. And never use the word *awful*."

The other side of the stereotype coin is Mary Poppins, immortalized in P. L. Travers's book and, even more so, in the Disney movie of 1964—an eccentric whipper-into-shape who is quite literally magical. It is she who brings light and life—as well as order—into a gray, dreary, and unsettled household in which the parents haven't time for their children and the children have never learned how to have fun.

Whether these stereotypes are true to life or sheer fiction, authentic or cartoons, they tell us something about the qualities that are universally thought of as describing the English nanny: brisk and gentle, nurturing and disciplined, soothing and sensible—all simultaneously. English nannies know how to calm and comfort, how to teach both manners and a sense of responsibility, how to make sure kids get nutritious food and fresh air and lots of fun—all the things that are good for them—while also insisting they behave themselves "properly." In short, if you're looking for the ultimate advice on raising happy, healthy, and well-brought-up children, look no further than the English nanny.

We represent the twenty-first-century version of the English nanny tradition. That version has been updated to include everything that has been learned about child care and child rearing in the past half century or more, and it has been adjusted for today's culture and today's families. While that 1941 matron was stiff and cheerless, we're informal and downright hip. While Mary Poppins used magic, we use intuition and common sense. But we admire and cherish the great English nanny tradition, and like the nannies of the stereotypes, we are child-care professionals, experienced in helping other people's children become healthy and happy as we support and reflect the values of the families we work with.

Although we both made our professional reputations in England, I—Kim speaking—was born and raised in Australia. In fact, my English mother had worked as a day-care leader and had very high standards for child rearing, which she believed ought to be a family affair. So when my parents started a business that occupied them round the clock, it was left to me and my younger sister to care for our much younger siblings. I can therefore say that I began raising babies as a young teenager—following the careful instructions of my mother—and learned to take care of toddlers and preschoolers before I went off to the University of Canberra to study communications. I worked my way through university with part-time nannying jobs, then was hired for my first full-time professional live-in nanny job by a fantastic family in Woollahra, a stately eastern suburb of Sydney, not far from beautiful Bondi Beach. I spent a year there, loving the two boys

I cared for, their family, and the situation—and I moved to London the following year to pursue my dream of becoming a true English nanny.

In London, I worked for several different families in a number of fabled neighborhoods—including a renowned Australian chef in West London. During my first week, I was one of nine nannies—plus all their charges—gathered for lunch in the kitchen of a large house, where all the nannies were talking about a former colleague who had since gone to the States. Her name was Justine, and I remembered her name.

It was the Australian chef who really awakened my passion for cooking. Under her guidance, I developed a reputation not just for terrific, fresh, home-cooked food, but for getting kids to enjoy shared mealtimes and to eat well. Working for such a busy boss and for other, similarly high-powered employers was an excellent education in self-reliance. Combined with my Aussie adaptability and with what I believe to be a natural intuition about children, I gained a reputation as being a pretty skilled nanny myself—and my global travels with the families I worked for made me a cosmopolitan nanny into the bargain.

After a number of years in London, I was wooed to New York by the single mother of two wonderful young boys. My reputation, I learned when I arrived, had preceded me, and my new employer's friends—as well as many fellow nannies—often turned to me for advice. My employer, meanwhile, soon introduced me to Justine, and it took just a few conversations before I made the connection: she was the nanny I had heard so much about in West London. But I'll let her tell her own story . . .

I'm Justine. I am London-born and London-bred—South London, that is—but, like Kim, I have taken care of younger children since I was a teenager. I'm one of nine children and helped to raise my five younger siblings, including a set of twins. It was the birth of my brothers and sister that opened my eyes to the wonder of children. I loved days filled with art projects and stories at bedtime, and I appreciated the way young children looked at the world with such curiosity and imagination. We never had a nanny ourselves, but I was fascinated by the nannies I saw at the park and at the school gate. I was struck by their cheerful manner and no-nonsense approach. They were a close-knit group who seemed to have all the answers to child care, and I longed to be one of them.

At eighteen I began my career as a professional nanny, a career that has taken me around the world—to London, France, Israel, the United States, and many places in between. Along the way, I had the opportunity to meet some fascinating people, to work in prestigious jobs, and to become a big part of many families' lives. It has been not only a career but an amazing journey, in which I have helped raise at least forty children, ranging from newborns to teens. I am proud to have helped so many parents with the often overwhelming transition a new baby brings. My reputation has been built on my ability to work with families, from changing diets and improving sleep habits, to solving discipline issues and helping set up schedules and routines. I am delighted to be an English nanny, just like the nannies I saw in the park all those years ago.

Over time, as Kim mentioned, I have become a well-known nanny, and I was secretly delighted when I discovered that Kim had heard a group of London nannies call me "the kind of nanny we'd like to be." I've also heard they still talk about my shepherd's pie recipe, which is always a favorite with both children and adults. (You can find the recipe in Chapter Five.)

On a trip to the Virgin Islands, I met the woman who is now Kim's employer. She introduced us to one another, and we got on straightaway: we had both cared for younger siblings, and had worked the London nanny scene; we both gave our whole hearts to the children we cared for, loved to cook, and moved in the same circles in New York. Above all, we both understood the particular role that nannies play in the lives of children and families, and we shared the same views regarding the nanny profession. Soon we went on to write *Nanny Wisdom* together.

The nanny role is unique. We love our charges, and they love us. We delight in the way children look at the world, and we find magic in caring for them. Therefore, whether you're the first-time parents of a newborn or you have a brood of half a dozen, you cannot parallel the unique attributes we bring to the child-care task. We have experience raising children in many different families, and we have an insider's view of both the diversity possible in family environments and of the universal issues that persist—family after family after family. Put it together with the great nanny tradition we've inherited, and you have a unique, unparalleled pool of wisdom on raising happy, healthy, well-behaved, responsible children—without hassles, and with love.

That's what we bring to you in this book: insider secrets, distilled not just from our own experience but from the experience of generations of English nannies—a complete compendium of nanny wisdom as it's been gathered through the centuries, and as we've used it day by day in families just like yours.

As we say time and again in the chapters that follow, we're presenting here "what works." Whether it's getting kids to sleep or getting them to eat well, teaching them good manners or a sense of responsibility, making sure they're having fun or that they're happy in school, here are the techniques, tips, and tricks that have proven effective and successful.

We've organized the book according to the issues that arise in child raising. After discussing our overall approach, we start with the first year of life, for that really is unique unto itself. Then we get right into advice on establishing a routine and schedule—in our view, the very heart of successful child raising—and we show you how to apply this good advice to sleeping, eating, discipline, fun and play, school, and traveling with kids. We even tell you how to pick a great nanny or babysitter, and we end with some words from the heart.

Scattered throughout the book you can find Nanny Wisdoms—tips or tricks we've picked up over the years, or practical strategies for dealing with a particular issue. In addition, where warranted, we've awarded the Nanny Seal of Approval to certain products we think deserve special mention.

We know how challenging child raising can sometimes be. And we know how much you love your children. Like you, we want to do the very best for them. That's why we've written this book. We offer it with our love and best wishes.

A Note about Names

Only in a couple of cases—we're not saying which ones—have we used the real names of the very real children you'll meet in this book. In fact, we have often called the same child by three, four, even six different names as we describe him or her in various situations. Our aim has been to guard the identity of the children we have cared for while illustrating our points with their stories.

Chapter One

It's All in the Approach
Nanny Speaks Up

Monday

"That's a posh house," the cab driver says as he pulls the boxy black London taxi to a stop in front of a five-story white Victorian row house. The address is a swanky one—just off the King's Road in Chelsea, in one of the better parts of town.

"Do you live here?" he asks as I hand him a ten-pound note.

"I do now," I reply.

With my much-prized and very stylish leather traveling bag in hand—a gift from my last employer—I proceed up the pathway and climb the steps to the bright red front door. Taking a deep breath, I push the shiny brass doorbell. From somewhere deep in the house I hear the bell ring, then a flurry of footsteps. Almost drowning out these sounds is the noise of children's voices alternately shouting and crying. I recognize the crying at once. It's the "I'm going to try for an Oscar, but really there is nothing the matter with me except that I want your attention" type of crying.

Perhaps I have my work cut out for me, I think to myself as the door finally swings open.

My new boss, looking much more frazzled and tired than at our previous meeting, embraces me gratefully and turns to her children. "Look, darlings," she says, "our lovely new nanny has come to take care of us."

With a look of relief on her face, she reintroduces me to four-year-old Ben and two-year-old Rosie. Ben has shaggy hair and is wearing a retro-style band T-shirt with faded jeans. Quite the little hipster, I smile to myself, but I also note the classic little-boy glint of mischief in his eye. I know what that look means: he will be a sweetheart, but I won't be able to take my eyes off him for a second. Rosie looks at me very shyly through long unbrushed hair and offers me a small, hesitant smile, which wins me over straightaway. She is wearing a beaded peasant dress, which I recognize as having come from a pricey London store called the Cross. Her face and most of her dress are splattered with her lunch—pasta with tomato sauce, if I have guessed correctly. And I'll bet the dress is "dry-clean only."

"Darlings, you remember Nanny. She used to look after your friend Rebecca before she moved to France." The children look up at me with new interest.

"We have heard such amazing things about you, and we are very excited to have you here," says Mum.

In truth, Ben and Rosie don't look at all excited that I am here, but I have no doubt we will be the best of friends in no time.

Inside the house, I am greeted by a sight of domestic disarray: the television is on at full volume, the children's pajamas are flung in the corner, half-eaten toast is trampled into the rug, and the sofa has a spreading wet patch where a cup of what appears to be apple juice has been tipped over.

"I'm so sorry about the mess," Mum tells me, as we make our way through to the kitchen, trying not to step on the discarded toys that seem to cover every surface. "We have been without a nanny for two weeks, and the housekeeper is sick today. Let's have a nice cup of tea," she suggests. I gratefully accept.

The tea, however, is not to be, as Rosie rushes into the kitchen clamoring, "I want sweeties, Mummy."

"Now, Rosie," Mum wearily replies, "you have had so many sweeties today, please don't ask for more. Really you have had quite enough candy already today."

"But I want it," whines Rosie.

"Darling, please don't start. Your teeth will fall out from all the candy you eat. Please just listen to Mummy this time."

"No!" Rosie screams and throws herself on the floor.

"Okay, fine then. Have it but stop that awful noise," Mum says, handing Rosie a packet of jelly beans. "Mummy's not happy about this," she adds as Rosie crams a handful into her mouth.

Mum turns to me. "Tomorrow I'm going to have to leave you to it. I'm so sorry, but I really do have to go back to work." She actually looks quite pleased at the prospect—not sorry at all. "Will you be okay with them?" she asks me.

"Of course, we will be just fine," I assure her.

The doorbell rings. "That will be Jack and Ella!" she says. "They are here for a playdate. Rosie and Ben, *please* play nicely today!"

"Does Rosie have an afternoon nap?" I inquire, as I watch the two-year-old rub her eyes and stifle a yawn.

"Oh no. It's too much of an effort to convince her that she is tired, so I gave up trying. Sometimes she nods off in the late afternoon," Mum informs me.

The afternoon quickly descends into chaos. Ben, as it turns out, is more interested in watching a video than in playing with Jack. Jack becomes upset when he realizes Ben isn't going to budge from his video for a second to play a game. Rosie battles through the afternoon, but sharing with Ella and Jack proves to be too much for her in her tired and cranky state. We experience one tantrum after another, until, mercifully, it is time for Jack and Ella to go home for dinner.

When the two guests are finally out the door, Mum turns to me and says, "Why don't you call it a day. I will give the kids their dinner and put them to bed. You can go and unpack." I gladly accept, although I suspect her offer has more to do with not wanting to scare me off than with any real concern for my unpacking.

Even from my quaint attic bedroom I can hear the carrying-on downstairs. When the rumpus has finally died down, I tiptoe downstairs, not wanting to disturb the little people who might be drifting off to sleep, and head to the kitchen for a glass of water. To my surprise I see Ben exactly where I left him, in front of the television. The only change is that now he is wearing his pajamas.

I note the time: nine o'clock. "I thought you were off to bed, lovey," I say to Ben.

"Mummy says I can stay up a little longer if I agree to go to bed with no fuss. But I think I want to watch another video after this one." He has not taken his eyes off the screen.

Oh dear, I think to myself. I am going to pay tomorrow with one tired and grumpy four-year-old on my hands.

Mum and Dad are in the sitting room eating dinner together—despite the extreme volume from the chirpy child's video. I am introduced to my other employer, and then Mum explains to me that "the kids have been waking up so early that I have decided to put them to bed later at night so that, hopefully, they will get up later in the morning." I look at her in horror. I've heard this line of thinking so many times before, and I know that it simply won't work: late bedtimes do not result in later waking.

Mum adds, "I know you're not supposed to start work till seven tomorrow morning, but do you think you could make just one exception and begin the day at six? I have decided I really must go into work early. Catch up on things, you know, before everyone else gets into the office." Her guilty expression tells me she will be off to the nearest café to have breakfast in peace before work.

"Don't worry," I assure her. "You go to work. We will be fine." Inwardly, I promise myself that things will be very different around here come Friday. To be sure of that, I know I had better have an early night; I'll need to pull all my nanny skills out of my hat for the task at hand.

Friday

The morning is calm—a pleasant time for all. Rosie and Ben kiss Mum and Dad good-bye, then come to the table for a breakfast of boiled eggs and toast. After breakfast, we head outdoors for an adventure in the park. The day is cloudy, but there's no rain yet. I announce to Ben and Rosie that we are going on a treasure hunt. They shriek with delight as I tell them about what they need to find, then run ahead of me as fast as they can in search of one stick with a bend in it, two red leaves, and three ducks in the pond. The hunt is topped off with turns on the slide and jumping in puddles.

At twelve-thirty, just before the rain comes, we're home again and tucking into a hot lunch of Easy Peasy Rice, which the kids gobble down. Then it's quiet time—for Rosie, a nap, and for Ben, a peaceful game of LEGO (the best opportunity, he has learned, to construct things he doesn't want little Rosie to knock down).

After their rest, the kids are ready for a rainy-day game. In the playroom, we set up chairs in a circle and cover them with a large sheet to make a tent—our "castle." We gather all the teddy bears together and invite them into our castle for a tea party. Afterward, we make some crafts with the leaves we found in the park that morning. We have been practicing clean-up time repeatedly since I started work on Tuesday, and now the children don't need to be asked twice to put things away. What's more, Ben hasn't suggested a video once today.

When Mum and Dad return from work, they find Rosie and Ben bathed, dressed in pajamas, and sitting on the sofa reading books with me. The TV is off; it has been off all day. Ben and Rosie jump up and, talking a mile a minute, tell their parents about our day of adventure and fun. Ben shows off the LEGO car he began yesterday and finished today. I had told him how proud he should be of it and had suggested saving it "to show to Mummy and Daddy when they come home. They will love to see it!"

I'm off for the weekend. As I kiss Rosie and Ben good night, Rosie asks me, "What are we doing tomorrow?"

"Tomorrow is Mummy and Daddy day, sweetie. I will be back when you have had three big sleeps."

I close the door behind me, but not before I have glimpsed Rosie and Ben cuddling with their parents on the sofa, excitedly displaying the day's leaf crafts.

Is this a fantasy? The script for a work of fiction? Advertising copy for a nanny employment bureau?

No. This is reality. The nanny in question is one of the authors—and could have been either one.

But is it possible? Can you really turn the chaos of this family's Monday into the reasonable and loving tranquility of their Friday—in a matter of days?

The answer is an unequivocal yes. We've both done it—time after time after time.

How?

It's all in the approach.

Raising Happy, Healthy Kids: Building the Foundation

Is there any life experience more fulfilling than parenting? And is there any job more important? How you raise your children will affect them their whole lives; it will affect how they raise *their* children. It will shape your family life—and your own life—for years to come. That's why the "how" of it is so important—and so absolutely basic.

Raising children is like building a foundation. Every brick counts. You cannot stint on materials or methods. Building a strong foundation will take time, commitment, and an awareness of what you are striving for. But it's important to build carefully. Why? Because when there's a house on top of the foundation, it's awfully hard to go back and fix what you excused or didn't pay attention to.

That's one reason so many people hire professional nannies like us. They trust the English nanny tradition in which we're steeped. They understand that we've had on-the-job training in that tradition. And they rely on our experience and the instincts we've cultivated from long hours of caring for other people's children in a variety of family environments.

Well, we are here to tell you what our tradition proclaims, what our training has taught us, and what our wide and diverse experience confirms—the one absolute truth about successful child care: it's all in the approach. We are talking about a course, a direction, a way to get to a particular destination—in this case, to the health and happiness of your children.

We are not talking about a rigid system. There is no single, uniform set of rules that can resolve all the challenges of parenting. There is no quick fix that works for all the sleepless nights, tantrums, sibling rivalries, and fussy eating. There are no magic incantations that get you to and through the many milestones your children will achieve along the way. And certainly there are no ready-made formulas for dealing with the new issues that constantly come up. The solution is in your approach to these issues.

Moreover, your approach cannot simply be child oriented; it must be family based to work well. An approach that works well for both children and parents, taking everybody's needs into consideration, is an approach that lets everyone enjoy their lives together. And that, after all, is the point.

We've cared for kids in a variety of cultures, families, and situations, and our experience has been that whoever and wherever they are, kids have the same needs. As we've seen time and again, those needs are easily met in a loving and calm environment, but they are met with difficulty, if at all, in a disorganized and inconsistent environment. With structure, day-to-day life runs smoothly. Without it, kids get confused, and their confusion can lead to chaos, frequent tantrums, conflict, and stress. It's simple: a calm, nurturing environment fosters happy, healthy children. A chaotic family life magnifies everyday child-care challenges, makes every issue that much harder to deal with, can burden family relationships, and can lead to both parents and children being unhappy.

First Things First: What's Your Approach? Do You Have One?

As illustrated in the story at the beginning of this chapter, Mondays are the perfect time to observe a family's approach to child care in action—and we've seen an awful lot of Mondays. Here are two fairly typical scenarios:

Family One: Everyone gets up at the last possible moment, and the kids immediately plop themselves in front of the TV instead of getting dressed. Dad desperately tries to locate last night's homework, while Mom begs the kids to come to the table for breakfast. Dad begins to shout at the children to listen to Mom; she checks the time and realizes it is way too late for breakfast now anyway. Stress levels are at an all-time high as Mom chases the kids around the house, wrestling them into their clothes. Finally, everyone is out the door—exhausted, stressed, and without breakfast.

Family Two: Everybody gets up with enough time for a pleasant morning. The children know their morning routine; they get up, get dressed, and come to the table for breakfast when called. After breakfast, the children have time to play a little, as their schoolbags have been packed the night before. There's a slight last-minute hitch when a teddy bear goes missing, but Dad cuddles teddy's owner while Mom goes and finds him. Now everybody is ready to leave the house.

The difference is in the approach. Family Two's approach means that there is no need to shout at the kids to get ready; these children *know what is expected of them.* The morning routine is well practiced, so that when there's a hiccup like a lost teddy bear—or an out-of-the-blue tantrum or a sudden bit of crying or an upset tummy—there is time to deal with it.

Not that any of this is easy. We have the insider's perspective on just how hard it is to raise children, and it's given us great understanding and no small amount of respect for parents. We know about the constant demands of everyday life; we understand the intense pressure you're under. It is not easy juggling the commitments of work, your child's needs, and a life of your own. Anyone can feel stressed and anxious as a result. Every parent has become frustrated with his or her children. Every parent has at one time or another felt overwhelmed at the thought of the children's mealtime, bath time, or bedtime. And even in the most organized, calm, and functional households, things do not run smoothly every day; that is simply the nature of child care.

The good news, however, is that by changing your approach—or perhaps by creating an approach, if you've been just getting through the day—*you can change what is going on.* And you can do this at any time. Children are incredibly adaptable. Whether they are babies, toddlers, preschoolers, or even preteens, it is never too late to go from chaos to consistency. We'll say it again: we've effected that very transformation time and again—gone into households with child-care problems, implemented our established approach, and turned even the most difficult family situations around.

What Needs Changing

But before you can change your approach, you need to know what you are changing. So the first thing to do is to look at your own parenting approach. If you feel you are having problems with your kids, sit down and figure out if anything you are doing may be contributing to those problems. This is not a blame-yourself exercise. Rather, it's an attempt to see if you have fallen into patterns that are creating problems.

What do we mean by "patterns" that may be "creating problems"? We know of one dad who would come home every day from work and leave his only set of car keys within easy reach of his two-year-old daughter. The next morning, panic would break out when the keys were nowhere to be found, and of course the two-year-old would have no idea where they were, so chaos and tears were practically guaranteed every morning.

Another example: a mother we knew virtually ran a restaurant in her kitchen for her three-year-old son. Each evening would begin the same way: Mom would cook a meal for her son. If he refused to eat it, she would proceed to offer him the contents of the refrigerator. "Darling, would you prefer a sandwich? What about a yogurt? A little plain pasta? Sweetheart, please eat something, what about some ice cream instead?" It wasn't long before her three-year-old demanded ice cream for dinner every night.

Five-year-old Lisa was a little old to be having daily tantrums, yet simple statements like "It's time for bed" would result in her throwing herself on the floor and screaming. Lisa's parents had an approach that they believed was entirely rational. So first, they would try to reason with her. Then they would plead. Neither worked. Finally, as the screaming intensified, they would promise her twenty more minutes if she would just stop crying. Immediately, Lisa's tears would stop, and she would continue playing as if nothing had ever happened. Her shell-shocked parents prayed they wouldn't have to go through it all again in twenty minutes.

In all of these examples, the parents' approach either created or abetted situations that were bound to have undesirable consequences. Dad could have simply kept the keys out of his daughter's reach; you can't expect a two-year-old not to be attracted to a set of shiny keys. The mother of the three-year-old certainly never dreamed that her child would end up eating only ice cream for dinner. But it is to be expected when fussy eating is approached this way. As for five-year-old Lisa, she had learned early on that having a tantrum was a sure way to get whatever she wanted. By consistently giving in to her tantrums, her parents had taught her quite clearly that tantrums were the way to go. Their approach encouraged her screaming; it was a message to her that such behavior was entirely acceptable.

Does your approach need changing? We have a suggestion. It starts with a bit of nanny wisdom, and it ends with ten absolute essentials for bringing up healthy, happy children.

The Nannies' Approach to Child Care

Our approach to child care is best expressed in terms of kids' needs. They need you to be loving, firm, and fun—all three—every day.

A parent's daily obligation: be loving, firm, and fun with your kids every day.

That sounds obvious, and perhaps it also sounds simple. But we think of it as a daily obligation that you, the parent, must act on. *Act* is the key word. There's nothing passive about this obligation or about doing it every day. In fact, it's so important that we've made it the first Nanny Wisdom of this book, worthy of its own special sidebar.

You need to be **loving** because love is the greatest need a child has and because kids thrive under constant loving care. There can never be too many cuddles, kisses, or cozy snuggles. Loving gestures, no matter how small, are essential: a hug first thing in the morning, a pat on the head as the kids pass by, a simple "I love you" as you tuck them in at night.

But there's more to loving care than that. Children need your encouragement, your patience, your time, your approval, your acceptance. Above all, they need to know that your loving care is constant and will never be withdrawn. Such unconditional love makes a child feel supported; it's the keystone of a rock-solid foundation for life.

You need to be **firm** because kids need clear boundaries if they are to feel safe and secure and if the world is to make sense to them. It is okay to say no to children, and when you have said no, you must mean what you say. That's how children learn respect for themselves and others, come to know what is safe and unsafe, and understand what is expected of them. It's how they gain a sense of responsibility and independence. Being firm with a child is just as important as being loving.

So is having *fun*. Childhood should be fun—for both your children and you—and kids offer so many opportunities for laughter, tickles, and silliness. And of course, the proverbial "spoonful of sugar" really does "help the medicine go down," for kids are always open to having a good time.

This means that you can use fun as a tool for getting things done. A child who refuses to get dressed is easily charmed by a silly game: "Look at these lovely shoes. Do we wear them on our heads?" He will be quick to point out they go on our feet, and before you know it, he will be dressed and you will both be out the door. A child who is dillydallying with tidying up his toys will get the job done if you make a competition out of it: "Let's have a race and see who can put the most toys away!" It's a game your child will enjoy.

It won't work to be just firm, or just fun, or even just loving. If you're good at being firm but weak at providing good old-fashioned fun or at demonstrating affection, the firmness won't really work. Firmness only gets respect when kids have experienced the balance of your approach and can accept that you aren't being mean or unfair when you enforce an established boundary. Kids need the whole trio—loving care, firmness, and fun. Anything less can cause problems.

How can you ensure that you are loving, firm, and fun every day? We've broken it down into ten absolute essentials.

The Nannies' Ten Absolute Essentials

These ten essentials are at the core of our approach. In our work caring for other people's children, we try to practice all ten every day. We consider them essential because they're indispensable to raising healthy, happy children. We consider them absolute because we have no doubt about their efficacy and importance.

In other words, we're positive these essentials work to make kids happy and healthy today and to give them a sound foundation for adulthood. We offer them as the basic guidelines for parents approaching the child-care task or ready to change their approach. Try to do all ten every day. And whenever things aren't working as smoothly as you'd like, go straight back to these basics and you'll come out all right. Here are the ten absolute essentials:

1. Enjoy your kids.
2. Be consistent.
3. Set a routine, put it on a schedule—and stick to it.
4. Impose discipline lovingly.
5. Insist on good manners.
6. Ensure there's fun and play every day.
7. At mealtimes, share fresh food and family conversation.
8. Nurture self-esteem and confidence.
9. Remember that all kids are different.
10. Keep your kids safe—always.

Let's go through them one at a time.

1. Enjoy your kids.

Your pace is hectic. Your to-do list is long. It is all too easy to miss out on spending quality time with your children, or to go through the motions so anxious and exhausted that you're not enjoying the time with them. The reality is that kids grow up really fast. If you don't take the time now to savor your children, not only are you both missing out, but your relationship won't be strong enough in those tricky teen years to come.

Forget about the dishes for a moment and put away the newspaper. Instead, sit down with your child to read a book, do a puzzle, or play with some toy trains. Kids adore playing with their parents, and a little imaginary play can ease the stresses of parents' lives too. You may discover something about your child or yourself that you may have forgotten.

You may also discover that a child who has been misbehaving was really just craving some undivided attention. To get it, he was quite happy to do something naughty; after all, even negative attention such as a reprimand is better than none at all. Parent-child quality time is one of the best antidotes we know to difficult or disobedient behavior.

If you are snowed under with household chores and work commitments, you might consider scheduling some time for fun and play at home or for a special outing—just as you would schedule a meeting or project. We know it can be challenging. In so many families, both parents work full-time, returning home from work late to find their children already in bed. This can be frustrating, and it places an enormous burden on weekends as the only time parents really get to see their kids. If that's the case in your home, make the most of it: on Saturday and Sunday, turn off your cell phones and enjoy your kids fully.

If there are chores that can only be done on the weekends, involve your kids in doing them. They can help you out with shopping, cooking, and errands. In fact, such involvement will give them a sense of importance and responsibility. Young kids love to help choose items in the grocery store. If you give them a duster they will quite happily work alongside you while you are cleaning. And when it's time to cook, get them to help with washing vegetables, mixing sauces, and setting the table.

Your kids don't need the yearly trip to Disneyland. Everyday activities in which you truly interact with your kids are the way to their hearts. It's not the overindulgent presents but rather the gift of yourself, one-on-one—the bedtime stories, the trips to the playground—that is most important. Allow your children to enrich and reward you every day; they are bound to enchant you, and it could be just the parenting refreshment you need.

2. Be consistent.

It's simple: when parents are consistent, kids know what to expect and what is expected of them. Kids thrive on it. That's why being consistent about such things as routine, schedule, sleep, diet, and discipline is an absolute essential.

The fact is that children quite naturally look to their parents for approval in what they do and guidance on how they should behave. In everything they do, they are in effect asking you what behavior is acceptable and what isn't. Scolding Emma for a certain behavior one day and overlooking the same behavior the next sends a mixed message. It's not just a confused answer, it's no answer at all. You can't expect Emma to know how to behave as a result, and that will make your own job of child care that much more difficult.

One of the keys to being consistent in child care is teamwork: everyone involved in the child's care—mother, father, and nanny, for example—should be on the same page, and each person must know and support the basic ground rules that have been set up. If not, you get the well-known "play one parent off against the other" syndrome—and you will get problems all around.

We have seen it time and again, and you probably have as well: James asks Dad for candy before dinner and Dad says no, so James immediately runs over to ask Mom. Mom says yes, thus sending her child an inconsistent message while also encouraging James to repeat the scenario.

Granted, consistency every day is a struggle, and for Mom, who has probably had a hard day at the office and really doesn't want any difficulties this evening, the easier route by far is to give in to the child's demands. Unfortunately, even one moment of inconsistency can set things right back, making tomorrow's challenges even harder to deal with. Tough as it may be, consistency is an absolute essential; keep at it, and success will not be far off.

3. Set a routine, put it on a schedule—and stick to it.

Every good nanny knows that a solid routine and an established schedule are the true path to contented kids. They're also the nanny's most secret and effective tools for making child care easy (as we'll discuss in detail in Chapter Three). Parents like having a routine and schedule: it ensures they get some time to themselves each day. But children like it, too: they feel comforted by the repetition (How many times have you read your child the same book? How often has she asked to see the *101 Dalmatians* video?) and they are reassured by knowing what is coming next in their day. Kids learn from the constant repetition of a routine and the security of a schedule; the structure gives them the balance they yearn for while they go through the many changes of growing up, making them feel safe and secure.

Set a routine, put it on a schedule, and it forms the basis of a child's day. Life is so much easier when children eat, nap, and go to sleep at roughly the same time every day. If a child's schedule is all over the place—if naps are irregular, if bedtime is different each night, if meals are served randomly—kids are unable to cope well with the demands of their day. They become overtired and overhungry and are prone to frequent meltdowns. You can't wait for a young child to tell you when he wants lunch or a nap. That's simply unrealistic; kids can't always recognize their hunger or tiredness. A routine and a schedule help kids anticipate their needs—and ensure their needs are met.

Within the framework of your child's routine and schedule, it's helpful to include simple rituals—little things you do every day at the same time that signal to your child what is coming next. Kids really adore rituals. It may be a story before bed, a song you sing every time you get your child dressed, a special phrase you always say as you tuck him in—"Sweet dreams" will do—or a request you always make (maybe simply handing your child his plastic cup and asking him to "put it on the table because we are going to have lunch now"). Whatever you choose to do, do it at the same time and in the same way each time. Kids will anticipate what is coming, and if you forget the exact particulars of the ritual, don't worry: they will be quick to remind you!

Parents sometimes tell us they don't want to be tied down to a regular routine and don't want their lives constrained by a schedule. They want life to be easier than that. Well, if you want family life to run smoothly, the only way is by establishing a consistent routine and putting it on a schedule. That really is the commitment you will need to make. Once a successful routine is established, there will be plenty of room for flexibility. A missed nap, a late lunch, an evening party is of no consequence; thanks to the strong foundation of the routine, you can simply go right back to it without fuss. Set your routine and schedule, stick to it, and we promise: you will see the benefits in your family life.

4. Impose discipline lovingly.

Parents often ask us what we mean by "loving discipline." Here's the answer we always give: discipline is love. Discipline is about positive reinforcement, not punishment. It is not a negative action; it is about building realistic boundaries, following through with standards you've set, and meaning what you say without making idle threats. It is never about bullying or scaring a child, and it shouldn't be a battle of wills. Rather, the goal is ultimately to teach your kids to find discipline within themselves. Loving discipline will support you when behavior issues do come up—as they surely will—and they will be that much easier to handle.

We know it is hard for some parents to put their foot down with their children. Many parents feel guilty because they work long hours, or perhaps because their child has experienced a family upheaval or the disruption of having moved or changed schools. Discipline, these parents feel, will only add to the stress the child is already feeling, and this, they fear, might also harm their own relationship with the child. "Will Jack resent me if I send him to his room?" parents have asked us, or "Am I spoiling little Sarah when I give in to her demands?" Many worry about being the bad guy, and they confuse that with telling their child he cannot do something: "How can I say no to my son, and still be his friend?"

In fact, it's the best friendship you can offer your child. Only by saying no when no is warranted can you teach your kids what behavior is and isn't acceptable. For example, a child must know it is okay to feel angry and frustrated but not okay to express anger or frustration by hitting someone else. He'll only know that if you teach him.

Without being told *no*, children will have a much harder time interacting with other children, playing in groups, and, later, listening to their teachers and getting their schoolwork done. Without loving discipline, everyday situations too easily spiral out of control, leading to behavioral issues, problems with diet and sleep, and often a family environment virtually at the mercy of the undisciplined child's caprices.

But *no* is only one side of loving discipline. The other side is an equally important reinforcing *yes*. If behavior that is unacceptable must be noted and dealt with, behavior that is acceptable must be underlined and applauded. "I was so proud of the way you acted just now" may be the most important words a child can hear.

Praise as well as disapproval, reward as well as responsibility, fairness in all things: loving discipline is an absolute essential for teaching kids the skills they need to function well in the world.

5. Insist on good manners.

Perhaps it's very British of us, but we must admit to being sticklers for good manners. To hear a child say "please" and "thank you" is gratifying and heartwarming; it makes the recipient feel appreciated. Good manners show a respect for others; they're an acknowledgement of your child's awareness that no one should be taken for granted. And like the other nine of the ten absolute essentials, good manners are also a gift you give your children, easing their way through just about any situation in life.

The way to instill good manners in children is to model those manners yourself. Kids learn by example; even a one-year-old baby will mimic "please" and "thank you." Talk to your children as you would like them to talk to you. If a child asks for something in a too-loud voice or with a rude tone, explain simply that "I don't shout at you, so please don't shout at me. Say it again in a proper voice and then I will listen to you."

Of course, children often need prompting to remember to use their manners. In fact, reminders usually have to be constant—at least at first. If you give something to your child and he forgets to thank you, remind him. Remind him again the next time. And the next. Overdo it, in fact, and eventually, it will become second nature to him.

And be sure to praise your child when he exhibits good manners. Telling your children "I love it when you say 'please,'" or "I'm very happy when I hear you ask your brother for the toy instead of just taking it from him" can be just as important for instilling good manners as the repetitive reminders.

Sometimes—especially with older children and especially if there have been a few days of woeful table manners—we'll launch a manners blitz. We will announce to the kids that we are having a manners competition. Then we'll draw up a chart and stick it on the fridge. When we see good manners—elbows off the table, eating with mouths closed, remembering pleases and thank yous without prompting—we reward the child with a star and let her put it on the chart. When the child achieves fifteen stars, she gets a small surprise present. Very small—stickers, crayons, bubbles, or coloring books are all good ideas. The idea is to use the present as positive reinforcement, not to overshadow the actual achievement.

6. Ensure there's fun and play every day.

Play is hugely important in a child's life. Through play a child learns about the world, discovers how things work, and practices interacting with others. He has the opportunity to explore his natural creativity, build his communication skills, and understand his own feelings. Fantasy play and role-playing unlock his imagination and let it run wild—an important way for a child to find his individuality.

Kids learn many skills and strengthen many abilities through play. Fine motor skills are developed through building LEGO cars and castles, stacking block towers, and solving puzzles. Going outside and kicking a football around is a great way to develop coordination as well as to foster a healthy interest in sports—and to have fun. Games can encourage educational growth from a very young age. Even an older baby will point to her own nose; a toddler will sing an alphabet song; a preschooler will play a card game of Uno or memory—and grow intellectually. Walking in the park, rolling around in piles of autumn leaves, and feeding the ducks are perfect ways to discover nature.

Individual play gives kids the chance to make discoveries on their own, but we are also keen believers in playdates. Playdates are the perfect opportunity for children to interact with each other—even babies enjoy being around other kids—while learning such invaluable life skills as sharing and self-expression. Playdates can introduce your child to a range of other people, each of whom becomes a potential friend.

But whether it's a playdate with other kids, individual play, or play with you, make sure there's ample time for play each day; it really is the defining activity of childhood.

7. At mealtimes, share fresh food and family conversation.

It's common knowledge that fresh food and a balanced diet are absolutely essential for a child's healthy growth and development. They're also one of the great pleasures of life. As nannies we know that good eating habits start in the cradle and that the food you offer your children now will have a powerful impact on their future relationship with food.

The best way to plant these good eating habits is through fresh food served at shared mealtimes. Yet such a scenario is becoming more and more rare. Because of today's busy lives and our convenience-food culture, children tend to eat an abundance of highly processed fast food. They often eat on the run or have their meals in front of the television. None of this is good for the child's health, development, or palate. In fact, in our experience, children who are raised on a fast-food diet quickly become fussy eaters; in due course, they won't even try a home-cooked meal. As for dining in front of the TV, it is a poor substitute for conversation over home-made food around the family table.

Preparing home-cooked food does not have to mean creating a huge extravaganza every night of the week. You need a fast meal? As nannies we have discovered every trick there is for fast, tasty meals that kids love—and we offer lots of recipes for such meals in Chapter Five, "Secrets from the Nannies' Kitchen." Quick pasta dishes, stir-fries, and omelets are all good options—easy and healthy.

The point is that you needn't make a big to-do of things in order to offer your kids a variety of fresh foods from a young age—especially if you stick to your guns through the fussy stages. Kids are quite capable of eating the same foods as the rest of the family, and running a catering service in your own home can be an exhausting habit—and one that's hard to break.

Above all, try to share meals with your kids on a regular basis. The simple rituals of a shared meal—setting the table, eating together, telling each other about the day—give children a sense of continuity and belonging. Yes, it's difficult for busy families to find time to sit down together for meals—especially with toddlers who may have to be in bed by seven. But if the whole family isn't able to eat together every night, then aim for once or twice a week. And when you do get together for meals, turn off the TV. This is the time for your family. It's a chance to hear from your kids—always important—and for them to hear from you. It's a time you can all enjoy. Taking the time to cook and share meals with your family is a simple but powerful expression of love.

8. Nurture self-esteem and confidence.

Let's face it: you won't be there to protect your kids every time they hit a bump in the road. But you can arm them now for any challenge they may confront, by nurturing a healthy self-esteem and confidence in their own sense of self.

The early years are crucial in building this invisible armor. A young child initially takes his sense of self from his parents; therefore, every interaction between you and your child will have a powerful impact. If you believe in the child, he will believe in himself—an invaluable conviction he can take through life.

In order for children to feel good about themselves, they need their parents to accept who they really are—with all their similarities to and differences from their parents. You might be outgoing and the life of the party—and the parent of a child who is naturally shy and retiring. No amount of pushing or criticism will change your child's personality, but the pressure may harm his sense of self and undermine his confidence.

Every child shines at some special thing; find that special thing in your child, and help him to develop it. To do that, you'll want to offer lots of opportunities for your kids to explore their strengths and interests. Offer sports lessons, dance classes, art workshops, and trips to the library—good ways for children to discover their potential. Whatever potential they find, help them realize it; achievement is a wonderful way to build confidence. Make sure, though, that your child understands that achievement means doing your best, not necessarily being the best. Children can easily become anxious and unhappy if they put themselves under too much pressure to be the winner.

Self-esteem can be nourished by giving children lots of praise and encouragement as they go through their day. Praise, however, is a precious commodity; it should not be squandered. Some parents fall into the habit of gushing over every little thing their kids do. Children see straight through empty praise, however, and it has the same effect as crying wolf: later, when the praise is deserved, children won't believe it. However, you do need to acknowledge not only their major successes but also their everyday achievements—getting dressed on their own, packing away their toys, or showing kindness to others. Telling kids you are proud of them sends a powerful message and makes them feel good about themselves.

One more thing about self-esteem and confidence: it's important to keep in mind that kids learn by your example. They are little sponges, absorbing everything around them. That means that if they hear you making self-defeating or self-deprecating comments—if you complain that "I really messed up today; I felt so stupid," or if you say that "this dress makes me look fat"—your kids will not only mimic the comments, they are also likely to develop the same negative attitude.

Happy, confident kids have parents who cheer them on, allow them to make mistakes, and are accepting of who they really are. Such parents build healthy self-esteem and confidence in their kids—invaluable tools kids will use all their lives.

9. Remember that all kids are different.

We are hardly able to count the number of children we have collectively cared for, but we can say with certainty that each has been completely unique and entirely special. Kids really do develop in their own time—and when they are ready. Some babies are walking at twelve months; others do not take their first steps until they reach sixteen months. Some children can string whole sentences together at eighteen months; others may not do so until they are at least two years old. Some three-year-olds are diaper-free at night, but other kids are five years old before they've reached this stage. Yet parents can easily fall into the trap of comparing their kids to everyone else's, the result of which can be harmful to the child's self-esteem.

Comparing kids' achievements can lead to an unhealthy competitiveness. We know of two six-year-old boys who were on the same after-school soccer team and had become the best of friends. In time, their parents also became friends. Unfortunately, it wasn't long before one of the parents began to boast about his son's success in scoring goals. The other parent would respond with his own exaggerated boast about his son's goal-saving techniques. This soon escalated into blow-by-blow arguments about whose son was better at soccer. Hearing these conversations, the boys began to criticize each other and to brag about their own performances—in perfect imitation of their parents. Soon both friendships were destroyed, and soccer was no longer the fun it once was.

Growing up is difficult enough without unnecessary pressure. Being a parent is about accepting the child you have. She'll do things in her own way and in her own good time.

10. Keep your kids safe—always.

Being a nanny is a huge responsibility in just about every way, but the hugest of its obligations is the safety of the kids in our charge. Safety is always on our minds, and we are constantly looking out for potential mishaps. That in itself can be a full-time job, for kids are naturally curious, and while they are discovering new things there can be accidents along the way. Naturally, a young child does not know what is safe and what isn't, so it's essential to pay constant attention to what children are getting into.

But paying attention is only part of the requirement. Kids need to learn safety as well. Certainly there are scores of childproofing gadgets that will help prevent kids from getting into the household bleach, touching the oven, or falling down the stairs. But we cannot solely rely on locks and gates to keep our kids safe. They need to learn why bleach is dangerous, why they shouldn't touch an oven, and why running on the stairs is not safe. Teaching those lessons is a parent's responsibility.

Kids are often impulsive and fearless; whatever their age, they are not entirely capable of foreseeing the consequences of their actions. You have to anticipate the consequences for them—and act on what you anticipate. If you leave a ladder out while you pop into the other room for a second, for example, don't expect your child not to climb on it. We knew a six-year-old who was a natural at karate and would often practice at home in front of the glass patio door. One day, he demonstrated a powerful jump-kick and ended up kicking in the glass and going right through it. No one had thought ahead to what could happen when the six-year-old practiced in front of the glass door. Caring for kids is about considering the possibilities of what could happen.

Of course, there is a fine line between being protective and overprotective. Kids need room to explore their world safely, and parents sometimes need to bite their lips when their kids experience the inevitable bumps and bruises as they learn to crawl, walk, and climb. A child will look to you for a signal on how to react when he hurts himself. If you run over to him at every little bump and scratch, make a huge fuss, and carry on as if he is desperately injured, all you're really doing is encouraging him to become stressed and upset. On the other hand, you cannot ignore a bump or scratch. Whether your child is a naturally tough little guy who never makes a peep when he hurts himself, or a more sensitive child who screams and cries every time he scrapes his knee, it's important to examine the hurt. Then offer a kiss and a sympathetic word, and keep your response balanced and realistic.

Be aware, be informative, be ready to step in, and teach your children how to protect themselves. That's the best way to keep your kids safe—always.

The Nannies' Ten Absolute Essentials are the foundational building blocks of our approach to raising happy, healthy children. We also believe that they are gifts you give your children now that will benefit them for the rest of their lives. No parent should do less; no parent can do more.

It's All in the Approach

★ Take some time to assess your current approach to parenting—and whether it's working.

★ Remember that you can change your approach at any time.

★ Be loving, firm, and fun every day.

★ Practice the Nannies' Ten Absolute Essentials.

★ Don't be too hard on yourself; it's not easy, so do the best you can.

Chapter Two

Babies:
The First Year
of Life

Start As You Mean to Go On

It is six A.M. on a bleak, drizzly Saturday in London, and I can hear my phone ringing. Who could be calling me at this hour on a weekend? I think fuzzily as I pick up the phone. "Nanny?" a woman asks tentatively in a distinctly American voice.

This is puzzling. "Yes," I answer. "Who is speaking, please?"

She tells me her name and the name of the mutual acquaintance who had given her my phone number. "I know all about you," she says. "I have been told you are the most fantastic nanny. I really want you to come and help me with my baby boy."

It takes me a moment to register the reality of who it is on the phone. To call her a well-known musician would be a silly understatement; she is a major star, and I have been a fan of hers for years. That she should be telephoning me is quite unbelievable, but I pull myself together as quickly as I can. "What kind of help do you need?" I ask.

"My baby is twelve weeks old," she says. "The baby nurse left us two weeks ago, and I haven't found a nanny yet. I am nervous with him; I don't feel like I know what I am doing and I feel so tired . . ." Then she bursts into tears. "Will you please come?" she begs.

"Where are you?" I ask.

"Los Angeles."

"I'm not really looking for a full-time position right now," I tell her. "My plan is to stay here in London for the next year or two."

"Please just come for a week," she quickly counters, "and you can decide later."

I look out the window. The first gray light of early morning now reveals not just drizzle but a steady rain. Warm L.A. sunshine seems awfully appealing. "Okay," I say. "When would you like me to come?"

"Tonight. My assistant has a flight on hold."

Twelve hours later, I am settled into my roomy first-class seat on the plane, watching movies, enjoying a seemingly endless round of beverages and snacks, and noting the famous faces in the cabin. On arrival in L.A., the warm sunshine is real, and I am escorted to a stretch limousine that drives me past beautiful, sprawling mansions and villas until we pull up in front of an imposing metal gate. Under the watchful eye of the security cameras, the driver buzzes the gate, which slowly opens to let us in. I have the feeling I am entering a celebrity hideaway and leaving the real world far behind.

The limo swooshes up the long drive to the house. I press the front doorbell, the door of the house flies open, and there stands the woman herself. Beside me, the limo driver gasps, and I must admit that I have to disguise my own shock at seeing her in person. Part of the shock is from actually confronting this star, and part of it is her appearance. She is wearing a nightgown and has the look common among all new mothers—complete exhaustion. I am taken aback at first as I try to reconcile the glamorous image I know with the tired-looking new mother standing before me. But her overwhelmed expression quickly snaps me back into nanny mode. I introduce myself and ask to meet her baby right away.

She leads me through the house to the nursery, where the baby is napping soundly. "He's sleeping now," she whispers, "but it has taken me two hours of rocking and singing to get him to sleep. And he won't sleep for very long. He'll wake up screaming in twenty minutes. He always does . . ."

We sit down in the kitchen over a cup of tea and talk about the baby, about how she is feeling, and about how she would like things to be. She wants a lot to be different, but she has no idea how to effect changes, and she seems utterly daunted by the prospect.

I encourage her to relax and remind her that this is an adjustment period for both her and the baby. "It's all in the approach," I tell her, "and the trick is simply to start as you mean to go on."

"Yes, but how?" she asks.

"By setting up good habits, introducing regular feeding and sleeping schedules, and teaching the baby to go to sleep independently. Starting now."

She sighs. "It sounds impossible," she says.

"It isn't," I assure her. "In the week I spend here, I can show you how to get started."

That's exactly what I do. And it's exactly what this chapter is about—helping you start as you mean to go on as a parent, right in that all-important first year of your baby's life.

Let's begin with your feelings about your new status as a parent. Whether they are rock stars or homemakers, all new parents share the same feelings of nervousness and exhaustion. The first year with a new baby is a major adjustment for all—for you, a precious new life to care for; for the baby, the challenge of settling into a new world. The first few months especially can be an intense and tiring time, but they can also be the most incredibly rewarding time of your life.

In the beginning, however, just about all new parents feel unsure of how to proceed—especially because they sense that the parenting choices they make in the first year have lasting importance. They're right about that: the decisions parents make and the precedents they set in these first months of life can establish some very basic habits. If the habits are good—if they make both the baby and the parents happy and healthy and able to enjoy one another—then the parents have done their child and themselves a favor. But if the habits are quick fixes like driving the baby around the block to get him to sleep, or overfeeding him every time he cries—even when he is not hungry—or weaning him with only sweet foods because he once rejected a tart taste, then parents may be setting the stage for family upset and upheaval later on when trying to change these habits.

So yes, the decisions you make in the first year about how and when to feed your baby, about what to do when she cries, and about where and when she will sleep are very important decisions to make.

In years gone by, parents were told that there was one way of doing things and one way only; strict, rigorous, and authoritarian advice prevailed. Nowadays, the trend is quite different, with new parents being advised to copy a lifestyle ill suited to the modern society in which we live. *Attachment* is the watchword of the day, and new parents are often pressured into eighteen months-plus of constant feeding, sleeping in the same bed as the child—which can result in her sharing the parental bed until she is eight or nine years old—and carrying the child at all times so that she will feel "attached" to them. We'd like to tell you that a healthy child who is well cared for and loved will feel secure and attached to her parents without being endlessly carried, fed at the first hint of fussiness, and put to bed with her parents.

In fact, we've found that parents who follow this style of child rearing often complain of exhaustion and anxiety. No wonder: these parents never get a break. At the same time, they're establishing habits that can keep them exhausted and anxious for a long time to come. They may end up having to rock their one-year-old for an hour or more before he falls asleep, constantly give their eighteen-month-old milk because he was never weaned properly onto food, endlessly entertain their three-year-old because he has never learned how to play independently, or lie down with their four-year-old for hours on end until he falls asleep because of the sleep associations they created in the first year of life.

We believe in a balanced approach to child rearing, a combination of structure and flexibility that works well for baby and parents. We do not aim to oppose any particular system or philosophy of baby care. Rather, we want to urge you to think about the choices you make now and to be aware of their long-term effects. In the first months of your baby's life, those choices will involve such basic matters as feeding your baby, responding when your baby cries, and getting your baby to sleep. Your approach now can affect the lives of your baby and your family for some time to come.

In the next chapter, and throughout this book, we talk in detail about our belief in establishing basic routines for your children and putting those routines on a schedule. In our view, the scheduled routine is the most solid basis there is for raising happy and contented children.

It really starts now. Providing structure in the most basic aspects of your baby's first year of life will make an enormous difference in your baby's overall well-being and contentment. Once you structure the meeting of your baby's basic needs into a routine, things will fall into place much more easily: your baby is likely to feed at regular times, sleep longer, and easily be weaned onto solid foods.

A structured approach also regularizes *your* life, and that makes you less prone to the anxieties and exhaustion that new parents often feel. Relaxed parents and a settled baby who is eating and sleeping well have a much better chance of enjoying one another—exactly what the first year of life should be about.

Just as we showed that rock star in Los Angeles, and just as we've shown scores upon scores of new parents, in this chapter we show you how to lay the foundation. Rather than discussing every aspect of the first year of life (there are lots of books that do that, not to mention your pediatrician), we focus on those basics of a baby's life—eating, fussiness, and sleeping—and we tell you what has worked for us in caring for lots and lots of babies in all kinds of families, homes, and situations.

Laying the Foundation

When your baby is as young as four to six weeks old, you can begin to lay the foundation for a structured routine. Just introduce a few regular activities into your day: a morning walk in the park, a group meeting of new parents, an afternoon visit with a neighbor. This gives some form to your life, and therefore to your baby's, and provides a foundation on which you can build a complete routine of activities, mealtimes, naps, and bedtimes—by and by.

We start with an overview of the first year of life, giving you a head start on knowing what's coming next.

Then we tell you how and when to introduce a flexible feeding schedule, and how to wean your baby onto fresh food. We believe very strongly that this method of weaning gives your baby a healthy start in life, encouraging wholesome eating habits for a lifetime. At the end of the chapter, we've included some of our favorite recipes for successful weaning with fresh food.

Next we discuss how to calm a crying or fussy baby.

And finally we tell you how to teach your baby to fall asleep independently, and how and when to introduce a sleep schedule.

As always, the advice we offer has been tested and proven effective in a variety of families with a range of babies. Whatever your individual decisions about your baby's first year of life, structuring the year as we suggest will prove to be your most important parenting tool, and will set you on the right path for a happy baby and family.

Overview: Your Baby's First Year

Months one through three are all about the parents and the new baby settling in and getting to know each other. For Mom, these first few months should also be about getting plenty of rest and learning to take each new phase in stride. We encourage you to feel things out, get to know your baby, and get used to relying on your intuition to know what works and what makes everyone happy.

During the first few weeks of life, your baby requires around-the-clock attention and loving care; she is on a natural twenty-four-hour schedule, which means she will need to feed and sleep a great deal. It is a time to become comfortable with your baby, to establish feeding, and to take good care of yourself—try to sleep when the baby sleeps, eat nutritious foods, and drink plenty of water. Try taking a relaxing bath while the baby naps. Ignore the housework for now; it will get done eventually. Don't be afraid to ask family and friends for help. If you do not have family or friends close by, join a new parents' group for support and for a friendly ear. You don't have to be SuperMom or SuperDad; just do the best you can.

The Daily Essentials

Here are two essentials to making your baby healthy and happy. Be sure you do them every day. First, surround your baby with love. Kiss her from the top of her head to her littlest toe. Babies thrive on kisses, cuddles, snuggles, tickles, soothing words, and songs. Your baby doesn't care if you don't sing like Julie Andrews in The Sound of Music; to her, you have the most beautiful voice in the world. Second, stimulate your baby's development by talking to her, reading to her, playing with her, and enjoying her.

After a few weeks, you can settle into the most basic feeding and sleeping schedule. Later, we suggest some simple rituals that will lay the groundwork for good feeding and sleeping habits, and eventually for a more structured routine.

Months three through six will find you and baby moving along nicely. The age of three months can be the perfect time to establish a real sleeping schedule, introducing regular daily naps and a consistent nighttime routine. Later we give you tips for putting your baby down awake, for ensuring he is content in his crib, and for laying the foundation for him to sleep through the night.

In months six through twelve you will see your baby growing and developing by leaps and bounds. He will soon be standing, crawling, and cutting teeth. He will be discovering the delights of eating solid foods, reducing milk feedings, and, if good sleep habits and a regular schedule have been established, he should be sleeping through the night. As you look back over this year, you will be astounded at how much you and your baby have changed since those first overwhelming days of your baby's life and your life as a new parent.

Eating

Feeding Your Newborn

How a mother chooses to feed her baby is of course her own very personal choice, but whether you breast-feed or formula-feed your baby, we advise getting on a feeding schedule as soon as you and your baby are ready. It will make for an easier life and a more settled baby.

We have seen it more times than we can count: once babies are put on a regular feeding schedule, they tend to be less fussy. They usually sleep better—and Mom can get some much-needed rest. She also has the ability to plan her day to a certain degree, and she can feel she has some control over her life; when she knows the times at which she will feed her baby, she can spend time catching up on chores or taking the baby on a walk.

If you are breast-feeding your newborn, the first few weeks of life are about establishing this method of feeding. By this we mean making sure your baby is latching on properly, feeding well at each feeding, and feeding on a regular basis. Take this time to get to know your baby. You may discover that your baby needs to be awakened for regular feedings, is tricky to burp, likes to be held in a certain position, or is fussy at certain times each day. Getting to understand her in this way will help you establish good feeding.

Once breast-feeding is well established, you can try to schedule regular

Starting a Feeding Schedule

At one of the new moms' meetings I regularly host, I was approached by a young mother who was having a really hard time with her four-month-old. The advice she had received had been to "demand feed" her baby and to feed him every time he fussed. Yet he would eat for only a few minutes at a time, sleep for short periods, and fuss a great deal. His mother was completely worn out and at the end of her tether. "When will my baby start feeding more regularly and sleeping for longer?" she asked me pleadingly.

I told her it was most likely something she would have to initiate. The key to it, I explained, was getting her baby on a basic feeding schedule. Once she wasn't constantly having to feed the baby, she could get some rest and get some control over her days. Then she'd have the resources to start establishing a basic sleep schedule. The plan was for her to start out by feeding the baby at regular intervals of two hours; once that was established, she was to increase the intervals to every three hours. I also gave her our Nannies' Top Ten Feeding Tips (see page 43).

In addition, I suggested that just because the baby was fussing didn't necessarily mean he was hungry. I advised her to try to settle her baby in other ways—offer him room-temperature water in a bottle, give him a pacifier, or take him outside for a walk in his stroller for a change of scenery.

Four weeks later, she told me how the change had improved their lives. She was feeding her son every three hours during the day, and because he was eating properly at each feed, he was also sleeping at more regular times and longer.

feeding times. The key is to make sure your baby feeds well and long enough at each feed. Babies who are nursing well can feed every two to three hours, while formula-fed babies can feed every three to four hours. Note that these intervals are timed from the start of a feed. When setting up a daytime feeding schedule, you may need to wake your baby when she is due for a feed. Do so by changing her diaper and/or gently tickling her feet, massaging her body, or changing her clothes. Once your baby is feeding well during the day, you can begin to extend the intervals between feeds at night.

Feeding schedules do not have to be strictly regimented, and your schedule may not be the same day after day. Your baby may want to feed more during a growth spurt, for example, or she may not feed so well if she is sick, overtired, or overstimulated. In either such case, the regular three-hour interval may only be a two-and-a-half-hour interval. Let your intuition be your guide, and be sensitive to your baby's needs; you'll know when she is hungry or tired, and you can adjust the schedule accordingly.

Giving Breast-fed Babies a Bottle

I was a young nanny working for one of London's top fashion models, who was breast-feeding her three-month-old son, Stevie. Fashion Week was madness as my boss dashed across town this way and that in a blur of clothes fittings and runway walks for one show after another—with me and Stevie close behind. Trying to breast-feed Stevie backstage at the shows—chaotic scenes of hair stylists, makeup artists, fashion designers, and photographers flashing their lights—was a major challenge, and neither my boss nor Stevie was entirely satisfied with the situation. After a while, I suggested that she pump her breast milk so I could feed the baby a bottle while she was working. Stevie took the breast milk from the bottle with ease, which thrilled both my boss and me. It freed her to work without worrying about feeding Stevie, and it gave me the option to stay home or go to the shows. Since then I have encouraged new mothers to give their babies the occasional bottle from a young age, simply so that the baby is used to taking a bottle if it is ever needed.

But having it work so well with Stevie was actually quite lucky considering that he was already three months old. Since then, I have cared for many breast-fed babies who will not take a bottle unless they have been given one before eight weeks old, and on a regular basis. This can be very challenging for both baby and nanny when the baby's mother goes back to work and a bottle is the only way to feed the baby. In such cases, it has typically taken me several days to get a baby to take a bottle successfully without a lot of fuss.

The lesson here is that it makes very good sense to start giving a baby a bottle somewhere between the ages of three to eight weeks. Please note, however: we don't recommend giving a breast-fed baby a bottle before breast-feeding is well established. If he is given a bottle any earlier, there may be nipple confusion.

To be sure, it will take a few days—or even a week or two—for you and your baby to settle into a feeding schedule, so don't expect it to happen at once, and don't worry if it takes time. It is helpful in the early days of establishing breast-feeding and setting up a feeding schedule to keep the environment calm and quiet. You don't want every single friend and member of your family dropping in, as nothing is more likely to disrupt your forming feeding routines.

The Nannies' Top Ten Feeding Tips

1. If you are having any trouble breast-feeding your baby, contact a lactation consultant, midwife, or postpartum doula (check out http://www.doulanetwork.com/ or http://www.dona.org/ for more about doulas). Ask family and friends who have nursed for advice and support, or join your neighborhood new mothers' group, if there is one. Getting some advice really makes a huge difference for breast-feeding moms. What you think may be something you have to put up with—sore nipples, for example—may actually be a hint of a problem (in this case, the baby probably isn't latching on properly). A consultant or experienced friend can help identify the issue.

2. Whether you are breast-feeding or bottle-feeding, make sure the environment is a calm one, and use the feeding time to bond with your baby. Speak in a soothing voice, make eye contact, enjoy this time together with lots of kisses and hugs.

3. It is very common for babies to become drowsy or fall asleep while they are feeding—on the breast or on the bottle—and therefore to fail to get enough milk. To make sure your baby gets enough milk, you need to keep her awake while she is feeding. To do this, first take her gently off the breast or bottle. If that wakes her up, fine. If not, try talking to her, tickling her feet, or changing her diaper. When your baby has enough milk at each feed, she will be able to go longer between feeds; it will then be easier to set up a regular feeding schedule. As the weeks go by, she will be able to stay awake for longer periods of time and to eat more at each feed.

4. If you are trying to set up a regular breast-feeding schedule and your baby still wants to nurse all the time, she may be feeding for comfort

rather than from hunger. One way to monitor this is to watch her throat to see if she is actually swallowing the milk or just sucking. If she is just sucking and not feeding, take her off the breast or bottle. She can suck for comfort instead on your clean finger, her fist or thumb, or a pacifier. (Do not substitute a pacifier for feedings, however, and be aware of the attachment that can be formed to pacifiers when used in the long term.)

5. Make sure you burp a baby well at least up to the age of four months. Burp her halfway through a feed and at the end of a feed. If she is not properly burped, she may become fussy and unsettled, and if you put her to sleep right after a feed and she has not been burped, she will likely wake up crying and uncomfortable within minutes. (For tricky burpers, see our colic tip on page 60.)

6. Share some feedings with your spouse or partner. If you are breast-feeding, pump some breast milk and put it in a bottle to give your partner the extra chance to feed and bond with your baby. (A baby often takes breast milk in a bottle better from somebody other than his mother; in fact, his mother may have to leave the room while her partner feeds the baby.)

7. If you are going to be returning to work, or if you would like your baby to drink breast milk from a bottle on a regular basis for some other reason, start giving the baby a bottle of your breast milk once a day between the ages of three and eight weeks. If you don't give the bottle before eight weeks, you may have trouble getting the baby to accept it. But once the bottle has been accepted, offer it on a regular basis. If you don't, it will not take long for him to forget about the bottle and he may refuse it.

8. It is common for new parents to be concerned about the amount of milk their baby is consuming—is she getting too much milk or not enough? Making sure she has regular feedings and that she feeds well each time should be sufficient, but the best measure is your baby's growth. If you're concerned that your baby is not gaining enough weight and is not taking in enough at her feedings, contact your pediatrician.

9. Make sure you nourish yourself with a well-balanced diet that is high in calcium; stay hydrated while you are breast-feeding.

10. Rest as much as you can and don't hesitate to ask for support from your partner, friends, and family.

Weaning Your Baby onto Solid Food

When your baby is about four or five months old, it is time to think about introducing her to solid foods. Weaning is a very exciting new phase in your baby's development. Up until now, her sole source of nutrition has been either breast milk or formula milk, because her digestive system simply was not ready for anything else. But now you may notice that you have a hungry baby on your hands, that milk no longer seems to satisfy her, or that she seems to take an interest in what you are eating. These are the sure signs that it's time to introduce solid foods into her diet. Of course, each baby is different, and you will have to rely on your instincts to tell you whether your baby is ready for this new stage of development.

Whenever the right time comes for weaning your baby onto solid food (between four and six months), what's important in our view is the kind of food you offer your baby; this can have a real impact on his future eating habits. That's why we advocate giving a baby fresh, nutritious food as much as possible—so that he will learn to love wholesome food and will be well on his way to a lifetime of healthy eating. That's a great gift you can give your child, which is why we urge parents to wean their babies with fresh food rather than with commercially made baby food in the jar—to whatever extent they can.

As we see it, commercially made baby food doesn't offer a baby's palate the variety of tastes and textures that allow the palate to expand. There's a blandness to food from the jar, and that's a limiting first impression that's hard to change later on. The more tastes and textures you can expose your baby to at this crucial time of weaning, the more open he will be to eating a great variety of foods. Actually, we've also found that jar-fed babies can become fussy eaters who will often reject fresh food when given it. Some commercially prepared baby food contains fillers, thickening agents, and sugar and salt—ingredients we really don't recommend offering to a newly growing baby. So we say, as much as you can, wean your baby onto fresh solid food. It's the best choice in every way for your baby's health, growth, and development.

If you do regularly feed your baby jar food, we encourage you to offer fresh food as often as you can. You might try mixing fresh cooked vegetables with the chicken dinner from the jar, or, if you have given your baby food from the jar for lunch, try offering him fresh fruit and/or yogurt for dessert. You can also share your own food with your baby—if it's baby appropriate and salt free. For example, you can easily give a seven-month-old a serving of your spaghetti marinara. Or you can add fresh vegetables, rice, or pasta to a can of salt-free soup or lentils; you can even serve it with a slice of toast.

If you do choose to wean your baby with fresh foods—and we hope you do—here's how to do it as easily and conveniently as possible.

You'll need some basic equipment for feeding your baby solid foods: plastic bowls, plastic spoons, and a large bib. You'll want a blender, food processor, or hand mixer—some sort of machine sufficient to puree food to a smooth consistency—and a pair of kitchen scissors, our preferred tool for chopping food for older babies. You'll also need a high chair or baby seat—a stabilized car seat will work—to put your baby in for feeding.

Sterilizing

You'll need to sterilize baby bottles until the baby is a year old; weaning utensils should be sterilized until the baby is six months old. Sterilizers that work using steam are found in most baby stores, or you can use an unmechanized method. Before using either method, however, be sure to wash bottles and utensils thoroughly in hot, soapy water, and rinse them well. Use a bottle brush to clean inside the bottles and the bottles' nipples.

If you are using a store-bought sterilizer, place the bottles and utensils inside the sterilizer with a little water and turn it on; the process usually takes about fifteen minutes.

If you do not have a sterilizer, use a large pot of water. Bring the water to a boil, then use tongs to place the bottles and utensils in the pot; leave them simmering for five minutes, then take them out, again using the tongs. Never leave this pot unattended, because the water will eventually evaporate, and the rubber nipples may melt.

Sterilized bottles and utensils may be stored for up to twenty-four hours before they need to be sterilized again.

Baby Food Made Easy

Below you'll find a complete stage-by-stage guide to weaning with fresh food, and you'll find the corresponding recipes at the end of this chapter. Suffice it to say that cooking for your baby doesn't have to be difficult or time-consuming. For example, it's easy enough to take a portion of unsalted vegetables from your own meal and puree or mash it, then serve it to your baby. And to make life even easier for you, we've included our favorite short-cut: the ice cube shortcut.

The Ice Cube Shortcut

If you're daunted by the idea of cooking a full meal for a baby who is only going to eat a small amount, try this ice cube freezer method for batch cooking ahead of time.

Cook portions of vegetables, fruit, fish, and meat, then freeze them in individual ice cubes. To create the baby's meals, just defrost a few different ice cubes, mix, and reheat thoroughly. For example, for lunch you might serve your seven-month-old a mixture of ice-cubed squash, potato, and fish. Or how about a combination of pear and apple for your five-month-old's breakfast? Here's how to do it, step by step:

1. Prepare the food, set aside a portion for baby to eat now, and spoon the remainder into ice cube trays. Place the trays in the freezer.
2. When the cubes of food are frozen, take them out of the tray and put them into a Ziploc bag. With a permanent marker, label the bag with the date and the contents.
3. When ready to use, choose individual cubes, defrost, and heat thoroughly over low heat, or heat in a microwave until evenly heated through; stir thoroughly and serve at room temperature.

A note on freezing: fruit and vegetables will keep for up to six months. Food cooked with milk or fish keeps for up to a month in the freezer. Chicken and red meat keep well for up to two months in the freezer. You should never refreeze defrosted frozen food.

How to Prepare Fresh Food for a Young Baby

It is very simple to prepare fresh food for babies using the following methods, and food prepared in this way is perfect for the ice cube shortcut.

While your baby naps one morning, you can easily prepare and freeze enough baby food for a whole month.

Fruit
(See listings for what age to introduce which fruit)

Apples, pears, peaches, plums, and apricots can be prepared in the following way. Peel and core the fruit, then place in a saucepan with enough water to cover. Place the lid on the pan and simmer over low heat for 8–10 minutes or until the fruit is cooked and soft enough for a knife to pass easily through it. Or steam the fruit over water for 10–12 minutes or until soft. When cooked, drain the water and puree the fruit in a blender. (Unpureed cooked fruit can be served to older babies and children with yogurt or oatmeal for a delicious nutritious breakfast.)

Vegetables
(See listings for what age to introduce which vegetable)

Potato, butternut squash, carrots, turnips, and parsnips will all need to be peeled, washed, and cut into cubes. Cauliflower, zucchini, and broccoli will need to be washed and cut into small pieces. Place the vegetable in a saucepan and add enough water to cover. Place the lid on the pan and simmer over low heat until the vegetable is cooked and soft, or steam over water until soft (a knife should pass easily through the vegetable). Place the cooked vegetable and a little water in a blender or food processor and puree.

Chicken
(From 6 months of age)

Poaching is the perfect way to cook chicken for babies. Trim the skin and fat from a chicken cutlet. Put enough liquid (use either water or salt-free organic stock) in a saucepan to cover the chicken once it is in the pan. Once the liquid is at a rapid simmer, place the chicken into the pan and cook covered on low heat until it is cooked completely through (the chicken should be white all the way through, with no pink flesh remaining). Place the cooked chicken with a little water or stock in a blender or food processor and puree for young babies; for older babies, chop with kitchen scissors.

White Fish

(From 7 months of age)

Poaching is a simple way to cook fish for babies. Use fresh fillets such as sole, flounder, or cod. Run your hand over the fillets to find any fine bones and remove. Put enough milk into a medium-size shallow pan to cover the fish. Cover with a lid, turn heat to low, and bring to a simmer. Once the milk is simmering, add the fish. Cook the fish for a few minutes until it is cooked through (it should flake apart easily). Remove the pan from the heat and, with a slotted spoon, scoop the fish out of the pan and onto a plate. Check the fish thoroughly again for any fine bones. Place the cooked fish and a little of the milk used in cooking into the blender or food processor and puree for young babies; for older babies, mash with a fork.

The Ten Times Rule

Our number one tip for feeding babies is our "ten times rule." Too often, a new parent will offer a baby a new food, see it rejected, and never offer it again. Yet it is common for a baby to reject a new food as many as ten times—and then decide he likes it. In fact, we've seen babies who go on to favor that particular food above all others.

So one of the best things parents can do for their babies is to keep offering them new foods. Encouraging them to be open to a variety of tastes ensures that they will receive all the nutritional benefits of a diverse menu—for a lifetime. Give a food ten tries at least before you take it out of your baby's food repertoire. And do introduce it again at a later time; babies' tastes aren't fixed.

Common Food Allergies

A note about food allergies, which can be inherited from a parent and often last for life: you can easily identify the cause of an allergy if solid foods are introduced one at a time. Families with a history of food allergies should consult their pediatrician before weaning their babies onto solid food.

The most common types of food to which babies are allergic are wheat, dairy, nuts, eggs, and gluten. Symptoms of an allergic reaction include rash, nausea, diarrhea, vomiting, breathing problems, and skin irritations. If any of these symptoms occur, call your doctor immediately.

The First Taste

THE FIRST BABY I ever weaned was Thomas, a little fellow with a healthy appetite and a sunny disposition. When he saw his spoon coming toward him, he would open up his mouth wide, like a baby bird, eager and ready to taste everything I offered him. After tasting, his expression would give away his response—"Mmm, not bad at all" or "Yes, that's good." His solid-food diet grew by leaps and bounds, and soon he was eating a wide variety of foods. I heard moms and other nannies talking about how hard it was to wean their babies, and I thought smugly to myself that it was my knowledge and expertise that had made weaning Thomas so simple.

Imagine my shock when the next baby I weaned proved to be just the opposite of baby Thomas. Lily was a tiny, delicate thing with big eyes always quietly observing the world around her. When she tried her first meal, those eyes opened wide in shock. With a horrified expression on her face she seemed to ask, "What are you doing to me?"

Unlike Thomas, Lily's solid-food diet grew very, very slowly. I spent the first month of weaning introducing her to solid food one teaspoon at a time. I knew it was just a new experience for her, and that she would take to solid food when she was ready. In time, of course, she did begin to enjoy food, and this thrilled me beyond words. As an experienced nanny, I now know that every baby is different, that there is no need to rush them into doing things they are not ready for, and that babies develop in their own time.

And here's sound advice about salt, sugar, and honey: don't give them to babies under a year old. Honey carries the risk of infant botulism. Salt and sugar aren't recommended for the under-ones; small babies don't need these seasonings, which aren't good for them.

The Stages of Weaning

We have weaned many babies onto solid food during our time as nannies, and we know that there is no need to feel overwhelmed. Weaning doesn't have to be hard; in fact, it's an exciting time, and we urge you to enjoy the experience with your baby, as he discovers the pleasures of solid food.

We have divided the weaning process into three stages; for each stage, we offer tips on what to expect, how to proceed, and which foods to introduce. Each stage builds a strong base for healthy eating and creates a taste for fresh, nutritious food.

Stage One: Four to Six Months

Timing plays a large role when introducing solid food to a baby. Begin in the morning or around noontime when your baby is neither overly hungry nor too tired to eat, and once you have found a time that works, stick to it. We suggest starting a solid-food meal after half a milk feeding, or thirty to sixty minutes after a full milk feeding, so that your baby is neither too full from milk nor desperately hungry.

As for the perfect starter food for weaning, it's baby rice.

Use a sterilized small plastic spoon and bowl, and make a very small amount of baby rice—about two tablespoons will do—of a smooth, wet consistency. Depending on your baby's comfort, feed her on your lap, in a high chair, in a baby seat, or in a car seat. Don't forget to use a bib and to have a washcloth handy; most of the rice will end up around her mouth.

In the beginning, babies tend to eat just a few spoonfuls of food. Feeding them solid food at this point is just an exercise to get them used to foods and to eating from a spoon; it also helps set up an eating schedule. Some babies do not take to eating solid food well straightaway. If this is the case, do not worry. If your baby gets upset or doesn't appear interested in food, just wait two or three weeks and try again; she will probably love it the second time around.

Once you have had success with introducing solid foods, start to work on building a solid food–diet schedule, aiming toward a goal of three solid meals per day by the age of eight months. At the same time, you should continue to add new foods to the solid-food diet. If you have older children, try to work the baby's meals around the rest of the family's mealtimes, so the baby can share mealtimes from the start. This probably won't work with evening meals when your baby is very young, however, as she may eat her dinner as early as four or five o'clock.

Savory Foods First

After weaning dozens of babies, I discovered that they often prefer sweet fruit purees to vegetable purees. This seems especially true for breast-fed babies, because breast milk is naturally sweet. When I was a novice nanny weaning a baby girl for the first time, I offered her mostly fresh fruit purees, as that was what she obviously preferred. I soon realized she wasn't eating a wide variety of foods and I wished that I had introduced her to foods with a sharper taste first. Since then, all the babies I have weaned have begun their diets with foods like green beans, broccoli, zucchini, turnips, and potatoes. I only add the sweeter vegetables like squash and carrots and then the fruit purees to the diet once the baby has accepted the savory foods and developed a taste for them.

My "savory-foods-first" rule ensures that a baby will like more than sweet foods; she'll like a variety of foods, and her diet will be well balanced.

Stage One: Foods for Four to Six Months

(in order of proposed introduction):

- baby rice (preferably organic)
- zucchini
- potatoes
- turnips
- green beans
- parsnips
- broccoli
- carrots
- butternut squash
- sweet potatoes
- avocado
- peeled and cooked apples
- peeled and cooked pears
- bananas
- peeled and cooked peaches

Stage Two: Six to Nine Months

At six months, a baby's main source of nutrition is still milk—with perhaps two pureed solid meals per day. Between seven and eight months, she should be eating three mashed solid meals and at least three or four milk feedings per day. By eight to nine months, she should be eating three meals a day (and a snack) of lumpy, chopped-up, or mixed pureed and lumpy food. At this age she will still need three or four milk feedings per day. Even if a baby has no teeth, or just one or two, she can chew with her gums quite well.

Once your baby is on a regular feeding schedule, she will anticipate her solid-food mealtimes. If your baby has been weaned onto solid foods by the age of six months, then now is the time to add new foods to her diet. It is a joy to feed babies at this age, as they are very keen and eager to taste every new flavor.

NOTE: *If you have just begun introducing solid foods at six months, go back to the section on Stage One and begin from there.*

Batch cooking—and our ice cube shortcut—come in very handy now; make it a habit to cook extra amounts of food for freezing. As your baby gets older, use small plastic containers for storing, instead of ice cube trays. Remember: you don't always have to cook a separate meal for your baby; try giving him a salt-free portion from the family's meal. It's a good way to accustom him early on to eating the same meals you eat. And by six or seven months old, your baby can drink from a sippy cup when he is in his high chair, to get him used to drinking from a cup.

Stage Two: Foods for Six to Seven Months

- Weetabix breakfast cereal (available in most organic sections of the supermarket or in health food stores)
- oatmeal (not pre-made or "instant";
- use traditional Irish or stone-cut)
- cauliflower
- peas
- barley
- brown/white rice
- quinoa/millet
- rice noodles
- pasta
- chicken
- plain whole-fat yogurt
- cow's milk (for cooking)
- mild cheddar cheese

Nanny Wisdom

Seating Arrangements

At nine months or so, babies become very curious and want to be included in everything that is going on around them. At mealtimes, that can mean a baby may feel left out when eating in a high chair, separate from the family dining table. The perfect solution to this is a baby chair that can be attached to the table. Your baby will love sharing mealtimes with her family and she will be more likely to eat better.

Stage Two: Foods for Seven to Eight Months

- white fish
- lentils
- couscous
- split peas
- tofu
- cooked and peeled apricots
- cantaloupe
- leeks
- celery
- asparagus
- corn
- cooked tomatoes
- peeled and cooked plums
- peppers
- cabbage
- finger foods (e.g., steamed vegetables, grated cheese, uncooked pears, salt-free rice cakes)

Stage Two: Foods for Eight to Nine Months

- red meat
- spinach
- eggplant
- mushrooms
- tropical fruit (e.g., mango, papaya)
- peeled ripe plums, peaches, apricots
- cottage cheese
- ricotta cheese
- garlic
- mild spices (e.g., cumin, coriander)

Stage Three: Nine to Twelve Months

By nine months, your baby's solid-food diet should be well established (although she will still need two or three milk feedings per day). It is now time to expand her diet. She can eat a much wider variety of foods and can be introduced to a whole new range of tastes and textures. In fact, your baby's diet can be very similar to your own—but without salt or sugar—and she can begin or can continue to enjoy sharing mealtimes with her family.

You may also find that at this stage, babies who never enjoyed pureed food will suddenly eat the same food, not pureed, with great enthusiasm. Finger foods—toast strips, cooked strips of chicken breast, steamed vegetables, peeled ripe avocado, peeled ripe pears, peaches, or plums, grated cheese, salt-free rice cakes, bite-sized pasta, bananas—are also ideal at this time, and they encourage self-feeding and independence at mealtimes. At twelve months your baby can begin to drink cow's milk or soy milk. You can stop giving formula, stop sterilizing, and cut back to two milk feedings per day to encourage a hearty appetite for her solid-food diet.

Nanny Wisdom

Too Much Milk

Twelve-month-old Patricia had not yet been weaned onto solid food properly, and her diet consisted solely of yogurt, crackers, and breast milk—which was given on demand. She slept with her parents and fed on breast milk many times during the night. When her mother tried to feed her breakfast she simply refused to eat, and by midmorning she would demand breast milk again. For lunch, she would eat a little yogurt, and she liked Goldfish crackers for an afternoon snack. In the evening, all she wanted was breast milk.

When I suggested cutting back on breast milk, her mother was incredulous. "How can I cut back on her breast milk when she is not eating regular meals?" she asked.

"Patricia won't eat regular meals precisely because she is too full from constantly feeding on breast milk," I answered. To make any headway with solid foods at all, I explained, Patricia would have to be hungry, and she wouldn't be hungry unless her mother cut back on the breast-feedings. We laid out a plan. Slowly, Patricia's mother cut back on milk feedings, and slowly we began to introduce regular meals as a replacement. We began with simple foods such as mashed potatoes, steamed vegetables, toast, white fish, chicken, rice, pasta, cheese, and fruit. After a few weeks, Patricia was hungry for solid food and accepted her new diet—a major breakthrough for both mother and daughter.

Stage Three: Foods for Nine to Twelve Months

- beans: kidney, black, butter
- chickpeas
- oily fish (e.g., salmon, tuna)
- peeled cucumbers
- beets
- cooked dates
- finger sandwiches
- nitrate-free turkey and ham slices

Stage Three: Foods for Twelve Months

- berries
- cow's milk
- soy milk
- honey
- whole eggs
- citrus fruits
- peeled and cut-up grapes
- kiwi
- pineapple
- lettuce
- uncooked tomatoes

Weaning Guide

Here's a one-day sample menu that puts it all together for you, giving you an idea of how many solid-food meals and milk feedings make sense at different stages of weaning. Recipes for all the meals begin on page 74.

AGE	WAKE-UP	BREAKFAST	MID-MORNING	LUNCH	MID-AFTERNOON	DINNER	BEDTIME
4–5 MONTHS	Breast milk or formula	Baby rice		Breast milk or formula		Breast milk or formula (optional: baby rice and zucchini)	Breast milk or formula
5–6 MONTHS		Baby rice and fruit				Nursery Puree	
7–9 MONTHS		Oatmeal and fruit	Breast milk or formula	Nannies' Chicken Dinner	Breast milk or formula	Delicious Minestrone	
9–12 MONTHS		Oatmeal and fruit, finger slices of toast	Breast milk or formula, or a snack	Orion's Lemon Salmon	Fruit and yogurt or grated cheese and steamed vegetables	Baby's Spaghetti with Meat Sauce	

Crying and Fussiness

How to Settle a Fussy Baby

In the first few weeks and months of life, it is quite common for a baby to become fussy and hard to settle, leaving parents feeling exhausted and wondering what they are doing wrong. The answer almost always is, you're not doing anything wrong. Crying is one way babies communicate. Even if your healthy baby continues to cry after you have fed him, changed his diaper, and burped him, don't panic: fussiness is normal!

Maybe he is overstimulated, or overtired, or getting used to body functions like digestion, or accustoming himself to light and noise. We suggest that you try to take it easy and stay calm; if you become anxious, your baby may sense your anxiety and become even more anxious himself.

Try not to overreact or panic when your baby cries or fusses. Of course, your first response is to want to put an end to whatever discomfort or unhappiness your baby may be feeling, and it is very common for concerned new parents faced with a fussy baby to spend hours rocking, feeding, or jiggling the baby, or passing him back and forth from person to person. But such excessive stimulation can have the opposite effect from what you intend, resulting in more crying and fussiness, making you and your baby even more exhausted.

Instead, try these suggestions to help your new baby settle and to keep yourself calm while he is being fussy:

- Alternate the positions in which you hold the baby.
- Play some soothing music.
- Carry the baby around the house in a sling. This leaves your hands free to do things, and the baby will like the constant motion and will be content being close to you. If the baby falls asleep in the sling, unhook the strap and lay him in his crib without waking him up.
- Try a pacifier. Pacifiers are very helpful when a young baby is fussy between feeds; the sucking comforts and soothes the baby.
- Give your baby a bath and follow that with a massage, using a little moisturizer or oil to help him relax.
- Hold your baby close to your chest, speak very quietly in a soothing voice, stroke his forehead, or calmly pat his bottom or back.

Hang-out Time for Babies

You don't have to hold your baby every second of the day. In fact, it is a good idea to let your baby lie on a blanket in his bassinet or under a baby gym, or sit in a baby-bouncer chair in a safe place near you. This will give your baby an opportunity to be comfortable without being held all the time, and that gives you a chance to cook a meal, play with your other children, relax, or catch up with chores. If you are putting on a one-man show for your baby all day long, he will quickly expect constant entertainment, he will fuss if he doesn't get it, and you will both become exhausted.

• Take a walk. Put your baby in a sling, Baby Björn, or stroller, and go outside. Get some fresh air and sunshine, or maybe meet a friend for coffee. The walk or chat with a friend will revive you, and your baby will be likely to fall asleep, giving you a much-needed break.

Is Your Baby Crying Because of Gas or Colic?

Some babies between two and eight weeks old may cry uncontrollably for hours on end, leaving parents feeling exhausted, stressed, and concerned about their baby's health. Such crying is usually worse in the afternoons and evenings and may be repeated for weeks at a time, yet the doctor visit typically results in a diagnosis of "nothing wrong, just gas or colic." Some babies are more prone than others, of course, and the baby's temperament as well as your way of dealing with the problem may affect how fussy the baby gets and how long the situation lasts.

Our Favorite Holding Position for Fussy Babies

Most babies love this holding position: hold your baby so he is horizontal and facing downward with your right arm under his chest and your right palm flat against his chest. Place your left arm between his legs so that your left palm is against his tummy and your fingers face each other. The positioning of your hands will depend on your size and the size of your baby. When you walk around holding your baby this way, the motion and position are likely to calm him.

If your baby is suffering from gas or colic, try your best to stay calm—we know this is easier said than done—and don't hesitate to ask for support from your family and friends. As for what to do about gas or colic, we have some suggestions, techniques, and a traditional "nannies' solution." Here are our suggestions.

First, are you breast-feeding your baby? If you are, let's look at *your* diet, because your baby may well be sensitive to something you are eating. Potential culprits are nuts, wheat, eggs, and dairy products. Other foods

Getting Out and About

We know that caring for kids at home all day long can be isolating. That's why it's so important to get out into your neighborhood. The local park, baby classes, and parenting groups are perfect places to meet fellow parents. Don't be shy about striking up a conversation with other parents; after all, you do have something in common, and other parents can be a great support system. Nannies are of course notorious for banding together in the park, but the truth is that when we start a job with a new family, we typically know nobody in the area. After a few visits to the park, however, we soon get chatting with other nannies and parents. It's useful, and we have made many great friends this way. So can you.

that might be linked to fussiness in babies are such high-fiber fruits and vegetables as beans, grapes, melon, peppers, cabbage, kale, and onions; garlic; and spicy foods. So our suggestion is simple: if you've been eating these foods, try eliminating them from your diet for at least seven days to see if there is any improvement in your baby's temperament.

Second, do you burp your baby sufficiently both during and after feedings? A baby who is not burped well may have swallowed too much air, which can cause considerable discomfort. But it is also true that some babies are just difficult to burp. So here are some techniques for a thorough burping, to be used as a preventive measure or as a remedy:

1. Always stop halfway through a feed to burp your baby. Be sure to burp her at the end of each feeding as well.
2. If it is difficult to get your baby to burp, get up from your chair and sit down again. Or carry your baby up and down a flight of stairs a few times. These brisk movements may just do the trick.
3. If your baby is formula fed, or if you give her breast milk in a bottle, replace her bottles with disposable-bag bottles. (We give the Nanny Seal of Approval to the Playtex brand.) These have a disposable liner bag inside the bottle, so once you fill the bag with milk, all the air is squeezed out. This helps prevent gas and discomfort.

As for the traditional "nannies' solution" for baby's gas or colic, here it is: gripe water. This has been used by nannies for more than a century, and it couldn't be simpler: it's just a combination of fennel and ginger delivered to the baby in a dropper before or after a feeding. You can buy gripe water in pharmacies, or look for it online—try http://www.babys-bliss.com/—and we recommend it; it can really ease a baby's discomfort.

Finally, of course, if you are concerned about your baby's fussiness, gas, or colic, do not hesitate to contact your pediatrician for a professional opinion.

Swaddling Newborns

Since newborns can wake themselves up through their own sleep movements, swaddling can be useful for putting newborns to sleep and helping them stay asleep. It should only be used with babies up to four or five weeks old, however. For some information on how to swaddle a baby, go to http://www.babycenter.com.

Sleeping

You know the expression "sleeping like a baby"? Well, the truth is that young babies don't always sleep very well—or for very long. Getting a baby to go to sleep and stay asleep is one of the biggest issues parents face. We are asked over and over: How do I get my baby to sleep? When will my baby sleep through the night? Why doesn't she sleep for very long?

And of course parents who are themselves sleep deprived tend to do anything they possibly can to get their baby to sleep. In the end, they can spend hours rocking, feeding, or walking the baby around the block to induce sleep. They simply do not know how to get their baby to go to sleep independently, and they worry that if they put the baby down while he is awake, he may feel anxious and begin to cry.

But here is the bottom line about putting babies to sleep: babies learn what you teach them. If you teach them not to like the crib, they won't. If you become anxious when you want your baby to go to sleep, your baby will become anxious too. In other words, what you do now, while your baby is new to the world, will set precedents for a long time to come, so this is the time to teach healthy sleep habits.

What do we mean by healthy sleep habits? A baby who can go to sleep without excessive feeding, rocking, or constant motion, who is content in her crib by herself, who wakes up in the night but knows how to put herself back to sleep, or who requires only that you go in and reassure her with a pat on the back and a kiss, is a baby with healthy sleep habits. When babies have learned good, healthy sleep habits, bedtimes are calm times that both you and your child can enjoy. What's more, babies with healthy sleep habits go on to become happy, well-rested toddlers and preschoolers who feel comfortable and secure when they go to sleep, and are less likely to have sleep issues in the future.

The other side of the coin, of course, is the wrong kind of sleep associations. Constant rocking or feeding, or driving the baby around the block so that he will fall asleep are habits that will eventually require difficult measures to remedy. These measures include controlled-crying methods, so that babies can learn how to go to sleep independently. In our experience, controlled-crying methods are not necessary if good sleep habits are taught early on.

Sleeping Positions

The recommended sleeping position for babies is on their back—never on their tummies, which raises the risk of sudden infant death syndrome, or SIDS. A prop-a-baby sleeping wedge is very useful in maintaining the recommended sleeping positions for young babies. Check out the Nanny Seal of Approval list (page 72) for prop-a-baby recommendations.

"Early on" means before your baby is three or four months old: that's when the good sleep habits need to be taught. Doing so takes commitment, time, and effort, and requires both consistency and persistence. But the return on this investment will be well worth it—for both you and your child.

Dormez Bien

I HAD BEEN LOOKING FOR a new adventure when I boarded the ferry and crossed the English Channel from Dover to Calais—but my new charge's sleep problems weren't exactly what I had in mind. I had just turned twenty-five, and my exciting new nanny position caring for eleven-month-old Eva was taking me to Brittany, on the northern coast of France. The family lived in a charming old French mansion that had been in their family for years. I was happy to have my own accommodations, an old cottage that had been the groundskeeper's house in years gone by.

Eva was a delight, and her parents were great to work for, so all in all I was thrilled with my new life and job. The one fly in the ointment, however, was that Eva was one of the trickiest sleepers I had ever come across. No wonder her parents were completely sleep deprived: the only way Eva would fall asleep was to be pushed around the house in her stroller for as long as forty minutes. Once she was asleep, the challenge was to remove her from the stroller very carefully, place her in her crib, and tiptoe away without waking her. If Eva did wake up—and she tended to wake up several times a night—this whole process would have to be repeated from start to finish.

Her parents were desperate to make a change, so I suggested a sleep plan I had used before, which involved a structured day, baby bedtime rituals, and the controlled-crying method. The idea was to teach Eva how to fall asleep by herself in her crib, how to put herself back to sleep if she woke, and how to sleep through the night. I knew we could change Eva's sleep habits, but I also knew it would be a challenge.

The next day, when Eva's parents were at work, I put my sleep plan into action. We had a calm, structured day at home, and when it was time for her nap, I popped Eva

What does it take to teach your baby healthy sleep habits? There are six basic steps:

1. Find the right place for your baby to sleep.
2. Teach your baby the difference between night and day.
3. Introduce baby bedtime rituals.
4. Put your baby to bed while he's still awake.
5. Establish a regular sleep schedule.

into her crib instead of putting her into her stroller. I used my baby bedtime rituals. I put her special blanket in her hand, turned on some quiet, soothing music, gave her a big kiss and cuddle, and left the room. After a few minutes, she began to protest, so I returned to her room and patted her on the back to reassure her that everything was all right. I did not pick her up. I retrieved her special blanket and placed it back in her hand once more. It was really hard to listen to Eva crying, but I knew it wouldn't last long and that soon she would be going to bed happily.

I kept this up, going back into her room to reassure her at intervals, but making each interval between my visits longer than the last. After half an hour, she finally dropped off to sleep. I peeked into her room and saw her sleeping peacefully. I was thrilled by this breakthrough: Eva had gone to sleep in her crib for the first time. I knew it was going to take several more days of consistent effort from all of us, but I also knew it wouldn't take long until Eva could put herself to sleep and feel content in her crib.

Eva's parents were overjoyed—and they were committed. That's what made it possible for us to persevere for the next week, which is how long it took before the old habits were broken and Eva was going to sleep independently and sleeping soundly through the night.

The only skeptic in the household was the housekeeper. She was never convinced, and she let me know what she thought of my methods by "losing" the English tea my family had sent over from home, by seeing to it that my sweaters came back from the laundry with buttons missing, and by leaving open all the windows in my lovely cottage in the middle of winter. My perfect job in France definitely had its quirks, but Eva had learned to sleep independently—and I was there to stay.

6. Get your baby to sleep through the night.
   Let's go through them one at a time.

1. Find the right place for your baby to sleep.
These days, there seems to be a fair amount of pressure on parents to co-sleep with their children. This is a personal decision, so our advice is to go with your own instincts and to do what suits you and your family best.

We remind parents who choose to co-sleep with their baby that they need to be aware they may face resistance when they eventually move the baby out of their bed. For one thing, the baby will be unaccustomed to sleeping alone. For another, he will not know how to put himself to sleep. So we recommend that parents who share their bed with their baby put the baby in his crib or bassinet for at least one nap a day; then, when he makes the nighttime transition to the crib, it won't be a completely new or shocking experience for him.

If you choose not to co-sleep, putting your baby in a crib or bassinet next to your bed for the first two or three months can work beautifully: the baby will be close to you for feeding during the night, and he will get used to sleeping in the bassinet and easily go on to a crib. You can still bring him into your bed for morning snuggles and the occasional nap without affecting his newly forming sleep habits.

2. Teach your baby the difference between night and day.

Since a baby doesn't know the difference between night and day, it's important to create an environment that helps make the distinction. Make sure your baby's nighttime sleep environment is dark and quiet, so that she gets the message that nighttime is not a time for activity. Invest in some curtains that block out light and will encourage the baby to sleep well. Use a dim light when feeding your baby at night instead of a bright overhead light. As much as possible, avoid playing, talking, or stimulation at night.

It's not uncommon for parents to play with their baby in the middle of the night—especially parents who have been at work all day—but this can become a habit that teaches the baby to wake up when she should be sleeping, and this habit can be very difficult to undo. So try to keep playtime and stimulation for the daytime only, and make nighttime a time of quiet and rest. In fact, unless the baby's diaper is wet or soiled, don't change it during the night, as doing so may wake her up fully.

3. Introduce baby bedtime rituals.

Baby bedtime rituals signal to babies that it is sleep time. They are simple procedures that you do the same way every time—and that you do persistently. Turning on the mobile over the crib before you leave the room, stroking your baby's forehead, saying "good night" in the same voice every night, night after night: all of these rituals add to your baby's sense of familiarity and security.

"What's the point in starting rituals now?" new parents often ask us; "my baby is too young to remember what she did yesterday." Yet the fact is that when rituals are repeated day after day, even very young babies come to expect them; the rituals tell the baby that something familiar is happening, and they alert the baby to what's coming next.

Introduce one ritual at a time, and keep adding to them as your baby gets older. Do them at the same time each day and in the same way. In our view, baths are the perfect ritual to start off with; a warm, relaxing bath at the same time each night helps signal nighttime and sleep time to your baby. Once a regular bath time is established, you can begin to add rituals to it: a massage after the bath, a song as you get the baby dressed for bed, gently placing him in his crib, then the addition of some soothing music, the spin of the mobile, and finally the kiss good night and your farewell words of "sweet dreams" or "night night"—the same rituals night after night. Such easy sleep-based rituals signal bedtime to your child.

4. Put your baby to sleep while he's still awake.

This is really the heart of healthy sleep habits. A newborn may nod off while he is on the breast or bottle, while you are taking him for a walk in his stroller, or while you have him in a sling or Baby Björn. That's all fine at first; these are not likely to become fixed sleep habits while your baby is still very young. As he gets older, however, pay attention to how he falls asleep. The reason? Even as early as eight weeks, a repeated method like rocking a baby to sleep becomes an association on which he becomes reliant. Soon, he won't fall asleep without it.

The best way to teach your baby to fall asleep independently, whenever possible, is to put him down to sleep while he's awake or drowsy. During the day, put him under a baby gym or in a baby bouncer while you are nearby; that way, he can sense your nearness and you can occupy yourself with a task—like cooking a meal. You will be sufficiently distracted from trying to help him get to sleep, and he will nod off by himself.

In the evening, make use of the aforementioned rituals: at bedtime, place the baby in his crib awake or drowsy, kiss him good night, pat his back, and speak softly. Then leave.

Or, at the very least, move away from the crib area; if you want to stay in the baby's room to assure yourself that he is fine and can settle himself, by all means go ahead. After all, this is not an exercise in making you feel anxious, so just stay there until you're sufficiently comfortable. Alternatively, you can leave the room and listen in on the baby monitor.

Either way, if the baby cries or fusses a little, stay relaxed, and stay where you are. It is very common for babies to fuss a little before they go to sleep; in fact, many children reject or fight sleep when they are tired, so there is no need to rush over to his crib if he is resisting a little. He is simply learning how to settle himself, and the best thing you can do for him is to give him the chance to drift off to sleep on his own.

 Pacifiers and Bottles as Sleep Aids

Pacifiers and bottles can play a role in helping very young babies get to sleep, but in the long run, their use can cause problems. When babies who rely on these sleep aids wake up in the middle of the night, they cannot get back to sleep without them. That means the parents are in and out of the baby's room time after time during the night replacing the bottle or pacifier. Later, when these children have to give up the pacifier or bottle, it can be very traumatic for them; we have seen four-year-olds who are still dependent on these sleep aids—just because it's too difficult to break them of the habit. In addition, bottles of milk at bedtime can lead to tooth decay, and excessive use of pacifiers and bottles can make growing teeth protrude.

If he continues to fuss, go ahead and reassure yourself that he is okay, pat his back for a few minutes, then leave his side again. You may need to do this a few times until he settles down, but it won't take long. If your baby has been fed and burped and if he has a clean diaper, there is no reason to worry.

When an Older Baby Wakes in the Night

The fact that a baby has learned to sleep through the night doesn't mean he won't one day begin to wake up again during the night. This waking is usually just a phase, and it will end soon enough if it's dealt with correctly. If it should happen that your baby wakes up crying in the night and nothing is amiss, go into his room, just pat him on the back to reassure him, and leave the room. Keep the lights off and do not engage in conversation. Do not pick him up. If you do, he could be up for the next few hours and will be more likely to wake up the next night, creating new patterns that are hard to break.

Hunger is almost surely not the cause of the waking. Instead, the baby has reached a wakeful moment in his natural sleep cycle and just needs some time to settle back to sleep.

However, if your child is sick or teething, he will need extra comforting, and you may need to stay with him until he settles back to sleep. Once the sickness is over, go back to your established approach.

It may take a few weeks—it may only take a few days—to establish these sleep patterns, but once you do, and once you combine them with a regular sleep schedule, you will have given your baby a big bonus: the ability to go to sleep by himself. Once the sleep schedule has been introduced, your baby will easily adapt to it. He will feel safe and secure in his crib or bassinet and will sleep more soundly now and in the future.

5. Establish a regular sleep schedule.

A baby on a regular sleep schedule will be less likely to fuss or to reject sleep. He won't be surprised when you pop him in his crib or bassinet; he'll "recognize" that it is his regular nap time or bedtime. But when should you start introducing a basic sleep schedule?

You can start when the baby is quite young. Granted, the sleep of newborns is scattered and variable, so while you may want to put a very young baby on a sleep schedule, it's usually a good idea to wait till the baby is about six weeks old. Use your intuition. If you've tried to impose

The Circle of Sleep

I BECAME KITTY'S NANNY when she was five months old. At that time, she had no regular daily schedule, and her sleep habits were all over the place. During the day she napped in the car, under her baby gym, or in her stroller, and each nap was at a different time every day. She usually napped for only twenty minutes, and when she woke, she wouldn't go back to sleep for at least another four hours. Once or twice a week she would sleep for two hours late in the afternoon and would be awake until at least 10:30 or 11:00 on those nights. At night she did sleep in her crib but was unsettled and woke many times. As a result, Kitty was often very fussy and overtired during the day. Although she was able to put herself to sleep independently, it was clear that she needed a regular sleep schedule to ensure sounder sleep, and for longer periods of time.

I explained to Kitty's parents my "circle of sleep" theory, which I had put into practice with many children before. A child that has regular daily naps will sleep more soundly at night, and solid nighttime sleep will lead to better daytime napping.

I began with the sleep schedule by first introducing an age-appropriate regular bedtime at night. I made sure that Kitty woke from her nap by four o'clock so she would be ready to go to sleep around seven. The first evening, after Kitty's bath, I began my baby bedtime rituals: I put her down in her crib, stroked her forehead between her eyebrows, and turned on her musical mobile. I left the room so Kitty could settle by herself as she usually did. Kitty now had a regular bedtime, and she would go to bed each night at the same time.

The next day the real work began. Once Kitty had been awake for two and a half hours, I put her down in her crib for what would become her regular morning nap time. I repeated my baby bedtime rituals and allowed Kitty to settle by herself. Although she slept for only thirty minutes, she had slept in her crib for her nap. I knew once we'd progressed further with the sleep schedule, she would eventually sleep for longer periods. I repeated the whole process again with her afternoon nap, so that now Kitty had two set nap times and a regular bedtime each day.

It took two weeks for Kitty to settle in to her sleep schedule, but once she did, she slept more soundly and for longer. She was less fussy, less tired, and altogether a happier baby.

a schedule and it's not working, let it go for a few weeks and try again when your baby is a little older.

By three months of age, if your baby is not on a basic sleep schedule, it is definitely time to think about introducing one. Her erratic twenty-four-hour schedule can now be turned into a more sociable and practical one closer to that of the whole family, allowing both parent and child more rest and greater consistency in their day. Regular napping is also the key to a good sleep schedule; a baby who doesn't nap well or at regular times during the day won't sleep well at night.

Background Noise

Do make sure that your sleeping baby gets used to some background noise. Otherwise, the slightest sound will wake him, and you will find yourself becoming a nervous wreck every time the phone rings or the dog barks.

To help teach him to sleep through background noise, do not tiptoe around him while he is sleeping, and do play some soft music—just loud enough for background noise. If there's conversation going on or if the television is on, it's fine; he'll stay asleep. If the doorbell rings during his nap, don't freak out; he'll get used to it, and soon the doorbell won't wake him at all.

Once you've decided you're going to introduce a regular sleep schedule, how should you go about it? Here are our four steps:

1. Establish a regular bedtime and lead up to it each night with the same routine—for example, a bath and a bedtime ritual.

2. Once your baby is happy in his bed, establish a regular morning nap time at home—typically, after a feed, or once he has been awake for two to three hours. At first, he may only sleep for twenty or thirty minutes, but the length of the nap will increase as the weeks go by. Do not attempt to put your baby down for a nap if he is screaming or very upset, however. To maintain calm, *for the first few times*, use a pacifier. If the baby spits the pacifier out once he is asleep, do not put it back in his

mouth; let him sleep without it. Here, the pacifier is a tool for relaxing the baby and keeping him calm while he gets accustomed to sleeping in his crib at regular times.

3. Once the morning nap time is established, add a regular afternoon nap time using the same approach.

4. Don't rush in too soon if your baby wakes up from a nap or in the middle of the night. Give him a chance to put himself back to sleep. A baby who goes down for naps awake has learned how to fall asleep independently, and will go to sleep at night more easily, will sleep for longer periods of time, and will know how to put himself back to sleep if he wakes—either during a nap or in the middle of the night.

Once you have followed these steps *consistently* for a minimum of three to four weeks, your baby should be on a regular sleep schedule. He should now go to bed while he is still awake in his crib—independently.

Eventually, your daily routine will include a feeding schedule, regular morning and afternoon activities, regular nap times, bedtime rituals, a regular bath time, and a regular bedtime. Once your schedule is well established, you will be able to be flexible when you need to be.

Sample Sleep Schedule   The table below is a sleep schedule for babies ages three to twelve months. We know it works because we've used it often in the past, but it is intended only as a guide. You may need to adjust it to suit your baby and your family's life.

AGE	WAKE-UP	NAP	NAP	NAP	BATH	BED	WAKE-UP FOR LAST FEED	WAKE-UP FOR NIGHT FEED
3–4 MONTHS		8–9 A.M. (1–1½ hours)	12:30 P.M. (1–2 hours)	Optional: short nap 4:30–5 P.M.			10:30–11 P.M.	2 A.M. (maybe)
4–6 MONTHS	5–7 A.M.	8–9 A.M. (1–2 hours)	12–1 P.M. (1–2 hours)		6 P.M.	7 P.M.	10:30–11 P.M. (maybe)	
6–12 MONTHS		9 A.M. (1–2 hours)	1:30 P.M. (1–2 hours)	N/A			N/A	N/A

6. Get your baby to sleep through the night.

"When will my baby sleep through the night?" is a common question from new parents. Every baby is different, and every baby sleeps through the night at a different age. Typically, babies sleep through the night once their birth weight has doubled, or anywhere between four and six months of age. In our experience, breast-fed babies usually sleep through the night later than bottle-fed babies because formula is more filling than breast milk. If, out of the blue, your baby suddenly sleeps through one whole night, it can be a sign he is ready to sleep through the night from now on. Usually, however, it is parents who make this happen.

The first thing to do is to make sure your baby is eating well and at regular times during the day. You are going to be cutting back on night feedings, so it's important that most of your baby's feeds are during the day. Cut back on his feeds one at a time and according to the recommended milk requirements for his age and weight. A bottle-fed baby shouldn't need to feed during the night past the age of five months, and a breast-fed baby shouldn't need to feed during the night past the age of six months. Often, giving a breast-fed baby a bottle of formula for his last feed may help lengthen his nighttime sleep.

If your baby is still waking to feed after the age of six months, it is time to drop the middle-of-the-night feeds. At this point, a healthy baby that feeds well during the day is only waking out of habit, not out of hunger. To drop the middle-of-the-night feedings, we recommend offering boiled cooled water instead of milk during the night; after a few nights of being offered just water, the baby usually stops waking up and begins to sleep through the night. However, we have cared for one or two babies who kept waking up to drink water in the middle of the night; if this happens, the only solution is not to offer the baby a drink. If the baby continues to wake up anyway, just go in his room, pat him on the back for a minute or two, then leave the room. You may have to go back a few times, but slowly increase the intervals of time before you do. It may take up to ten nights for the baby to stop waking up and start sleeping through the night.

Many of the babies we have cared for have begun to sleep through the night once solid food has been introduced. This isn't so much because the

Baby Items

For Feeding:

- Baby's Bliss Gripe Water
- Fisher-Price booster seats
- Graco clip-on chairs
- My Breast Friend cushions
- Playtex disposable-bag bottles or Avent bottles
- Prima Papa or Fisher-Price high chairs

For Sleeping:

- Bowron sheepskin (in bed, or for baby to lie on)
- Fisher-Price Sounds 'n Lights baby monitors
- Sassy Prop-a-Baby sleeping wedges for back sleeping
- 7am Concepts sleeping bags for strollers

For Getting Around:

- Baby Björn baby carriers
- Britax car seats
- Graco combination stroller–car seat
- Graco portable travel cribs
- Maclaren or Silver Cross strollers
- Parenting Concepts slings
- Petunia Pickle Bottom diaper bags

For Development and Play:

- Boppy Donut cushions (for babies learning to sit up)
- Fisher-Price or Graco baby bouncer chairs
- Fisher-Price baby gyms and stroller toys
- Sassy teethers

For Bath Time:

- Mustela or Burt's Bees baby bath products

Nanny
Seal of
Approval

solid food fills them up. Rather, it's because the introduction of solid foods takes place at a time when everything is coming together—the baby is on a regular eating schedule, is going to sleep independently, and has been placed on a regular sleeping schedule. Together, these things create a structure that makes life with baby easier, smoother, and more comfortable for all.

The First Year of Life

★ Relax. Take it slowly; allow yourself time to adjust. Get to know your baby.

★ Establish a feeding schedule.

★ Establish a sleeping schedule.

★ Wean with fresh food.

★ Start as you mean to go on: set up good habits in the first year of life.

Nanny Recipes

Weaning
Stage One: Four to Six Months

BABY RICE AND ZUCCHINI

1 baby serving

There are many myths about what to feed babies. One Irish grandmother I knew insisted that babies should have a dash of Guinness in their evening bottles. Another well-known belief is that filling a baby's bottle with a mixture of baby cereal and formula will prepare the baby for solid foods and help him sleep longer. Thankfully, following these myths and old wives' tales is chiefly a thing of the past. Instead, follow this recipe for the perfect starter meal, once your baby has accepted baby rice. It has a mild flavor, and the zucchini is rich in carotene, potassium, and vitamins A and B.

> ¼ zucchini, cut into slices
> 3 tablespoons milk (formula or breast)
> 2 tablespoons baby rice

Steam the zucchini for 3 minutes or cook in a small amount of water until soft.

Heat the milk until warm, mix with the baby rice.

Puree the cooked zucchini in a blender (use a teaspoon of the zucchini water to aid blending if needed); the consistency of the zucchini should be very fine.

Mix the zucchini into the rice mixture.

Allow to cool to room temperature and serve.

NURSERY PUREE

8 baby servings

This puree combination is a favorite with young babies; they love the sweet taste of butternut squash. The squash is great to combine with a new, possibly bitter vegetable—like broccoli—as it sweetens and mellows out the tart taste of the vegetable. This recipe is perfect for the ice cube method.

> *1 medium potato, peeled and chopped into small pieces*
> *1 cup butternut squash, peeled and chopped into small pieces*
> *1 head broccoli, washed and chopped into small pieces*
> *Optional: 1–2 tablespoons vegetable liquid for pureeing*

Place the potato and squash in a small saucepan. Cover with water and a lid, bring to a boil, then turn the heat to medium and cook for 10 minutes. After 10 minutes add the broccoli and continue to cook until the vegetables are soft. Or, steam the potato and squash together and place the broccoli in the steamer 10 minutes before the end.

Once cooked, combine all ingredients together with some of the liquid, puree, and serve.

HENRY'S AVOCADO AND BANANA

1 baby serving

Henry was six months old when I began caring for him. At our first meal together, I offered him a dish of homemade vegetables and baby rice. He took one mouthful and immediately spat it out. I learned from Henry's mother that his solid-food diet had consisted only of baby food from a jar, so he was not used to the flavor and texture of fresh foods. Henry's parents became enthusiastic about switching his diet from commercial baby food to homemade fresh food, however, and eventually, Henry did too. My recipe for avocado and banana soon became his favorite meal.

> *2 tablespoons avocado, mashed with a fork*
> *¼ banana, mashed with a fork*
> *1 teaspoon milk (breast or formula)*

Put all three ingredients into a bowl, mash together with a fork, and serve.

Stage Two: Six to Nine Months

NANNIES' CHICKEN DINNER

8 baby servings (2 adult servings)

Once your baby is six months old, you can begin to add many more foods to his diet. The best meat to introduce first is chicken; it has a bland taste and is easy to digest—perfect for a young baby. I have recommended this recipe to many parents who were having trouble getting their baby to eat solid foods; for several this was the turnaround meal, the one where their babies really began to enjoy eating solid foods.

> 1 small onion, sliced
> 2 tablespoons olive oil or butter
> 1 large carrot, peeled and chopped
> 1 leek, sliced
> 2 celery sticks, sliced
> 1 boneless, skinless chicken cutlet, sliced into long strips
> 4 cups chicken stock (homemade or organic)
> 1–2 cups water
> 1 bay leaf
> 1 sweet potato, cut into cubes
> 1 white potato, cut into cubes
> Handful fresh parsley or chives, finely chopped

Sauté the onion in oil or butter in a medium-sized pan until soft; add the carrot, leek, and celery, and cook covered for 3 minutes.

Add the chicken breast and sauté for 3 minutes over medium heat.

Add all the remaining ingredients. Make sure the liquid covers the ingredients, and add water if necessary.

Bring to a fast simmer, then reduce heat and simmer partially covered for 30 minutes, or until vegetables are tender.

Discard the bay leaf, and puree the chicken mixture in a blender; there's no need to blend for older babies.

Note: Freeze any leftovers.

JACK'S CAULIFLOWER CHEESE

8 baby servings (2 adult servings)

When Jack was seven months old, I would hold a weekly gathering of babies and nannies at his house for lunch and playtime. I would serve this delicious recipe of cauliflower cheese to the babies—it was always a real favorite with them. Full of flavor and rich in calcium, it is very simple to make. You can begin to use cow's milk in cooking once the baby is six months old.

> 1½ cups cauliflower, washed and cut into pieces
> 3 tablespoons butter
> 2 tablespoons flour
> 1 cup whole milk
> ½ cup grated cheese (mild cheddar or Monterey Jack)

Steam or boil the cauliflower for 5–8 minutes, or until tender.

Melt the butter on low heat in a heavy saucepan.

Once the butter has melted, take the pan off the flame and add the flour; mix to a smooth paste using a wooden spoon.

Return the pan to a low flame and cook the flour mixture, stirring continuously, for 1–2 minutes. Gradually add the milk, stirring to prevent lumps, until the mixture begins to simmer and thicken. Note: you can use a hand whisk to prevent lumps from forming, although I prefer a wooden spoon.

Remove from heat, add the grated cheese to the sauce, and pour the sauce over the cooked cauliflower.

Serve pureed or chunky.

NANNIES' NURSERY FISH PIE

Nursery fish pie is a classic recipe that English nannies have been cooking for hundreds of years. Many generations of British babies had their first taste of fish with this heavenly dish. Creamy fish and soothing mashed potato—your baby will gobble it down, and you will love it too.

When serving this dish to a young baby, there is no need to bake it: just puree and serve. The rest of the family will enjoy it cooked the traditional way, baked until golden brown. Another option is to place baby portions of the fish pie in ovenproof ramekins, cover them with foil, and freeze them for a later date. When you're ready to serve the fish pie, remove the ramekin from the freezer and bake, covered, for 30–45 minutes at 400°F, then puree or mash with a fork if necessary.

POTATO TOPPING
4 Idaho potatoes peeled and cut into cubes
1 tablespoon butter
¼ cup milk

FISH
4 fillets or 1½ lbs white fish—sole or flounder—with the skin and bones removed
1 cup milk

WHITE SAUCE
3 tablespoons butter
2 leeks or 1 onion, chopped very finely
2 tablespoons flour
2 cups milk (you can use some of the fish liquid to make up the 2 cups)
1 cup peas, frozen or cooked fresh
2 tablespoons fresh parsley, chopped finely
½ cup grated cheddar cheese

Preheat oven to 450°F (if baking the fish pie).

Place the potatoes in a medium-sized saucepan and cover with water. Place lid on pan and cook over high heat for 15–20 minutes, or until potatoes are soft. Drain the water, and mash the potatoes with butter and milk until soft and creamy.

Meanwhile, cook the fish. Pour the milk into a medium-sized shallow pan with a lid, turn on low heat, and bring to a simmer. Once the milk is simmering, add the fish, cover, and cook for a few minutes until it is cooked through (it should fall apart easily). Remove the pan from the heat and with a slotted spoon scoop the fish out of the pan onto a plate. Check the fish thoroughly for any fine bones. Do not discard the fish liquid if you are using it for the white sauce.

To make the white sauce, melt 1 tablespoon of butter in a medium-sized saucepan over medium heat, add leeks or onions, and cook until soft. Add the remaining butter, and as it melts add the flour and stir vigorously with a wooden spoon, cooking for about 2 minutes. Slowly pour in the milk, stirring constantly. Add the peas and parsley. Continue to stir until the sauce begins to thicken, and cook until the sauce is very thick, stirring occasionally.

Remove the sauce from the heat and add the fish to the sauce.

If feeding a young baby, combine a portion of fish, sauce, and potato and puree.

If cooking the traditional way, pour the fish sauce mixture into a buttered ovenproof dish and top with the mashed potatoes. Sprinkle the grated cheese on top.

Bake at 450° F for 20–25 minutes, or until browned.

 Nanny Wisdom

"Put my dinner in the fridge!"

This little trick saves me every time I have a hungry, screaming baby on my hands whose dinner is too hot to eat. I put the bowl of food in the fridge or freezer for quick cooling; after a minute or two I give the food a good stir to distribute the heat evenly, and dinner is ready to go. With this simple trick a hungry child will be eating much faster.

DELICIOUS MINESTRONE

8–10 baby servings (4 adult servings)

Eight-month-old Melissa never took well to the transition from pureed food to lumpy food, until I offered her my version of homemade minestrone. She quickly devoured its bite-sized soft pasta and the colorful vegetables, which help make it the perfect transition meal. I like to chop up the ingredients with kitchen scissors. Add extra kidney beans and extra fresh basil, and serve to the entire family as a wholesome lunch with some fresh bread.

> 1 onion, chopped
> 2 cloves garlic, crushed
> 1–2 tablespoons olive oil or butter
> 1 leek, washed and finely sliced
> 1 celery stick, sliced
> 3 carrots, peeled and sliced
> 1 zucchini, sliced
> One 15-ounce can crushed tomatoes
> 5 cups chicken or vegetable stock
> 4 cups water
> ½ cup pasta (shells or fusilli)
> ½ cup fresh parsley, chopped
> ¼ cup fresh basil, chopped finely
> Salt and pepper to taste (for babies older than one year)

Sauté the onion and garlic in olive oil or butter in a large saucepan on medium heat for 2–3 minutes, or until soft, being careful not to burn the garlic.

Add the leeks, celery, carrots, and zucchini, and sauté for a further few minutes.

Add the tomatoes, stock, and water and bring to a boil. Cook over medium heat, partially covered, for 25–30 minutes, or until vegetables are cooked. Add the pasta and fresh herbs and cook, partially covered, for a further 15 minutes, or until pasta is done. Extra water or stock may be added as the pasta soaks up liquid. Season to taste.

GROWING-STRONG SPINACH PASTA

4 baby servings (2 adult servings)

Babies love this simple, tasty dish, and you will love that it's full of vitamins and ready in a snap. The smooth, creamy sauce and delicious spinach make this dish fabulous for all the family to share.

> 6–8 ounces pasta shells or fettuccine
> 1 clove garlic, crushed
> 1½ tablespoons olive oil
> 1 heaping teaspoon flour
> 1 cup cream
> 2 cups baby spinach, finely chopped
> Optional: 1 tablespoon fresh basil
> 2 heaping tablespoons freshly grated Parmesan cheese

Cook pasta as directed on package.

Meanwhile, in a medium-sized saucepan, sauté the garlic in olive oil for 1–2 minutes over medium heat, being careful not to brown the garlic. Sprinkle in the flour, mix well, and cook for another 1–2 minutes.

Reduce the heat to medium low and very slowly pour in the cream; stir continuously until sauce begins to simmer, and cook for 2–4 minutes, or until the sauce has thickened slightly.

Add the spinach and basil (if using) to the sauce and cook for 3 minutes.

Turn the heat off and stir in the Parmesan cheese. Mix the sauce through the pasta and serve.

Season adult portions to taste.

BABY'S SPAGHETTI WITH MEAT SAUCE

8–10 baby servings (4 adults servings)

As a live-in nanny, my weekends were my own, and I would spend most of my time out. One Sunday afternoon, however, I popped my head into the kitchen to say hi to my boss. She was feeding nine-month-old Jake and looking very distressed. "What's wrong?" I asked her. "Jake will never eat more than three mouthfuls of food," she said. "What am I doing wrong?" I explained to her that whenever I fed Jake his meals, I always ate my meal at the same time; Jake would become excited when he saw me eating, and he would often mimic me. Sharing meals with Jake, in fact, took the focus away from him, and he would often even try to feed himself. From that day on, my boss made sure Jake shared meals with the whole family.

> 1 pound spaghetti
> 1 small red onion, chopped very finely
> 2 cloves garlic, crushed
> 2–3 tablespoons olive oil
> 1 pound ground beef
> One 28-ounce can Italian whole tomatoes
> 2 medium-sized carrots, peeled and finely chopped
> ½ zucchini, finely chopped
> ¼ cup fresh basil, finely chopped
> Parmesan cheese to serve

Cook spaghetti as directed on package.

In a medium-sized saucepan, sauté the onion and garlic in the olive oil over medium heat for 5–6 minutes, or until the onion is soft. Stir to prevent the garlic from burning.

Add the beef and cook until browned, about 8 minutes. Add the tomatoes and stir to combine. Add the carrots, cover, and cook sauce over medium heat for 15–20 minutes. Stir occasionally.

When the sauce has thickened and the carrots have cooked through, stir in the zucchini and basil and cook for five more minutes.

Serve over spaghetti, and sprinkle freshly grated Parmesan cheese on top.

Season adult portions with salt and pepper.

Stage Three: Nine to Twelve Months

RATATOUILLE

4 adult servings

I learned to cook this recipe while working as a nanny in France and caring for four-year-old Madeleine and eleven-month-old André. To collect all the ingredients for the meal, the three of us would head to the local market and walk around, squeezing the ripe tomatoes and picking out the best eggplant we could find. Madeleine and André enjoyed smelling the fragrant bunches of fresh oregano and basil; Madeleine would choose the herbs and carry them home in her very own basket. When we returned home, Madeleine and I would prepare this dish while André was taking his nap. Later, the whole family would share this delicious French vegetable stew accompanied by some rice, chicken, and a fresh, crunchy baguette.

> *1 onion, chopped*
> *2 cloves garlic, sliced or crushed*
> *2 tablespoons olive oil*
> *1 medium-sized eggplant cut in small pieces, or 2–3 small eggplants, sliced*
> *Salt and pepper (for babies older than a year)*
> *1 medium-sized zucchini, sliced*
> *1–2 peppers, preferably red, orange, or yellow, sliced*
> *One 28-ounce can whole tomatoes*
> *2 cups water*
> *1 tablespoon dried or fresh oregano*
> *Handful of fresh basil*

Sauté the onion and garlic in oil in a large pan for 3–5 minutes until soft. Stir to prevent the garlic from burning.

Add the eggplant and sauté for a few more minutes. Add all the remaining ingredients except the basil and bring to a boil. Cook partially covered over medium heat for 45 minutes to an hour, or until eggplant is tender and no longer tough. Add some extra water to the pan during cooking time if the vegetables soak up the liquid.

Add fresh basil, stir, and serve.

ORION'S LEMON SALMON

2 adult servings

When Orion was a young baby, he never really enjoyed eating pureed food. To my surprise, once I began to cook him unpureed foods, he took to eating with a passion. He soon ate everything he was served, and he would happily try new foods. When he was just about a year old, we went to a restaurant with outdoor seating where we shared a plate of grilled salmon, roast potatoes, and asparagus. Orion amazed the passers-by; many stopped to comment how great it was to see a child so young enjoy such "sophisticated" food. It reconfirmed for me that providing fresh food from the beginning of a child's life pays off, setting up a lifetime of good eating habits. Salmon is still one of Orion's favorite foods.

> *Two 2–4-ounce fillets of fresh salmon, skin and bones removed*
> *½ lemon, juiced*
> *Optional: 1 teaspoon fresh parsley or dill*
> *Pinch of salt and pepper (for babies older than a year)*

Preheat oven to 450°F.

Place the salmon on a large piece of foil in a baking dish, with the lemon and herbs on top. Wrap the salmon in the foil and seal it tightly like a parcel.

Bake for 15–20 minutes or until cooked through.

Serve with Creamy Lemon Sauce, potatoes or couscous, and vegetables.

> ### CREAMY LEMON SAUCE
> *1 tablespoon butter*
> *½ cup heavy cream*
> *Lemon juice to taste*
> *Optional: 1 teaspoon fresh parsley or dill*
> *Salt and pepper*

Melt butter in a small saucepan over medium heat. Reduce heat to low and whisk in cream, stirring continuously for 4–5 minutes, or until sauce has thickened.

Remove from heat and add lemon juice, herbs, and salt and pepper (if using). Stir and serve.

MY FIRST DAHL

2 adult servings

Dahl, the lentil dish that is a staple of the Indian diet, became a staple of my diet as well while I was traveling around India for three months. When I got back to my nanny job in London, I was inspired to cook it myself. I was looking after eleven-month-old Rebecca at the time, and this became her favorite meal—something she liked to have at least once a week. It is packed with protein, and it also introduces young babies to subtle spicy flavors. I add just a little ground cumin and coriander—flavorful spices, yet not too overpowering for a baby. Dahl freezes very well.

1 cup rice, brown or white basmati
1 small onion, finely chopped
1 clove garlic, crushed or finely chopped
1 teaspoon ground coriander
1 teaspoon ground cumin
2 medium carrots, chopped into small pieces
1–2 tablespoons olive oil or butter
2 cups vegetable or chicken stock
1 cup red lentils

Start to cook the rice, as directed on package (brown rice can take 40–50 minutes to cook).

In a medium-sized saucepan, sauté the onion, garlic, spices, and carrots in oil or butter for 3–5 minutes, over medium heat.

Add the stock and lentils; bring to a boil.

Reduce heat and simmer, uncovered, for about 45 minutes, or until mixture becomes thick and lentils are soft.

Season adult portions with salt and pepper. Serve with rice.

Chapter Three

The Scheduled Routine

Child Care Made Easy

I t is a typical weekday morning in London, and in parks all across the city, English nannies are exchanging stories, child-care secrets, and gossip as they watch over their charges. Kids chase each other noisily around the circle of nannies or whiz down slides squealing with delight. Nannies soothe babies to sleep, gently kiss away toddler scrapes and bruises, offer a cuddle or reassuring word where needed, and encourage sharing and kindness. It's a busy scene, one that radiates the wonderful noise and energy of happy children at play.

Then, virtually on the dot of noon, the parks begin to empty. By 12:10, the playgrounds are completely deserted. The reason is simple: the nannies have taken their children home for a hearty lunch. By 1:30, all across London, virtually every child under the age of three and in a nanny's care is tucked up in bed for his or her afternoon nap. And that's the way it is every day.

Creating a routine and putting it on a schedule: it is the classic formula that has been practiced by English nannies for centuries. The scheduled routine ensures that children will be well rested and content, and it is the key to keeping households running smoothly. When children have a regular routine, their needs are easily met, life is as stress free as possible for everyone, and everyday challenges are more manageable.

Today, the scheduled routine is still at the heart of the English nanny tradition. It's the formula that enables us to be organized, loving, and patient. In fact, it's the foundation of successful child care.

What do we mean when we talk about routine and schedule? By "routine," we mean the organization of the key elements of a child's day every day: waking up, eating, napping, playing and doing other activities, bathing, going to bed. By "schedule," we mean the planned times when those things should occur, give or take thirty minutes or so. Creating a routine and putting it on a schedule are not only important for a child's well-being and valuable for a pleasant family life; in our view, they're the key to raising a contented, well-behaved, independent child.

The scheduled routine is good for children because they thrive on consistency and structure and yearn for stability. You often hear young children asking "Where are we going today?" or "What am I doing next?" Max, aged two, offers a perfect illustration of this need to know, this yearning for structure and stability. His mother works three days a week, and each night when she tucks him into bed, he asks her whether she is going to wear jeans or a skirt the next day. If the answer is "jeans," he knows she is staying home, and if it's "a skirt," he knows she is going to work. He is happy either way, but he wants to know at night what to expect the next day. Knowing what is coming makes children feel safe and secure.

Structure does this; it rationalizes and clarifies what is otherwise just aimless chaos in the perspective of small children. After all, they do not control their world, and if they never know when it's time to eat or sleep or play or be still, the world can be confusing and unsettling. The consistency and structure of a scheduled routine ensure that kids know what to expect and what is expected of them. It anticipates kids' needs: when they are on a schedule, kids get enough sleep, have regular mealtimes, and receive recognizable signals about what is coming next.

Parents' lives, too, are dramatically improved when kids have consistent routine. Precisely because it lets children know their boundaries, the scheduled routine is a parent's basic support system. Suppose your child's established morning routine allots playtime *after* he is dressed and ready for school. That means that on a morning when you find him engrossed in a game while he is still in his pj's, all you need to do is remind him of his regular morning routine. "Sweetie, you know what we do every morning: first you get ready for school, *then* you play games." You don't need to issue a lengthy explanation; all you have to do is restate the standard routine. He will understand, and chances are he will run off to get ready for school on just that single reminder.

Parents who contend that schedules are "old-fashioned" or who think life would be easier if the children were on the same schedule as the adults in the family are laboring under a misapprehension. It is the reliably consistent kids' routine that liberates parents. Are your kids throwing tantrums or squabbling with each other? When they're on a scheduled routine, there's light at the end of the tunnel: you know you will get a break when they are put down for a nap at one o'clock or when they go to bed at seven. With a scheduled routine, you can actually plan activities for yourself, relax when the kids are napping, and look forward to evenings and some grown-up conversation because the kids are tucked in bed at a regular bedtime.

Good for your kids, good for you: the scheduled routine is the foundation of child raising and of a pleasant and peaceful family life. In this chapter, we tell you how to create the right routine for your family and put it on a workable schedule that will benefit both your children and you.

Repetition: The Heart of Routine

I had agreed to look after my friend Sharon's three-year-old and eighteen-month-old boys, and we had arranged to meet for lunch, after which I would take over. "What is the boys' routine for the rest of the day?" I asked Sharon.

"Well, they eat their dinner at 5:30. After that, they have a bath together, get into their pajamas, read two stories, and are in bed and asleep by 7:15."

Setting Precedents

Because kids easily cling onto any repetition, you must be sure that the routines you establish are a help and not a hindrance. If you read your child ten bedtime stories instead of two for three nights in a row, be prepared for her to request ten stories on the next night. At that time, however, you may be too tired or it may be too late to read the ten stories, and you may regret this new addition to your established routine. Before you know it, your child's bedtime routine is no longer effective and bedtimes are pushed back.

During this explanation, I noticed three-year-old Simon listening intently to what his mother was telling me and nodding in agreement. It was clear to me this was a child who was very proud of his daily routine.

"Mom," Simon piped up after Sharon had finished spelling out the routine. "What about our dance after dinner?"

"Oh, yes. I forgot to mention that after dinner we put on some music and dance for a few minutes. They boys love this so much, how could I have forgotten to tell you?"

The rest of the afternoon went like clockwork. The boys knew exactly what to do and what was coming next. We ate dinner at 5:30 as usual, we had our dance around the living room, the boys got out of the bath without protest, and then cuddled up with me on the bed to read their two stories.

When I gave them both a glass of milk, Simon asked me, "Why are we having milk?"

"Mommy asked me to give you milk after your bath," I replied. His puzzled expression made me wonder if I had heard his mother correctly, but I was sure she had told me to give the boys milk after their bath.

When Sharon returned home that night, I asked her about the milk. "I left in such a hurry I guess maybe I wasn't clear," she said. "The boys have milk with their dinner, and water after their bath."

Simon's quick questioning of why things were different demonstrated how well established the family's routine was. Clearly, he relied on the consistency of the routine, and my inadvertent break in the established order of things had puzzled and confused him.

Repetition plays a key role in a child's life and is at the heart of the routine you establish. Maybe it's because kids are going through great developmental change that they find comfort in repetition. Certainly, every parent is well aware that nothing makes a child happier than reading the same book over and over, or using the same bowl at breakfast every morning. In addition, it is through repetition that a child learns such basic skills as putting a puzzle together or drawing a circle. By the same token, the repetition of a routine on a consistent schedule is exactly what a child needs to feel safe and sound.

A Standard Routine on a Consistent Schedule

- Does your family life run as smoothly as you would like it to?
- Do you find yourself constantly stressed and easily frustrated with your kids?
- Are you absolutely exhausted from the everyday work of child care? Do you have downtime during the day and evening?
- Does your child appear to be overly tired? Does he fall asleep at erratic times?
- Does your child have an appetite at mealtimes?
- Does your child have frequent tantrums or meltdowns, especially in the late afternoon?
- Do you frequently have problems getting your kids to do simple, everyday tasks like getting dressed or leaving the house in the morning? Do they reject bath time, bedtime, or mealtimes?

If you answered yes to some or all of these questions, your family's life could probably benefit from the introduction of a standard routine on a consistent schedule. In fact, a scheduled routine may well change your family's life. We've seen it happen many times. And while it's best to create a routine and schedule that work for your family sooner rather than later, it's also true that you can create a scheduled routine at any time—and see it make a difference.

About a year ago, the father of a two-year-old named Beatrice approached us at a party and complained that his daughter was turning the household—and her parents' marriage—upside down with tantrums, crying, refusal to eat, and resistance to sleep.

"Do you think there might be something wrong with Beatrice?" he asked us. "Do you think she might have a behavioral problem or something?"

"Hang on a minute," we cautioned. "First, tell us about her routine and schedule."

"Routine? Schedule?"

"The structure of her day," we explained. "When does she wake up? Nap? Play?"

"It changes every day," said Dad, and while he explained the busy and varied lives he and his wife led, and how they tried to adapt Beatrice to their irregular ways, we scribbled down a simple schedule appropriate for two-year-olds.

"Put this somewhere where both you and your wife can see it," we urged. "Follow it consistently, and please let us know how it's going."

Two weeks later, Dad called to report that they were following the schedule faithfully and were astonished and overjoyed with the positive changes that had occurred: Beatrice's tantrums were fewer and farther between, her appetite was improved, and her spirits were high.

Six months later, he called again—this time to tell us very simply that

The Nannies' Terrific Timer

As you can see again and again in this book, one of our all-time favorite tools for introducing and maintaining a scheduled routine is a simple kitchen timer. If your child negotiates and procrastinates over everyday requests, the timer will be a clear signal that she will easily understand. Set the timer and let your child know she has ten more minutes for play; then it's time to do what needs to be done—leave the house perhaps, or get into the bath, or go to bed. When the timer goes off, that's the signal: your child knows that it is now time to end whatever she is doing. The Terrific Timer also encourages a child to listen; that alone can prevent the fuss that might otherwise ensue when you ask her to stop playing. The key to making the Terrific Timer work is consistency: if you ignore the timer when it goes off, so will your child.

structuring a routine and putting it on a schedule had changed all their lives for the better. In fact, he and his wife now saw why so many of their friends were having Beatrice-like problems with *their* kids: no routine, no schedule. They, by contrast, had become committed to their newly structured family life.

A scheduled routine can change and improve your family life, too. Before creating one for your family, however, it helps to get a clear picture

WHAT'S HAPPENING NOW?

AGE:	WAKE-UP	BREAKFAST	ACTIVITY	NAP	LUNCH	ACTIVITY	NAP	ACTIVITY	DINNER	ACTIVITY	BATH	BED
MONDAY												
TUESDAY												
WEDNESDAY												
THURSDAY												
FRIDAY												
SATURDAY												
SUNDAY												

of what is happening now. On page 92 is a sample chart on which you can note down your child's mealtimes, nap times—if applicable—activities, bath times, and bedtimes over the course of a week. Be sure to include *all* activities: school, playdates, home play, scheduled classes—swimming, ballet, soccer, etc.—even errands with Mom and Dad. And make sure you jot down the duration of each activity.

After filling out this chart faithfully for a week, take a look to see what kind of routine, if any, is at work—and on what sort of regular schedule. Is your child sleeping, napping, and eating at the same times each day? Is there a regular bath time? Playtime? Does your child's bedtime give you a chance for an evening?

Schedule variances of thirty minutes or so from day to day are not a problem—that's the way the real world works—but if your chart is all over the place, it's time for a real routine on a solid schedule.

Nanny
Wisdom

Over-scheduling

If your child has frequent meltdowns by the time Thursday morning rolls around, is too tired to eat well at most mealtimes, or is uninterested in attending his activities and frequently asks if he can stay home and play, it may be that he is over-scheduled, and the chart should make that clear.

Children need downtime just as much as they need stimulation and exercise, and if you find your child's activities are pushing back nap times and bedtimes on a regular basis, it may be time to cut back his busy schedule. Start by dropping one or two activities and pay attention to the positive changes in his mood, appetite, and energy. Drop some more activities if necessary—until he is no longer melting down, refusing to eat, or asking to stay home instead of doing an activity.

What a Standard Routine on a Solid Schedule Looks Like

Here we come to the heart of the matter. The following charts are samples of age-appropriate scheduled routines we have used many times. Obviously, different families have different commitments and responsibilities, so be aware that the times listed here are variable. For example, parents who tend to arrive home late from work during the week may want to push dinnertime back; that, in turn, may mean you schedule bedtime at eight o'clock instead of seven. So please look upon these samples as general guidelines only, and use them to help establish the routine and schedule that are right for you.

Scheduled Routine: Twelve to Eighteen Months

WAKE-UP	BREAKFAST	PLAY	NAP	LUNCH	ACTIVITY OR ERRANDS	NAP	PLAY	DINNER	BATH	BED
6–7 A.M.	7:30 A.M.	8–9 A.M.	9–11:30 A.M. (1½–2 hours)	11:30/ 12 P.M.	12:30– 2 P.M.	2–3:30 P.M. (1–1½ hours)	3:30– 5 P.M.	5:30 P.M.	6:15 P.M.	7 P.M.

Scheduled Routine: Eighteen Months to Three Years

WAKE-UP	BREAKFAST	ACTIVITY OR ERRANDS	LUNCH	NAP	PLAY	DINNER	BATH	BED
6–7 A.M.	7:30–8 A.M.	9:30– 11:30 A.M.	12/ 12:30 P.M.	1–3 P.M. (2 hours)	3–5 P.M.	5:30 P.M.	6:15 P.M.	7 P.M.

Scheduled Routine: Three to Five Years

WAKE-UP	BREAKFAST	PRESCHOOL	LUNCH	SHORT NAP OR QUIET TIME	ACTIVITY OR PLAY	DINNER	BATH	BED
6:30–7 A.M.	7:30 A.M.	9 A.M.	12/12:30 P.M.	1:30–3 P.M.	3–5 P.M.	6 P.M.	6:30 P.M.	7/7:30 P.M.

What do you do when there is more than one child in the family? In the next chart, we put it all together, showing you a schedule for a family with three children—all under the age of five. It's a way of fitting three different schedules into one that works for the whole family.

To whatever extent possible, it's highly beneficial to have all your children on the same or similar schedules. A regular schedule for all will let you organize your time and will allow the whole family to be content and well rested. The one we show here leaves room for flexibility; for example, while the five-year-old is at morning preschool, the toddler can run errands with Mom or Dad, and the baby can have his morning nap in his stroller.

This way, no one has to stay at home every morning. In fact, as you'll soon see, once you have your basic routine and schedule well established, there will be plenty of room for flexibility.

Your Family's Routine and Schedule

Now that you have an idea of what a scheduled routine should look like, here's how to make it happen. This is the way we do it when we go into a new family that doesn't have a successful routine and schedule—yet.

1. Establish the scheduled routine that works for you.
2. Display the schedule for everyone to see and follow.
3. Implement your scheduled routine.
4. Now that you've got it, you can be flexible.
5. Make it work long-term.

THE COMBINED SCHEDULED ROUTINE: THREE CHILDREN UNDER THE AGE OF FIVE

	TWELVE-MONTH-OLD	TWO-YEAR-OLD	FOUR-YEAR-OLD
6–7 A.M.		WAKE-UP	
7:30 A.M.		BREAKFAST	
8:30 A.M.		TAKE 4-YR-OLD TO PRESCHOOL	
9:30–11:30 A.M.	NAP	PLAY AT HOME; PLAYDATE; ERRANDS	PRESCHOOL
12 P.M.		PICK UP 4-YR-OLD FROM PRESCHOOL	
12:30 P.M.		LUNCH	
1–3 P.M.	NAP (1–1½ hours)	NAP (1½–2 hours)	QUIET TIME; FRIEND OVER
3–5 P.M.		ACTIVITY: PARK; PLAYDATE; ERRANDS	
5:30 P.M.		DINNER	
6:15 P.M.		BATH	
BED	7 P.M.		7:30 P.M.

1. Establish the scheduled routine that works for you.

The first step in planning a realistic routine on a workable schedule is to make sure it is age appropriate. Check our charts on pages 94–95 for the age-appropriate guidelines, and use these as your basis for working out your own routine and schedule. Make sure your child's bedtime sleep and nap time sleep meet the minimum sleep requirements—see Chapter Four—and that mealtimes and snack times are regular—see Chapter Five.

It's important that your scheduled routine be one that everyone can realistically follow. For example, if you pick your kids up from day care every evening at six, a seven-o'clock bedtime simply will not work. By the time you get home, feed the children, bathe them, and get them into bed, it will be at least seven-thirty. In this case, it is realistic to set bedtime for seven-thirty or eight.

Similarly, a schedule that doesn't offer enough cushion time in between events and doesn't allow for any delays—like the children eating

Getting Organized

It's often the simplest tricks that save you time in the long run. Being organized is a habit, and it begins with thinking ahead. Here are some tips we've found invaluable in keeping life smooth and simple, especially in busy households:

- Make school lunches and pack schoolbags the night before so mornings are less chaotic.
- Keep a diaper bag packed and ready to go by the front door, and keep a second in the stroller. Replace the contents immediately after use, so you are never without a diaper, clean bib, or spare change of baby clothes.
- Keep kids' coats, shoes, gloves, and hats in the same place so you don't have to search for things. This also helps children become more independent, as they can easily locate their own things without assistance.
- Teach kids to put their ballet shoes or baseball mitts back in their bag, ready for next week's class.

Children who are encouraged to be independent—and well organized!—from a young age acquire valuable life skills earlier than kids who have had everything done for them. An organized household can save everybody many headaches.

slowly, or the need to look for misplaced shoes, or a request for just one more turn on the swing or just one more cuddle before bed—is unrealistic. The scheduled routine isn't there to run your life, and it shouldn't be at the sacrifice of spontaneity. It's there to support and improve family life, not hinder it or drive you nuts trying to stick to it. This is not the army; this is your family. If the schedule is leading to high stress, exhaustion, and defeat, it's too crammed. Cut it back and relax a little.

2. Display the schedule for everyone to see and follow.

Now that you have worked out a realistic routine and have put it on a schedule, draw it up on a large piece of paper and tape it to the fridge or write it on a blackboard where the entire household can see it. For a scheduled routine to work successfully, everyone who cares for your child—moms, dads, nannies, grannies, aunts, and uncles—all need to follow it consistently, and they can do so only when they can easily and quickly refer to it.

Displaying the schedule also lets everyone know how serious you are about it. Tell them that a deviation of thirty minutes or so is okay, but overall you would like the schedule to be followed. Keep the schedule up-to-date and adjust it as your child gets older and his needs change.

3. Implement your scheduled routine.

Implement your new routine in phases, one day at a time. Start fresh in the morning so you can implement the changes through the course of the day. Set nap times and new bedtimes for the same time each day, and do this consistently for one week. When you have the sleep schedule up and running, begin to introduce snacks and mealtimes at set hours of the day, and do this for a week also. Finally, introduce activities and playdates that fit in around the new sleep times and mealtimes.

We recommend introducing a sleep schedule first because a well-rested child is more likely to eat well. Activities come last because sleep times and mealtimes are the most important element of a child's day.

When introducing the new routine and schedule, you'll find that small rituals will be the key to success. By "rituals," we mean simple activities or practices that signal to your child what is coming next in his day: reading him a short story before bedtime, or asking him to help set the table before meals, or requesting that he pick up his backpack when it's time to go to preschool or day care. Such rituals provide the repetitiveness and stability that kids really love. What's more, such rituals encourage kids to listen better and help prevent resistance to basic requests.

For example, two-year-old David hated getting out of the bath; his mother usually had to pluck her crying boy out of the tub mid-tantrum. To implement the new scheduled routine, therefore, I devised the following ritual: David's mother would tell him five minutes in advance that it was nearly time to get out of the bath. When the five minutes were up, she would ask him to pull out the plug. David was thrilled with his new task, and after Mom had made her five-minute announcement, he was happy to "pull out the plug" without a fight. His new responsibility became a well-loved ritual.

A Tale of Two Schedules

Here's a story of Luke and Ellie. Two-year-old Luke was highly energetic and needed plenty of exercise in his day; otherwise, he would become restless and cranky. I used the basic schedule for a two-year-old as a framework, and within it, I made sure I incorporated plenty of physical activity into Luke's day. Instead of playing at home, we would spend most mornings in the park where Luke could race his tricycle around the winding pathways. Then, after Luke's afternoon nap, we would go swimming at the local pool or have playdates in the garden, where he could run about with his little friends to his heart's content. By the end of his active day, Luke was tired out, calm, content, and ready for bed.

Two-year-old Ellie was very different; she needed a lot more downtime in her day. She had the same basic routine and schedule as Luke, but her activities were fewer and usually took place in the morning. She loved spending her mornings on a playdate or going to music class or swimming class. But I quickly learned that another round of activities and playdates in the afternoon was just too much for her. Even with a nap, Ellie lacked the patience to share and play well with other children later in the day. So instead, I made sure Ellie's afternoons were spent quietly and calmly playing at home with her toys or doing a craft project. That level of activity suited her just fine and made Ellie a lot happier and less tired. The routine and schedule you establish need to take each child's individuality into consideration.

Nap Time and Quiet Time

WHEN A CHILD is not on a regular daily routine that includes a scheduled nap time or quiet time, it may be a real struggle to introduce one into the day. But it can be done. Remember two-year-old Rosie and four-year-old Ben from Chapter One? Here's how I made it work with them:

It was clear to me in my first week of caring for Rosie and Ben that they needed some downtime each afternoon. So after lunch on my very first day, I announced, "Rosie, you are going to have a little nap now, and Ben, you are going to have some lovely quiet time."

"It doesn't sound very lovely," mumbled Ben.

I smiled to myself and said to them, as cheerily as I could, "Come on, let's go up to your rooms now."

The children followed me upstairs, protesting all the way.

"I don't want to nap," Rosie whined.

"Well, sweetie, let's just have a little lie-down and rest for a while," I suggested, "and I will tell you a story by drawing pictures on your back."

"Pictures on my back? What do you mean?"

I popped her into bed and sat on the edge. Ben came and sat next to me; I could tell that he too was now intrigued by this "drawing on backs" business. "On your tummy," I instructed Rosie. Then with my finger, I began to "draw" pictures to accompany the fairy tale I was telling her, tracing them through her T-shirt onto her back. Rosie lay calmly as she listened to my story, and as I knew she would, soon fell asleep.

"Please," said Ben, "can I have a story too, and can mine be about Superman?"

"Of course," I whispered, gently leading him away from his sleeping sister and into his room.

After the Superman story, I got Ben started on a quiet game of LEGO. He was soon absorbed in the car he was building, and I was able to slip out of the room for my own hard-earned quiet time—a nice cup of tea and a shortbread biscuit.

The next day and every day thereafter, Ben and Rosie went happily and without protest to their rooms for their nap and quiet time.

Quadruplets at a Fashion Shoot

I WAS HELPING OUT with a photography shoot for a big fashion magazine. Fashion shoots often tell a story, and this particular story, set in an elegant Manhattan town house, was about a socialite mother and her twin girls. "Mom" in this shoot was a professional model dressed in the latest designer evening gowns and glamorous high-heeled shoes; she was to be pictured in various domestic situations with her identical twin girls.

To create this illusion, the magazine had hired three-year-old identical quadruplet girls. The plan was to use two of the quads in one picture, then the other two in the next picture so that the little girls didn't become too tired or bored and get distracted during the shots.

As a nanny, I was eager to chat with the mother of these four about her experience of raising quadruplets, and I was impatiently awaiting their arrival. Their call time was 9:00 A.M., but I fully expected them to be late. I knew how hard it was to get one three-year-old out the door on time, let alone four!

To my astonishment, at precisely 9:00, the quads and their mother arrived: four identical little girls with curly brown hair, sparkling brown eyes, and big smiles scampered into the house. They produced an instant whirlwind of continuous movement and noise that seemed to be everywhere at once. Asking questions and looking at things, chasing dogs, climbing on chairs, the four won over everyone's hearts in seconds. I looked at their mother in awe, amazed at how well she coped with four three-year-olds, especially looking well rested and well put together as she did. How does she do it? I wondered to myself.

The little girls wore identical jeans and sweaters, but each girl's sweater was a different color—yellow, purple, red, and green—with the same color shoes to match.

4. Now that you've got it, you can be flexible.

Once your routine and schedule are well established, there will be plenty of room for flexibility when needed. A scheduled routine need not introduce rigidity or boredom into your life; rather, it should complement your lifestyle in a positive way. There will always be days where you need to deviate from your established routine and schedule, either out of necessity or choice.

When Mom said, "Girls, take your shoes off, please, and put them over here," the quads did so at once. I noticed that each little girl's socks matched her sweater and shoes.

"Is red your favorite color?" I asked the one closest to me.

"Red is *my* color!" she answered, in a tone that declared she couldn't believe I didn't know that already.

Her mother explained. "Each of the girls has her own color, and most of her belongings are in that particular color: socks, shoes, sweaters, jackets, pants, cups, bowls. Or, I'll sew a ribbon of that color somewhere on an item, so that each girl can recognize her own things. I used this method when they were babies, and it just seemed like a good idea to continue it."

"You are really organized," I said in admiration.

"I have to be," she said, as she helped one of the girls take her sweater off.

"Do the girls have a regular routine and schedule?" I asked, curious to know how their household worked.

"Absolutely!" She gathered two little girls onto her lap for a cuddle. "There is no other way. If I hadn't had them napping and feeding at regular times, there is no way I would have gotten through the first two years. I never would have had time to do anything at all, chores would never have gotten done, and I wouldn't have had a spare moment even to take a shower.

"The girls rely on their schedule," their mother went on. "If bedtime is delayed by ten minutes, usually one of the girls will come to me with her teddy bear in one hand and a story in the other. They notice any deviation, and they don't much like it."

"That's impressive," I told her, but what really impressed me was that she seemed calmer than mothers I knew who had just one child. This was a mother who clearly knew the benefits of a routine and schedule.

Look at the Watsons. Dad worked full-time and Mom worked three days a week in their furniture store, and on the days that Mom worked she would bring one-year-old Mary along with her. At nap times, Mary slept in the back room of the store in a portable crib. While her mother kept to the structure of Mary's routine and schedule the best she could, Mary's naps and meals were often a little late, as they had to fit in with Mom's work.

The Weekly Agenda

Life with kids can be pretty hectic. Appointments, activities, school events, and family commitments can easily be missed if you don't have a good working system. It can become even more confusing if there are a number of different people involved in the day-to-day care of the children. Here are two tips for keeping things superorganized:

We've already suggested you put the schedule on a blackboard. Now we suggest making it a large blackboard and putting it in the kitchen or family room where everyone can see it. Then, using a different color of chalk for each child, write each child's regular activities for every day of the week and the time they occur. This way everyone will know which child needs to be where and at what time. It will also help you when scheduling other appointments so you don't double book.

The next suggestion is to get a big daily calendar—that is, one with a page per day—and place it near the phone in the kitchen or family room. Write in all appointments, playdates, school events, babysitter vacations, birthdays, and the like. At the start of the week, take a moment to view the week ahead and let everyone know the week's details. Specify everything—from when the dog's heart pills should be administered to when the gutters should be cleaned.

If you get both of these systems working, everyone will know exactly what's going on and what needs to happen when. It's also a good habit to get into before your kids become teens; at that point, they can write in their own schedules for games, school trips, and medical appointments.

On the days when Mary's mother wasn't working at the store, she made sure to put Mary back on her standard schedule. Because she was so committed to maintaining the schedule, the "irregular" days at the store had no real impact, and Mary was still able to benefit from the structure established for her.

5. Make it work long-term.

For your routine and schedule to be effective in the long term, consistency and reinforcement are essential. When an everyday occurrence like sickness or a vacation upsets an established routine, get back to basics as soon as possible; otherwise, your hard work can disappear all too quickly.

Twenty-month-old Ingrid went on a vacation with her parents from New York to Europe for two weeks. While they were away, Ingrid, already suffering from jet lag, got in the habit of missing naps and going to bed late at night. Her mealtimes were also at different times each day. Once the family returned home, Ingrid's parents knew they had two choices: they could either continue to let the schedule go, or they could reestablish her pre-vacation schedule. Since they already knew the benefits of a scheduled routine—Ingrid had thrived on it—it was an easy decision for them to make. After a couple of weeks of consistent bedtimes, mealtimes, and rituals, Ingrid's routine was reestablished.

The Scheduled Routine

★ Establish and implement an age-appropriate routine on a solid, consistent schedule.

★ Make sure your routine and schedule are realistic in terms of both your children's individual personalities and your family's needs, principles, and commitments.

★ Build rituals into your child's daily life.

★ Be consistent; it's the key to successfully implementing a scheduled routine.

★ Once you've established a realistic routine on a schedule, you can be flexible.

Chapter Four

The Well-Rested Child

Sweet Dreams

L isa Richardson checks her watch—6:00 P.M.—and experiences the same sinking sensation she always feels at this time of day. Just ahead lies the Battle of Bedtime, the hardest part of her day. The struggle to get four-year-old Meg and two-year-old James bathed and into bed has been a battle of wills since both children were babies. There is no winning or losing this battle. There's only Lisa wondering to herself daily, What am I doing wrong?

It is a question she can't begin to answer. All she can do is take a deep breath and prepare for the challenge ahead. She takes that deep breath now, thinking to herself that maybe tonight will be easier. Then she calls out to the kids, "Okay, it's time to go upstairs now."

Engrossed in their game of LEGO, Meg and James simply ignore her.

Lisa tries pleading. "Meg and James, please come on now. Mommy really means it this time. It is time to go upstairs. Won't you please stop playing now?"

"No, Mommy," says Meg. "We're not tired."

"No, we're not tired!" James repeats.

This is a new wrinkle. Now even two-year-old James has become an expert at resisting bath and bedtime, just like his sister. He's already copying Meg's habits, Lisa notes to herself.

She tries again. "Come on, darlings. Please listen to Mommy tonight."

"No, Mommy, we're busy," Meg declares.

Lisa decides to bargain. "All right then. But just five minutes more."

But as is usually the case, the five minutes stretches into a half hour of Lisa pleading, and it isn't until she promises an after-bath treat that the kids actually head upstairs. Lisa rushes them into the bathroom, closes the door, sits down on the toilet seat, and congratulates herself.

From her perch she watches lovingly as her children race their toy boats across the water and make soap-bubble beards on each other's faces. Few things bring her as much joy as seeing them play together in this way, but her joy is slightly tempered by the knowledge that getting them out of the tub could well be as hard as getting them in was. This current calm and happiness, Lisa well knows, can easily turn to tears and hysterics when bath time is over.

Lisa decides on a strategy of bribery, proposing, "It's time to get out of the bath and have your treat now." This is greeted with excited shouting and a blissfully quick exit from the bath. Stark naked and shrieking with delight, Meg and James race downstairs to the kitchen and tear into the treat jar.

Lisa grabs the towels and pajamas and chases after the kids. But even as she reminds them, "You must get into your pajamas before you have your treat," she realizes that she must not only get the children back upstairs to their bedrooms, but, once there, must also deal with her mistake of having given them sugar right before bed. The children are wired and climbing all over the sofa when they announce, "We are ready for our movie now."

Lisa's watch reads 9:00. She has been at this for hours already. "Darlings, it's really late. I am not sure a movie is such a good idea tonight."

"But Mommy," Meg protests, "we always watch a movie before bed." This is true.

"Yes," Lisa says, "but you have swimming class early tomorrow. I don't want you to be tired for it."

"*Please*, Mommy."

She looks at her children. Their lips are trembling. At any moment they are going to burst into tears. Lisa's heart goes out to them. "Well, all right," she replies, "but it must be a very short movie."

That is the signal for Meg and James to rush over to the TV and start arguing over which movie they want to see. Meg gets her way, as she usually does, with her choice of *Snow White*.

The kids, who by now are yawning and rubbing their eyes, sit down on the sofa to watch the movie and are soon captivated by it—until Snow White gets hauled off into the woods by the huntsman, at which point James's look of excitement turns into a look of terror. Overriding Meg's objections, Lisa fast-forwards through the scary part, then pops out to the kitchen for a moment. When she returns, both kids are fast asleep on the sofa. She sinks into the chair and breathes a sigh of relief. She will leave it to her husband to carry the kids up to their beds when he returns from work.

Her watch reads 10:00. In another twenty-plus hours, she will have to fight the Battle of Bedtime all over again.

We doubt there's a parent anywhere who hasn't experienced Lisa Richardson's frustration and confusion. Not one of the many families we've worked with has avoided the Battle of Bedtime—whether they experience it as a minor hiccup or a constant nightmare. Resistance to going to sleep and problems staying asleep are completely natural and normal in babies and young children. Even the best sleeper has the occasional lapse, and all kids go through stages or phases of difficulties with sleep. So at some point, all parents may confront the same challenges as Lisa Richardson or they may face a sleep challenge that is even more difficult to deal with. Many parents worry about their children's sleep habits. It's not surprising at all, in fact, that the question we get asked more than any other is, "How can I get my child to fall asleep and stay asleep?"

We understand the concern. Of course you want to make sure your kids get the sleep they need to stay healthy and to grow and develop properly. Besides, we've dealt with sleep-deprived kids, and we know it's no picnic. A tired child is prone to bad behavior and tantrums; she can have a meltdown in the middle of playing with others or by herself. And tired parents tend to be impatient and to act inconsistently, which only makes the situation worse.

We've also seen firsthand how good sleep habits can be the key to the child-care puzzle. A consistent sleep schedule that both you and your kids rely on makes all the child-care pieces fit together so that everything becomes easier. A well-rested child is likely to eat well, tends to have a well-balanced temperament, and in general is a pleasure to be around. Her parents are likely to be more at ease, too.

In our experience working with so many different families, we've encountered just about every possible sleep scenario—from delightful, calm bedtimes to a never-ending cycle of lack of sleep and exhaustion. We have faced all the common bedtime struggles: nighttime routines that are out of control, awakenings in the middle of the night, sleep disrupted by illness and teething, and kids who are unable to fall asleep on their own. We know that none of it is easy. But over time, we have learned what works and what doesn't work when it comes to kids getting the sleep they need, and we've used what works to turn around the challenging situations we've confronted.

In this chapter, we talk about how much sleep young children should typically have, and about how their sleep can be divided up into nighttime sleep and daytime naps through the first years of life. Then we offer what we call the basics of sleep: ways to teach children to fall asleep independently and stay asleep through the night—even if they have problematic sleep habits now. We also tell you how to break those sleep habits, while assuring you it's never too late to do so. Finally, we talk about how to deal with those inevitable occurrences that disturb your children's sleep now and again.

How Much Sleep Makes a Well-rested Child?

Every child is different, but all children need plenty of sleep: thirteen or fourteen hours a day for one-year-olds to three-year-olds, and a minimum of eleven to twelve hours a day for preschoolers. Kids who get irritable, who nod off in the late afternoon, or who fall asleep every time they get into a car or stroller are probably not getting enough sleep—either because the fourteen hours still aren't enough for them, or because they're not even getting the minimum twelve hours.

We believe lack of sleep is a real problem for many kids—we estimate that some children are missing out on as much as four hours of the recommended sleep requirement—and that their parents do not realize it. Either young kids have bedtimes that are simply too late for their age group, or, innocently enough, bedtime gets later and later each night. A couple of "special" late nights, "just one more" TV show or computer game: each exception pushes back the bedtime hour, but wake-up time stays the same, and soon enough, kids are sleeping less and less.

Sleep Equals Sleep

One of our nanny mantras is that "sleep equals sleep," and our two anchors for securing enough sleep for kids—nighttime and daytime—are early bedtimes and good naps.

We strongly believe that children need an early bedtime. The reason is simple: kids tend to wake up early in the morning—whatever time they go to bed. Putting them down early ensures they'll get enough sleep.

It is unrealistic to wait for a child to tell you he's tired or to wait until you see signs of tiredness. That burst of energy some kids suddenly get in the evening is normal, and delaying bedtime till it plays itself out only leads to overtiredness.

Some parents believe that a later bedtime will ensure that their child will wake up later the next morning. It doesn't work. Instead, the child ends up fatigued—and in a pattern of late bedtimes that is hard to change. Typically, the late-bedtime pattern begins in infancy, with the young baby's last nighttime feed. This last feed usually guarantees at least five or six straight hours of sleep—for both baby and parents. It's when the baby gets a little older and is able to sleep for more than five or six hours at a stretch that parents often make the mistake of failing to move the bedtime forward. Yet moving to an earlier bedtime is easy to do. Start gradually. Put your child to bed fifteen minutes earlier on the first day, then increase that time by ten minutes on succeeding days, until a more age-appropriate bedtime hour has been reached.

And just what constitutes an age-appropriate bedtime hour? Here's a typical sleep schedule for ages one through five—a sample plan only, but one we've successfully used as a guide. Basically, if your kids are more or less in these ranges, you can rest assured—literally—that they are getting the sleep they need.

AGE	WAKE-UP TIME	NAP TIME	BEDTIME
12–18 MONTHS	5:30–7 A.M.	Morning nap: 8:30–9:30 A.M. (2–3 hours) Afternoon nap: 1–2 P.M. (1–2 hours)	6:30–7 P.M.
18 MONTHS		Nap time: 11 A.M. (2–3 hours) (no second nap)	6–7 P.M.
18–20 MONTHS TO 3 YEARS		Afternoon nap: 12–1 P.M. (2–3 hours)	7–7:30 P.M.
3–5 YEARS	6–7 A.M.	Quiet time (occasional catnap)	

Marathon Naps

While long naps are common if children are sick or having a growth spurt, a three- or four-hour nap every second or third day is a strong indicator that your child is overtired and needs more sleep. Maybe his bedtime is too late at night, or perhaps he is waking up during the night; in any event, he clearly needs these extra-long naps to catch up on the missed sleep. Such marathon napping is your cue to examine your child's sleep habits and schedule—and to make some changes.

We've seen firsthand what can happen when kids don't get the sleep they need and when there's no sleep schedule at work. Eighteen-month-old Elizabeth stands out as a notable example. I arrived in her household to find an irritable little girl, with little appetite and poor sleep habits. When Elizabeth was playing with other kids, she easily became upset. Even the suggestion that she share a toy would start her hitting or kicking the other children. Her tantrums were out of control and frequent; on some days she had as many as ten or twelve. Simple everyday things like getting dressed or brushing her teeth would quickly lead to tears and hysterics. And at dinnertime she would refuse to eat anything and would only drink milk.

Elizabeth did not take regular daily naps, and her bedtimes were erratic and late, so it was clear to me that she wasn't getting enough sleep for her age and that this was probably the root of her behavior problems. I advised her parents that a regular sleep schedule was the answer to improving her behavior, appetite, and mood, and they agreed to try it. On cue, once she started having regular naps during the day, Elizabeth began to sleep more at night. We introduced a regular early bedtime, and after two weeks of good nighttime sleep and daytime naps, the changes in Elizabeth's behavior, appetite, and mood were dramatically evident. Of course, she still experienced the ups and downs common to any toddler, but at least now she faced these ups and downs well rested—much better able to cope with her frustrations and enjoy the milestones of her own growth.

To see if your child's sleep habits are affecting her behavior and appetite, it's a good idea to draw up a chart tracking her current sleep schedule over a period of seven days. Write down her bedtimes and wake-up times, and note how much sleep she had, and what her mood and behavior were like before and after her rest. After seven days, you should be able to see clearly how much sleep she is getting and how sleep affects her mood. If she is frequently overtired before and after sleep, is grumpy and irritable during the daytime, and has an extremely erratic appetite, she's clearly not sleeping enough, and we would definitely suggest introducing an earlier bedtime.

Below is a sample sleep chart we've used to monitor the amount of sleep a child is actually getting, and to illustrate the connection between sleep, behavior, and appetite.

SLEEP CHART

	BEDTIME	WAKE-UP TIME	LENGTH OF NAP(S)	TOTAL HRS SLEPT*	MOOD**
DAY 1					
DAY 2					
DAY 3					
DAY 4					
DAY 5					
DAY 6					
DAY 7					

* nighttime plus naps
** measured on a scale of 1–10, where 10 is the best-rested child; note irritability, tantrums, overtiredness, erratic appetite, etc.

Daytime Naps

For children up to about the age of three, naps are essential. Kids this age are on the go all the time. They are also churning their way through substantial emotional and physical development. They really do need plenty of rest.

Their parents need them to nap as well. Kids' daytime napping is a chance for grown-ups to relax or catch up on chores. It's a time parents justifiably look forward to.

Some parents wrongly assume that if a young child doesn't nap during the day, she will sleep better at night. Nothing could be farther from the truth. Remember the nanny mantra that "sleep equals sleep"; the truth is that a child who naps well during the day will sleep even better at night. All told, a good daytime nap and an early bedtime are the perfect foundation for a hearty appetite, proper concentration, a happy mood, and healthy growth and development.

From Two Naps to One

Around the age of eighteen months, your little one may find it hard to get to sleep at her regular afternoon nap time—a good sign that she is ready to drop her morning nap and transition to one afternoon nap a day.

It's a simple transition, and you'll probably find it easiest to see through in two stages.

In stage one, gradually move the morning nap to a later time. Change a nine-thirty nap to ten-thirty or even eleven. It will take a few days, and some perseverance—and of course some children will make the transition easier than others.

One useful tip for easing the transition is to schedule an activity during your child's usual nap time. Take her to a music class or for a walk in the park—make sure she stays awake on the way home—then put her down for a later nap in her crib or bed. She'll be more than ready for sleep and should stay asleep for the usual length of time. You will probably need to give her a little something to eat before the nap, because she will be waking up from this later nap time at an hour that may overlap with her normal lunch schedule. And if she's hungry when you put her down, she is more likely to rest badly and wake up too soon. Also, since she is not getting a second nap, she will probably need to go to bed earlier at night during this first phase of the transition.

In stage two, simply move what is now a late-morning nap to the early afternoon. Continue with the morning activities—the classes or walks in the park—and your child will soon have the energy to stay awake all morning and have just one good early afternoon nap. This way she will be well rested but still ready for bed at her usual bedtime.

Naps for Toddlers

Two-year-old Charles takes his afternoon nap at one-thirty every day, but today he is having a lovely time playing with his brand-new toy train and is perfectly happy to keep on playing. He doesn't seem tired, so his mother makes the decision to let him skip his nap today—just this once, she says to herself. After all, he is having so much fun it just seems a shame to interrupt him.

But by the time four-thirty comes around, Charles is in a terrible state. His eyes are red, every little thing upsets him, and soon he is throwing a tantrum. By dinnertime, he is unable to eat at all; instead, he cries and whines without taking a bite of food. His mother decides to give up on dinner, and, realizing that Charles simply isn't coping at all, she quickly scoops him up for an early five-thirty bedtime. He's asleep within minutes. But it's an awfully early bedtime, and Charles is unlikely to sleep through the night as he usually does.

Like most toddlers, Charles is not yet ready to miss his naps. He's still at an age at which kids require at least twelve to fourteen hours of sleep each day, so the loss of a two-hour nap is significant. Charles's tantrum and poor appetite are typical results.

That's why we believe it's essential to stick to the routine of the afternoon nap right up until, at least, the age of three. Make sure, however, that the naps end no later than three-thirty. If your child is still sleeping past three-thirty, he will likely not be able to go to bed until after nine or ten—much too late for a young child to get enough rest.

From Nap to Catnap: Quiet Time for Preschoolers

Usually somewhere between the ages of two and a half and three and a half, preschoolers will ease out of their daily nap. If your child is not tired until late at night even after an early afternoon nap, that could well be the signal that he is ready to drop the nap altogether. During the transition, he may only need to nap two or three times a week—for shorter periods of time with each nap—until eventually he drops his nap completely.

If your child gets overtired during this transition, we suggest making his bedtime earlier and temporarily cutting back on his afternoon activities. We also recommend giving him his main meal at lunchtime, as he may be too tired to eat well at dinnertime.

Even when your child is no longer sleeping during the day, it is a good idea to encourage a daily quiet time. Try to get him to see this as a special time for himself—a time when he is in his own room or special space, where he can play quietly, look at some of his favorite books, or listen to books on CD or cassette. Quiet times reinforce the importance of independent play and, of course, are a real lifesaver for parents as well, offering some precious downtime during the day. In short, quiet time is great for both children and parents.

On the days when your child is a little extra-tired, short catnaps in the stroller or the car are a blessing. But make sure the catnaps end before three-thirty, or your child will not be ready for his bedtime that evening.

Sam's Quiet Time—And His Mother's

FOUR-YEAR-OLD SAM KNEW IT WAS quiet time every day after lunch, and he looked forward to it.

"What are you going to do in your quiet time today?" his mother would ask him at lunchtime. Sam would ponder the possibilities before answering. "I am going to draw in my new Superman coloring book," he replied one day, "and can I listen to a story on tape at the same time?"

"Sure. That sounds lovely, Sam."

"And what are you going to do in your quiet time today, Mommy?" Sam asked.

"I am going to read the newspaper for an hour," she said, as she put the kettle on for a cup of tea.

"You do that every day!"

"I do, don't I, darling? It's my special time to relax and catch up with the world, and it's your special time to play on your own. And after we've both had our quiet time, we are going to meet your friend Joseph in the park."

"Okay, Mommy," said Sam, as he got his crayons and got ready for coloring.

Sleep Basics: Learning to Sleep

We know kids who need to be rocked or driven around the block before they'll fall asleep, who won't fall asleep anywhere but the living room and must be carried to bed once they're asleep, who can't go to sleep without multiple bottles of milk, who need to have someone by their side until they fall asleep. Almost certainly, these kids have worried parents who, understandably, will do anything in order to get their child to sleep. Despite their best intentions, however, such parents actually teach their children to be completely dependent on Mom and Dad to get to sleep.

Falling asleep on your own is a basic life skill, and parents are the best people to teach their children this skill. All children are quite capable of going to sleep on their own; they just need to learn how. They need to learn how to go to bed awake, how to be comfortable in bed alone, how to like sleep, and how to fall asleep independently and go back to sleep if they wake during the night. Teaching your children these sleep basics is the key to peaceful bedtimes—and it's a gift that will benefit your children for their lifetimes.

Sleep basics are really about creating the right sleep associations. Sleep issues often result from wrong sleep associations learned very early on. For example, parents quite naturally feel distressed when they hear their child crying; they rush to pick her up, feed her, rock her to sleep. The child then associates sleep with being picked up, fed, and rocked, and is unable to go to sleep otherwise. Unknowingly and with the best intentions, parents can thus become a sleep aid for their child.

Maybe you're the parent of a child who rejects sleep regularly. You feel helpless, and you're beginning to feel the situation is hopeless as well. When your child falls asleep easily on the sofa while watching TV, you're more grateful than anything. But if the child continues to fall asleep this way, the result will be that he simply won't be able to go to sleep *without* watching TV. Once a habit like that is formed, it is hard to break, and your child will be missing out on the security and comforts of a structured bedtime.

Whether you need to break old habits, or want to nurture good sleep habits, here's how to teach your kids the basics of sleep.

Create the Right Environment

Easy bedtimes start with a happy, positive sleep environment. For a child to sleep well, he needs to like his room, be comfortable in his bed, and feel secure and content in his surroundings.

A child's bedroom needs a night-light, curtains that block out the sun and streetlamps, and good ventilation. It does *not* need a television. We feel strongly that a child's bedroom should never have a TV. Not only does the thought of watching television distract a child from sleep, but a TV's presence will make getting a child to bed that much harder, as negotiation for TV becomes a factor in the bedtime routine. In our experience, television is the wrong preliminary for sleep; it is too stimulating for many children, especially at a time when they need to be calming down.

In fact, as much as possible, the environment of a child's room should be calm and soothing, cozy and comfortable. That's why we feel that psychedelic swirls of paint on the walls, scary pictures, or menacing puppets have no place in a child's bedroom. Such "decorations" can sometimes make the imagination work overtime; a child will have trouble drifting off to sleep if her brain is busy conjuring up images to be frightened of.

Too many toys in a child's bedroom can also muddle bedtime for some children—although others aren't distracted at all. If the toys in your child's bedroom are too enticing for him when he should be sleeping, make a place for them somewhere else in the house.

One way to encourage your child to be happy in his bed is to take him shopping for his very own special sheets and bedspread. Bob the Builder or Spider-Man (or your child's favorite character) can make your child excited about bedtime, and a positive attitude goes a long way toward creating the right atmosphere for bedtime.

We believe parents can help create that positive attitude. When you tell your child to "hop into your lovely, warm bed," or when you comment that "your bed looks so cozy—as comfy as a cloud," you're letting him know you have positive feelings about bed, and you're guiding him to feel positively about bed, too. The other side of that, of course, is that a bed should never be used as a place for punishment or for a time-out. It needs to be a calm, happy, and inviting place.

Set a Regular Bedtime

We're convinced that one of the best ways to teach children good sleep basics is to set a regular bedtime. It's confusing to kids not to have a sense of the end of their day, and it makes it hard for them to settle down when the end of the day is suddenly announced to them. By contrast, when bedtime is on a set schedule—the same time every night—children know what to expect, and they won't be surprised to find out it is bedtime even if they are playing. Pleas of "just another cartoon" or "I want to finish playing" are easily denied when you can remind kids of what they already know: "It's seven o'clock—your bedtime." The kids may be unhappy to miss the cartoon or unwilling to stop playing, but they'll be prepared to pack it in and go to bed when it is a regular and recognizable part of their day.

Develop an End-of-day Routine

Precisely because sleep is essential for kids, parents, and family harmony, the bedtime routine is probably the most important routine in the household. It's really an end-of-day routine, a carefully considered wind-down that will lead to a peaceful bedtime and a good night's sleep.

Of course, every family is different; every household runs on different rhythms and holds different values. But here's the routine we try to put in place in every household in which we work. It's a "nanny classic"—a tried-and-true methodology that has been proven effective. It has worked for centuries—on children who grew into prime ministers and poets and peers of the realm, as well as on lots of just plain folks. Here's the way we do it:

The Nanny Classic End-of-day Routine

1. dinner
2. bath
3. into the bedroom
4. pj's
5. bed

The winding-down routine starts with dinner, and once dinner is over, we recommend getting the kids right into a warm bath. Its relaxing, calming effect is the perfect lead-up to sleep.

After the bath, it's important to keep the kids calm as you prepare them for bed. This is not the time for boisterous play. Although we love the energy that fathers so often bring to playtime, before bed is not the time for the roughhousing and energetic games that can wind the kids right back up into a frenzy of hysterical giggles. Older siblings can also upset bedtime routines, encouraging younger ones to run around and go crazy right before bed— leaving the little ones virtually shaking from the stimulation and excitement.

 ### Siblings at Bedtime

An older sibling can sometimes add to the challenge of creating a peaceful bedtime. Big brother or big sister may see your attempts to put the little one to bed as an opportunity for play—the kind of play that gets both kids overexcited and can lead to squabbles and disruption. Try separating the older kids from the younger ones at bedtime. Let your older child play quietly, look at books, or watch an age-appropriate TV show in another room while you put your younger child to sleep.

That's also why we advise that at bedtime there should be no action TV, no computer games, no sugar or sweet drinks—and that includes juice. Any and all of these things are too stimulating before bed. It is nearly impossible for children to make a swift transition from an overexcited state to the calm that's needed for sleep. Buzzing kids won't want to get into bed and will have a tough time falling asleep once you manage to get them there.

So our suggestion is to take kids straight into their bedrooms after the bath, dry them off, and get them right into their pajamas—ready for their bedtime story and tucking in. And stay in the bedroom; don't let the kids go back to the playroom, living room, or kitchen. Wandering back into areas associated with play can undo the calming effects of the end-of-day routine, and may mean starting all over again to get your child in the right frame of mind for sleep. Certainly, children may like a little bit of play in their room after bath time, but generally, the bedtime ritual should follow swiftly once they're out of the tub and into the bedroom. This works beautifully, as it eliminates any messing about and prevents distractions and possible conflict. And you're ready for one of the most significant childhood experiences you can give your kids: a loving, sweet bedtime ritual.

Establish a Bedtime Ritual

Ritual is essential for a peaceful bedtime. Rituals reassure a child, signal that it's time for sleep, and provide a sense of security and belonging. That's why the principal rule regarding the bedtime ritual is to do the same thing in the same way every night. Our suggested bedtime ritual is another "nanny classic"—although, of course, you may want to vary it to meet your own family's needs. The important thing is to keep it the same every night.

The Nanny Classic Bedtime Ritual

1. story
2. tuck-in
3. kisses and snuggles
4. your special goodnight—the same words night after night

The most successful bedtime rituals are short and sweet. A bedtime ritual that drags on for over an hour, involving story after story, isn't a ritual: it's a lengthy process that delays sleep.

Choose one or two short stories or a chapter of a book. Get comfortable. Sit your child on your lap in a comfy chair in her bedroom, or snuggle her into her bed. Read the story with your child, tuck her in, pull up the covers, pat her on the back or lightly stroke her forehead with soothing motions, and kiss her good night. Create your own special set of words for your good night farewell, but keep in mind that it works best to say the same thing as you leave the room night after night; that's your signal to your child that it's time for sleep. Your good night doesn't need to be elaborate. "Sweet dreams" or "See you in the morning, sweetie" or simply "I love you" will do just fine. It's the sameness of the ritual that counts. It makes your child feel taken care of and reassured, so that she can go to sleep feeling loved and content.

Three-year-old Penny followed the same bedtime ritual night after night. At seven, her bedtime, she could be found standing in front of the bookcase choosing a book for her Dad to read to her. A moment later, she would have decided on her favorite, *The Very Hungry Caterpillar*.

Every night, seeing the book, her father would say with a smile, "I had a feeling you would choose this one."

Penny would settle into the comfy old armchair in the corner of her bedroom, and every night Dad would say, "Don't forget Bertie," as he picked up the teddy bear and joined Penny on the chair. Then Dad would read, and Penny and Bertie would listen intently to the story.

And at the end of the book, when the caterpillar had turned into a beautiful butterfly, Penny knew it was time to hop into bed. Up from the chair, under the covers, snuggle up with Bertie, a hug from Dad—and then it was "good night, Penny," and "night night, Daddy." Every night without fail.

The Spare Bear

Whether your child's security blanket is a real blanket, a teddy bear, a soft pillow, or something else he adores, it is probably essential for contented sleep. Its very familiarity makes your child feel secure at bedtime, and it's something he can cuddle up to reassuringly. That's why we suggest having one or two spares around in case of loss. And to prevent loss, it's a good idea to keep the original in the child's room and leave it there.

The bedtime ritual needs to be meaningful. This is a special time for you and your children; they need to have you all to themselves, and you need to give them the message that this time together is a priority. So allow no interruptions. Don't answer the phone, and tell other family members to wait a moment. "Not now, I am putting Josie to bed" will communicate to your child just how important bedtime and sleep are. Long after they're grown and gone, your children will remember the bedtime ritual and the safe, warm feeling they felt when you tucked them in, kissed them good night, and said your special words.

And ideally, your child's "good night" is the last peep you will hear until your "good morning" snuggle. Turn on the night-light, turn out the main light, and pull the door halfway or completely closed behind you—a signal it's now time to go to sleep.

Callbacks

But of course, it doesn't always work that way. There are often a few "callbacks." Children like to test their limits, especially at bedtime, so be prepared for such tactics as "I need a drink," "I'm not tired," or "I can't get to sleep." Unless you're quite firm about these callbacks, you'll be in and out of the bedroom ten times before you know it, and that will set back all the progress you have made in establishing the sleep basics.

That's why our strictest "nanny bedtime rule" is that we allow only one callback. One only, and that is it! We do respond to the first "I can't get to sleep," or "I need a drink of water," or similar call. It's essential, after all, to check to see if there really is something amiss—anything from an upset tummy to a pillow that "fell out" of the crib or bed. If it's just a testing of the boundaries, however, we assume our most nannyish no-nonsense tone and address the request swiftly: "Sweetie, that's it now. I'm not coming back in again. Go to sleep. I will check on you when you are asleep." If the child calls out again, we do some calling out ourselves: a very definite "No. It's sleep time now." And that's it. Responding further only delays and reduces the child's valuable sleep time.

Obviously, this rule does not apply if children are sick or if they have been experiencing a major change in their lives—a move to a new home, perhaps, or the start of school, a new baby in the house, visitors, traveling—anything that might produce anxiety. That's altogether different; at such times, callbacks may well be genuine cries for needed attention. Parents will know if that is the case or if a child is testing his boundaries. If it's the latter, let him know the boundaries are firmly in place; it will reassure him, and he'll sleep just fine.

Undoing Bad Habits

No parent consciously or deliberately teaches his or her child the wrong kind of sleep habits. On the contrary. You love your kids, you know that sleep is important for them, you don't want to see them unhappy, and you're willing to do just about anything to stop their tears and help them fall blissfully asleep. It's the doing "just about anything" that can have the opposite effect of what you're hoping for, because kids who grow accustomed to being kept in motion or endlessly stroked, patted, or rocked before they'll fall asleep are kids who aren't learning how to fall asleep independently. One way or another, their parents are becoming their personal sleep aids.

The habit of parental intervention is a tough one to undo, and when you do attempt to make changes to established sleep habits, cries of shock and protest are pretty much guaranteed. It's a challenge we've confronted many times, and we know how difficult it is for parents—for us, too!—to make the necessary changes. It takes real commitment and perseverance by both parents, but we can tell you that if you keep at it, the situation *will* improve, and new healthy sleep habits will be learned. These sleep habits—learning to go to bed awake, to be comfortable in bed, and to fall asleep independently—are a positive step forward for your children and for the family as a whole, so it is definitely worth making the commitment to lessen your intervention.

That's how it worked with eighteen-month-old Tom. The only way he could fall asleep was to have his back patted, and his parents said this had been the case since Tom was an infant. It was hard to watch these two, hunched over their son's crib for hours on end, rubbing his back until he fell asleep—and until they were exhausted. Yet they had accepted this bedtime routine as normal.

Changing this routine was difficult precisely because it had gone on for all of Tom's life. But here's how we did it:

At Tom's usual bedtime, when he was in a calm and relaxed state anticipating the back-patting to come, the person designated for that night—mother, father, or nanny—would place him gently in his crib with his favorite teddy bear, say a few reassuring words, and leave the room. At first Tom was shocked by the change and immediately began crying. It was terribly hard for his parents to resist running back in there and patting their boy's back again, but I kept reminding them why they had decided to change Tom's sleep habits, kept asserting that this was part of the process, and kept assuring them that only their commitment would make change possible.

So for those first few bedtimes, instead of getting his back patted again, Tom's crying would bring the designated person into his room briefly—just to speak to him reassuringly, lay him back down, and place his teddy by his side. No one picked Tom up, and certainly no one patted his back, even though it took about forty minutes for him to fall asleep those first few nights. On succeeding nights, we let him cry for a bit longer before anyone went into the room, and when one of us did enter the room, there was no talking at all; it was simply a matter of letting him know someone was there. It took fourteen challenging nights of Tom's protests and not a few moments of doubt on his parents' part, but we finally did it. By the end of the fourteen days, Tom's new habit of independent sleep was well and truly established.

Nanny Wisdom

Where Bedtime Rituals are Concerned, Similar Is Not the Same

Emily, fifteen months old, had trouble settling at bedtime. Her parents had a good routine going, with a regular bedtime, and with a bedtime ritual they followed each evening—the parents alternated evenings—but Emily still grew restless and fussy when she was put into her crib at night. It took considerable and careful nanny questioning to figure out why. Here's the story:

When it was Mom's night to put Emily to bed, Mom would sit in a chair and read Emily one story, then put Emily down in her crib and tuck her in. When it was Dad's night to put Emily to bed, he would lie down with her on his bed, read her as many as six stories, and only put her into her crib after she fell fast asleep.

Similar rituals, but not the same. Nanny suggested that both parents do exactly the same thing night after night. It worked. After night after night of the same thing, Emily knew what to expect and could settle easier at night. Suggestion? Make sure everybody involved in putting the child to bed is on the same page when it comes to a bedtime ritual.

Saying Good-bye to Bottles and Pacifiers

If your child needs bottles of milk or a pacifier to get to sleep, and he wakes up frequently during the night for another bottle or pacifier, it is time to say good-bye to these sleep aids. Without realizing it, you are rewarding your child for frequent waking.

Instead of motivating him to stay asleep, you are actually giving him reason to wake up. The solution is to remove the attraction of waking up by getting rid of the pacifier or bottle—either on a cold-turkey basis, or by gradually cutting back on the frequency with which it is offered. You will certainly hear protests from your child, but remember that you are breaking a habit: there is no way it is going to be easy. You'll sometimes need to stretch your creative imagination to figure out ways to end a bottle or pacifier habit. With three-year-old Zoe, who had been falling asleep with a bottle of milk ever since she was a little baby, some fairly elaborate planning and a bit of theatrics did the trick.

Zoe not only needed the bottle to fall asleep in the first place, she also woke frequently during the night and would need another bottle in order to fall back to sleep again. Zoe's mother had long wanted to change this situation but wasn't sure how. What's more, the time had never seemed right to try to get rid of the bottle; the family had moved to a new home, and then there had been a new baby. Now things were more settled—and Zoe was still dependent on her bedtime bottles of milk.

Zoe didn't like it when her mother told her, "You're such a big girl now, you don't need bottles anymore." She looked up from her coloring book with an expression of absolute horror. "Yes, I do!" she cried. So I asked Zoe if she knew about the bottle fairy.

"Is she like the tooth fairy?" Zoe asked, immediately interested. Her six-year-old cousin had recently been visited by the tooth fairy, and Zoe had become obsessed with the idea.

"She is like the tooth fairy," I explained, "except that she collects bottles for the little babies that need them, and she gives presents instead of money to big girls and boys who give her the bottles they don't need anymore."

"What kind of presents?"

"Well, that depends. I once knew a little girl who was given a beautiful dolly in exchange for her bottles," I replied.

Zoe considered this new information only briefly before announcing, "I think I will give my bottles to that fairy!"

That night, before Zoe went to bed, we gathered all the bottles in the house and put them on the kitchen table. We wrote a note that read: "To the bottle fairy, I am a big girl now, so please take my bottles to the babies that really need them. Love, Zoe."

But as I was tucking Zoe into bed a bit later, her lip began to tremble.

"I think I want my bottle," she said softly.

"I know, sweetie," I replied, "but I have an exciting surprise for you that will help you go to sleep tonight."

"What is it?"

I had put a little portable stereo in her room and had borrowed a fairy tale on cassette from the library. "It's a fairy tale for you to listen to while you fall asleep. And as you do, you can think about what your present might be from the bottle fairy."

I pressed the play button on the stereo and sat on Zoe's bed to listen to the story. She lay with her hand resting on mine, listening intently to the story about fairy adventures in an enchanted garden. I thought she was being very brave to attempt to fall asleep without the bottles she loved so much. Fortunately, the fairy tale distracted her just long enough for her to nod off to sleep. I gently kissed her good night.

Then, on my way out of her room, I sprinkled a trail of glitter and colorful stars from her windowsill across the bedroom floor, through the door and down the hallway to the kitchen table where the bottles had been placed. I put all the bottles firmly in the garbage can and replaced them with a beautiful doll in a sparkly pink dress—everything a three-year-old girl could wish for. I sprinkled the doll with the remaining glitter and stars and propped a note next to it. "Dear Zoe," it read, "Thank you so much for giving your bottles away to the new babies. You are a very brave big girl. Please take good care of this very special dolly. Love, The Bottle Fairy."

The next morning Zoe ran into my room shouting. "Look! Look! The bottle fairy gave me this dolly! And come and see the fairy magic she sprinkled all over my room, with her little fairy wand!"

Still, that night at bedtime, she had a brief moment of regret. "I want my bottle," she said.

"We don't have bottles here anymore," I said firmly. "Instead, you have your lovely dolly. Let's tuck her into bed beside you."

Zoe turned to her new doll, patted its hair, and shut her eyes, ready for sleep.

An Out-of-Control Bedtime

After four hours of watching my very pregnant friend Julie attempt to get her four-year-old son, Damien, into bed and to sleep, I knew it was time for a few words from the heart. At midnight, when Damien finally nodded off to sleep on the sofa, I approached the subject of his out-of-control bedtime.

"Julie," I said gently, "you really need to sort out Damien's bedtime. It seems to be a very stressful time for you both, but it doesn't have to be this way. And how will you cope when the twins are born?"

"Damien's always been a difficult sleeper, but I really thought he would have grown out of it by now," she replied earnestly.

"You and Damien both need a bedtime routine that works and doesn't take hours each night," I told her.

"What am I doing wrong, and what can I do about it?"

"First you'll need to change your approach. For the situation to change, Damien needs a short and sweet bedtime routine, he needs to learn to enjoy bedtime and to be happy in his bed, and most of all he needs bedtime boundaries," I explained. "He needs to know that his delay tactics will no longer work, that you won't be running back into his room every two minutes when he calls out, and that there is no more getting out of bed and roaming around the house for hours on end. Right now Damien knows that at the end of his antics every night, you will eventually give up and let him sleep on the sofa."

"How do I set up bedtime boundaries when we have never had any?" she asked

"You can change the situation, but it will take commitment and consistency. Once you start to make the changes to Damien's bedtime, you will need to follow through. Otherwise, it will be very confusing for him.

"You can do it," I concluded. "Tomorrow night I'll come over and walk you through it."

The next evening Julie began with Damien's new peaceful bedtime routine: after his bath she read him two stories, tucked him into bed with a kiss and a cuddle, and said goodnight. After switching on the nightlight and turning on a quiet story on the CD player, she left the room.

After a few minutes, Damien called out, "I need another story, Mommy."

As I had instructed, Julie went into Damien's room and said, "No more stories. It is sleep time now. Goodnight—I'll see you in the morning." Then she left the room again.

Damien shouted, "Mommy, I need you!"

"Damien, it's time to go to sleep. No more calling out."

Moments later, Damien appeared at the living room door. "I don't want to go to sleep," he said.

Julie looked at me for support, and I quietly reminded her to lead him back to his room, not to engage in conversation but to simply tell him it was bedtime, and to put him back into bed. Then Julie sat outside his bedroom door. I had explained earlier that this would help them both during the transition. Every time Damien got out of bed, Julie would be there to take him straight back into his room, and he would feel more secure knowing she was close by.

Damien, of course, was surprised and upset by the changes being made, and it was difficult for his mom not to give up. That first night, she had to take Damien back to his bed many times before he realized she meant business and there would be no more sofa sleeping or running around the house after bedtime.

After that night, Julie continued to follow the calm bedtime routine, and to stick to the boundaries we had set. Every night the process became a little easier, and eventually Damien was happy to go to bed—and stay in bed—for a good night's sleep.

Sleeping in "My Own Bed"

Some parents make the choice to share a bed with their child, both for the convenience and for the closeness it offers. But when parents are ready to reclaim the bed for themselves, co-sleeping can be a hard habit to break.

Parents have told us that they believe their child will be the one to decide when to move to a bed of his own. In our experience, however, children who are used to sleeping in their parents' bed don't want to move out till they're eight or nine years old; once children are in the habit of doing things a certain way, they don't like to change.

So when you want your child to sleep in a bed of his own, it's up to you to initiate the end of co-sleeping. Start by teaching the child to feel positive about his own room and about having his own bed. Talk to him about how he is big enough now for his own bed, and encourage him to feel excited about the move. When you're ready to make the move, go back to the basics covered earlier in this chapter, and especially to the Nanny Classic End-of-Day Routine and the Nanny Classic Bedtime Ritual.

Nanny Wisdom

A Star Chart for Staying in Bed All Night

Star charts can work wonders with children older than two and a half, providing a real incentive for staying in bed—either to break the co-sleeping habit or to ease the transition from crib to big bed. Here's what a typical star chart looks like:

SLEEPING IN MY OWN BED: MY STAR CHART

MONDAY	TUESDAY	WEDNESDAY	THURSDAY	FRIDAY	SATURDAY	SUNDAY
*		*	*	*	*	*

Draw up a sleep chart, and put it in your child's bedroom. It's a good idea to tape it to the inside of the bedroom door, where the child can see it every day.

Discuss with your child why you are doing the star chart and what you are trying to change. Then tell her how it works: "You are a big girl now, and it's time for you to sleep in your very own big girl's bed all night long. When you do, and every time you do, you can put a star on the chart the next day. And when you have five stars—when you have slept in your own bed the whole night for five nights—you'll get a special present for trying so hard." Talk to your child about what present she would like; you might even cut a picture of it out of a catalog to paste onto the chart. Remind your child of her goal each evening, and praise her in the morning if she warrants a star.

It is common for children to do well the first night, then suffer a setback the next night. If this happens, don't award a star, but don't make a big deal out of it, and of course don't punish or criticize her for the setback. But do stick to the system, and let your child know you're sticking to the system: "Love, you did so well the night before, and I know you will be able to do it tonight so that I will be able to give you another star tomorrow morning." Positive words lead to progress.

Praise your child when he stays in his bed, using a star chart as positive reinforcement. Explain the rules about staying in bed all night: when he wakes up in the morning and can see sunlight out his window, it is morning time, and he can then come into your bed. When he does wait till morning to come into your bed, give him a cuddle and tell him how proud you are that he slept the whole night in his bed. Keep special storybooks in your room that you read only in the morning.

If he continues to come into your bed in the middle of the night, the only solution is to take him back to his room every time. And we do mean *every time*. In the middle of the night, when a little person climbs into bed with you, the very last thing you want to do is get up and take him back to his own bed. It is all too easy to think, "Well, just this once." But "just this once" can undo weeks of progress you have already made.

Dealing With Inevitable Sleep Disruptions

Sometimes, despite the best intentions, the most solid routines, and the healthiest sleep patterns, your child's sleep gets disturbed. Such disturbances are not uncommon in small children, and even the easiest sleepers become difficult when they are sick, or teething, or going through developmental changes and normal growth phases. So here are some typical sleep occurrences—and suggestions for how to deal with them.

Moving from a Crib to a Big Bed

The transition from a crib to a big bed is a breeze for some kids, a difficult adjustment for others—one of those junctures when good sleep habits can disappear and established routines can fall apart. It's not surprising. The child who has been comfortable in her crib now faces a whole new sleep environment, and that may suggest a whole new sleep agenda.

You may find, for instance, that your child feels unsure for the first few nights. "Lie down with me," she may suggest. If you do, you will have to wait until she is asleep before you can leave the room. If you try to leave the room before she is fully asleep, or if she wakes as you are tiptoeing out, you will just have to start the process all over again. Before you know it, that process will have become the new established bedtime routine—just

Our Favorite Bedtime Stories

For young kids:

- Goodnight Moon by Margaret Wise Brown
- Guess How Much I Love You by Sam McBratney
- Harold and the Purple Crayon by Crockett Johnson
- Pat the Bunny by Dorothy Kunhardt
- The Runaway Bunny by Margaret Wise Brown
- Snoozers by Sandra Boynton
- Time for Bed by Mem Fox
- The Very Hungry Caterpillar by Eric Carle

For older kids:

- Alfie Collection by Shirley Hughes
- The Cat in the Hat by Dr. Seuss
- Eloise by Kay Thompson
- The Faraway Tree Stories by Enid Blyton
- Make Way for Ducklings by Robert McCloskey
- Possum Magic by Mem Fox
- Relax Kids: Aladdin's Magic Carpet and Other Fairy Tale Meditations for Children by Marneta Viegas
- Winnie-the-Pooh by A. A. Milne

Nanny Seal of Approval

because your child and you treated the big bed as an "exception." Instead of staying until she falls asleep, reassure her that everything is fine and that you are close by. Then pop your head in every now and again to make both of you feel comfortable with this change.

We have found that the best way to make the transition from crib to bed a smooth one is to keep your approach the same from one environment to the next—same end-of-day routine, same bedtime ritual—and to act positively about the new environment.

What's really new about the big bed, however, is that kids now have more options if they wake in the night. They can get out of bed, leave the bedroom, and wander around the house in the middle of the night, whereas back in the crib, their only real choice was to fall back asleep. One of the places kids can now wander is into your bedroom and your bed. This could create a whole new set of sleep problems, and your child could end up in your bed every night.

In general, if your child has trouble adjusting to the new bed, we recommend going right back to the basics of creating good sleep patterns: calm environment, early and regular bedtime, the right sleep associations—in other words, the Nanny Classic End-of-day Routine and the Nanny Classic Bedtime Ritual.

Here are some additional tips to ease the transition:

- Make the change from crib to big bed only when your child really seems ready for it. Use a birthday or special occasion to proclaim that the child has reached this milestone.
- Do not make the change during other major events—for example, a new baby, a new house, the start of preschool, toilet training.
- Be clear and firm about the "big-bed rules":
  - No getting up: children must sleep in their own bed all night until they see the morning sunlight.
  - No coming into your room—except for a morning snuggle once they've seen that sunlight.
- Consider letting your child share a room with an older sibling; this can make the transition a lot easier, as the transitioning child will love being in the same room as her older sibling, while the older sibling presumably has already mastered the big-bed rules.
- Place a guard on the side of the bed so your child won't fall out.
- If your child becomes anxious in the big bed, reassure her, but do not lie down with her until she falls asleep, and do not let her leave her room. Try playing a tape or CD of a bedtime story or soft music while she goes to sleep.
- If your child gets out of bed repeatedly, gently take her back to bed each time, with minimal talking or interaction. Tell her it's sleep time now. If she becomes very upset and begins to cry, pat her back to calm her. If she asks you to stay with her until she falls asleep, tell her you will sit outside the bedroom door and check on her once she is asleep. Then sit outside her door until she is asleep. If you use this approach consistently, she will soon stay in her bed, and once she feels comfortable you won't need to sit outside her door.
- If your child gets up in the middle of the night and climbs into your bed, take her back to her room and put her back in bed straightaway.

Yes, we know it is hard to do this in the middle of the night, but it pays off if you do it consistently. If you let her share your bed even one time, it will become a hard habit to break. Limit the bed-sharing to morning snuggles.

- Make sure the house is locked up and safe just in case your child goes wandering while everyone else is asleep.
- If you're purchasing a new bed, bring your child shopping with you, and involve her in the choice of bed.

Jack and His Big-boy Bed

Nanny Tales

JACK WAS THRILLED to be making the transition from crib to big-boy bed—just like the one his older brother, Max, slept in—but it would take the help of both Max and Jack's teddy bear to make the transition smooth and successful.

Jack had picked out his very own big-boy bed in the mattress store the day after his third birthday. Right there in the store, I asked him if he remembered the big-bed rules we had gone over so many times. He was letter-perfect: "I have to stay in my bed all night and not get out of bed until morning, and then I can go into Mommy and Daddy's room for a morning snuggle." Jack was clearly proud of his new big-boy status.

But that night, he looked awfully tiny in the spacious new bed. As I tucked him in, he announced in an uncertain tone, "I'm a big boy now. I have a big-boy bed, just like Max." He looked at me with an anxious expression.

"Yes," I said, "you are. Let's tuck your teddy bear in bed with you. Teddy is very excited to be sleeping in a big bed, too."

"But he's a little bit scared. He always slept in my crib before."

I sat Teddy on my lap and spoke directly to him. "Teddy, I know it's a big change, but there's no reason to feel scared. Max is sleeping in his bed next door, and Jack's mommy and I will be right downstairs." I turned to Jack. "Does Teddy feel a bit better now?" I asked.

"Yes," he assured me. "Teddy feels much better now."

When a Good Sleeper Becomes Unsettled, Stick to the Basics

Even the best sleepers go through unsettled times. It is not uncommon for little ones to wake up for what seems to be no apparent reason, and as always, it is how you deal with these sleep disturbances that counts. If you run into your child's room at the first sign of waking or restlessness, you can easily create bad habits that will disrupt sleep over the long term.

Eighteen-month-old Jimmy was on a great sleep schedule: he went to bed awake, fell asleep on his own, and slept through the night. Then one

"Okay, then. Sweet dreams, darling. Mommy will be up to tuck you in soon." I kissed him on the forehead.

But shortly after he had been tucked in, when his mother and I were downstairs chatting about plans for the next day, the intercom began to crackle with the sounds of activity upstairs. Jack was getting out of his new bed and running into his brother's room. We stopped our conversation and listened in.

"Jack, what are you doing in my room?" Max sounded outraged. "Go back to your room or you'll get in trouble for being in here!"

"I don't want to."

"You know the big-bed rules. We have to stay in bed until morning, and then when it's sunny outside we can go into Mommy and Daddy's room." Then he added: "Sometimes Daddy lets me watch cartoons in their room, and sometimes Mommy reads me special stories in the morning."

Jack had been unaware of this secret morning activity and was clearly impressed. "Will Daddy let me watch cartoons, too?" we heard him ask.

"Only if you sleep in your own bed all night," Max said with a knowing, big-brother tone.

Jack considered the issue only briefly. "Okay. Nigh-nigh, Maxey," we heard him say. Then came the sounds of Jack scampering back to his own room and climbing into his new bed.

And then, all was quiet.

night, out of the blue, Jimmy woke up in the middle of the night crying. I went into his room at once and was relieved to see that everything was as it should be. There was no real reason why he should be awake at this time of night. I picked him up to comfort him, and he went right back to sleep in my arms, but once I attempted to put him back in his crib, Jimmy woke up and began to cry again. I spent the next twenty minutes patting his back until he fell asleep again. Then I sneaked back to my own room, tiptoeing carefully so as not to wake him.

The next night I awoke to hear him crying again and wondered why my easy little sleeper was waking up in the middle of the night—coincidentally, at exactly the same time as the previous night. I waited a few minutes to see if he would stop crying, but he didn't, so off I went to his room. This time, just the sight of me in the doorway stopped his crying.

This seemed a critical moment. I knew that if I picked Jimmy up, he would expect it every time he woke up in the middle of the night. So I went back to the basics. I laid Jimmy down in his crib, turned on his musical mobile, patted his back, and left the room. Jimmy did begin to fuss again, but this time I did not go into his room. I knew that doing so would encourage him to wake up every night, creating new habits that would be hard to break, and encouraging him to rely on someone else to get to sleep.

It wasn't easy not to run back in the room and pick him up, but I knew that would only make it harder to break the habit, and then we'd have to teach Jimmy the basics of sleep all over again. After a time, he grew quiet, and when I tiptoed back into his room to check on him, he was indeed sound asleep.

Climbing Out of the Crib

Around the time a child learns to climb, he may also figure out how to climb out of his crib. This may be a signal that he is ready to move to a big bed, but it may just mean he likes to climb, and you don't want to move a child to a big bed too soon.

If you do not think your child is ready for the move to a big bed, you will have to nip the crib climbing in the bud by putting your child back in his crib *every time* he climbs out. Do this with minimal interaction and a firm facial expression, and your child should soon stop the climbing.

An Early Morning in New York

IT WAS FOUR-YEAR-OLD HANNAH who taught me to turn early mornings into quality time with a child. Her father had told me about their first-light walks—a godsend to a father who routinely worked late—but it wasn't until Hannah's parents were away celebrating their anniversary that I learned just how lovely these walks could be.

It was six o'clock on a crisp April morning in New York when, through the baby monitor, I heard Hannah chatting to her doll. I sat up in bed, rubbing my tired eyes and regretting last night's late bedtime. Then I got out of bed, pulled on my dressing gown, and climbed the spiral staircase to Hannah's room to see what was going on. Everything was fine. When Hannah saw me she gave me a big kiss and suggested that we get dressed and head outside for what she called "an early morning walk."

For the next two hours, she introduced me to a New York most of us rarely see. On the street, we were greeted by bright New York sunshine and fresh morning air. A yellow taxicab cruised by, and Hannah stuck out her arm and shouted in her loudest voice: "Taxi!" The cab screeched to a halt. "You're a real New Yorker," I told her. We relinquished the cab and walked on, witnessing all sorts of sights and sounds: a woman running with her twin babies in a jogging stroller, a few Wall Street business types in immaculate suits briskly heading downtown, a woman arranging bunches of flowers at the corner deli that was just opening for the day. "Good morning, Esperanza," Hannah said to the woman.

"*Hola!* Hannah," Esperanza replied, handing her a small daisy.

"Thank you," said Hannah. "See you tomorrow."

Then she said, "I'm hungry," so off we went to her favorite café for eggs, bagels, and glasses of warm milk. Hannah tucked into her breakfast with enthusiasm, then picked up a newspaper that had been left on the next table and announced she was "catching up with the news."

I checked my watch: eight o'clock already. The morning had flown by. I now understood why these early morning outings were so important to Hannah and her father. It was their special time together, and they had made a ritual of it.

Another suggestion is a crib tent. It attaches to the crib with Velcro and makes a roomy tent over the crib, making it impossible for a child to climb out and potentially injure himself in the process.

We have used crib tents with great success. Yes, the sudden appearance of a crib tent may confuse your child a little; after all, this is an addition to—and therefore a change in—his sleep environment. But we have found that kids quickly get used to the tent; by about the third use, it becomes an accepted part of the bedtime ritual. In fact, kids really like to see the crib tent go up and will often want to help you zip it up. It's the perfect solution for crib climbers who still aren't quite mature enough for their own beds.

The Early Riser

Most children go through a stage of very early awakenings, but if your child consistently wakes up at 5:00 A.M., you may want to do something to help him sleep longer.

First, check the sleep environment. Are the curtains blocking out enough light? Sun streaming into your child's room at first light will start his day no matter what time it is. What's available to your child on awakening—a toy, a book, something to engage him? A child who enjoys being in his room will be more likely to hang out there when he first wakes up. You can encourage this by suggesting he read a story, or play with a special toy, when he wakes up before coming into your room.

An alarm clock and a star chart are often enough to encourage children three years and older to stay in their room for a while in the morning. If your child has been regularly waking at 5:00 A.M., set the clock for 5:15 and tell your child he needs to stay in his room until he hears the alarm go off. When it does go off, he can come into your room for morning snuggles. Put up a star chart and award a star every time the child waits for the alarm. Then, over the course of a number of weeks, set the alarm for a few minutes later each day. We've found that after a few weeks, kids actually begin to wake up a bit later. But while a later wake-up isn't guaranteed, the clock technique usually guarantees a later get-up.

It should be said, though, that some children will be early risers, up and ready to go at the crack of dawn no matter what you do. All you can do is be prepared for the early risings—perhaps by going to bed earlier your-self. Try to take turns with your spouse or partner to manage the morn-ings. For parents who are at work all day, in fact, early mornings with their child can be a very special way to enjoy quality time together.

Of course, as we've mentioned before, what you should avoid with an early riser is attempting to keep her up significantly later than usual at night in the hope she will wake later. Children usually rise at the same time each morning irrespective of when they have gone to sleep.

Vacations

Vacations can easily disrupt your child's sleep habits. If you travel to a dif-ferent time zone, or if you are sharing a room or bed with your child, all of your routines and schedules can simply fall apart at the seams. There's noth-ing for it but to try to keep to a routine and schedule as much as possible while away, then to go back to the sleep basics as soon as you get home. It may take a little while to get back on your old schedule, but keep at it.

Terrible Teething

Cutting a tooth can be terribly painful, and that can affect sleep. Keep in mind that the teething will not go on forever—even though it feels like it—and do what you can to comfort your child. Teething rings and gel can help ease the pain so you can all get some much-needed rest. As soon as the teething episode has passed, return to the sleep basics so your child's sleep habits aren't too affected by the trials of teething.

Sickness

If your child is sick—and children are certainly prone to catching every-thing around—all bets are off when it comes to sleep routines and sleep schedules. In fact, sickness typically affects sleep; an erratic sleep pattern may be a symptom of whatever is wrong. Your sick child will probably need to take extra naps during the day and may be awake with a fever or vomit-ing during the night. She will certainly need lots of extra love and care, and this may include your staying in her room until she falls asleep, or even sleeping in her room. Once she's better, however, be sure to go back to your old sleep routine, or peaceful bedtimes can become a thing of the past.

A Spooky Night in a Scottish Castle

"**S**NAP!" SHOUTED SIX-YEAR-OLD JAKE triumphantly, as he smacked his hand down on the pile of playing cards. His four-year-old brother, Harry, and three-year-old cousin, Millie, looked on glumly, not happy to be beaten at their favorite card game yet again.

"No more Snap tonight, children," I announced. "It's past your bedtime. So let's hop into bed for a story."

We were staying at the children's grandparents' castle in the heart of the Scottish Highlands. A very grand party was going on downstairs to celebrate the grandparents' ruby wedding anniversary. Since we were ensconced in the old nursery, in a remote wing of the castle, I wouldn't catch a glimpse of the party myself.

"Millie," I said as I lifted her into one of the high, rickety beds and pulled the blankets up around her chin, "you can have the bed next to mine."

The children were getting cozy in their beds, so I turned off the main light, leaving two small lamps on. In the dim light, the old nursery immediately took on an eerie feeling.

I suggested to the children that we read the next chapter of *Winnie-the-Pooh*. But before we could find out what Pooh Bear was up to, Jake turned to his brother. "Harry, did you see those old suits of armor in the hall?" he asked mischievously.

"Yes. Why?"

"There is a dead person in the armor. That's where they used to put dead people in the olden days."

Oh no, I thought to myself. Let's not start down that path. "That is not true, Jake. Hundreds of years ago, knights wore that armor for protection in battle, so knives and lances couldn't hurt them."

Hoping that would be the end of that kind of talk, I opened *Winnie-the-Pooh*.

"Harry, did you see those big paintings in the hallway?" Jake now asked.

"Yes," Harry whispered unsteadily.

"Well, ghosts come out of those paintings at night, just like in *Harry Potter*."

"Jake," I said as sternly as possible, "you know that is not true! Harry, he is just teasing you."

"I'm scared!" Millie cried out.

"I don't like it here," Harry wailed. "I want to go back to my own room in London."

"What was that?" Jake asked, now scared himself.

I knew that if I didn't turn this situation around quickly, there would be three hysterical kids running into the ruby anniversary celebration. I decided to try a guided meditation to get the children's minds on something pleasant.

"Sweeties," I began, "there is really nothing to be frightened of, so I am going to tell you a very special story." That got their attention.

"Now, everyone lie down in your beds, please. Close your eyes and let's all take in a big breath of air." I heard their little chests filling with air, then exhaling.

And so I began. "One day, Jake, Harry, and Millie went to the beach for a picnic."

"What did we eat?" asked Jake.

"Cheese sandwiches," I said, as that was his favorite lunch.

"Did we have cake after?" asked Millie.

"Yes, darling, you had chocolate cupcakes."

"I can see those cakes in my head; they have sprinkles on top!" Harry called out.

I went on: "The beach was made of soft white sand. Warm sand that felt delicious as the children walked on it. Can you feel the sand between your toes?" I could just make out the children nodding. "Just as Jake, Harry, and Millie were finishing their cupcakes, they heard a voice calling out to them from the ocean. 'May I have a cupcake, please?' asked a beautiful mermaid.

Jake walked down to the water's edge and gave the mermaid their last cupcake. The mermaid told them that it was the most delicious cupcake she had ever tasted, and, to thank them, she would like to show them her mermaid home at the bottom of the ocean."

"But how would we breathe in the ocean?" Jake asked, yawning.

"She would sprinkle us with magic mermaid seaweed and then we could breathe like fish," Harry told Jake sleepily.

A few moments later, I noticed all was quiet in the room. I looked over to see Jake, Harry, and Millie sound asleep. One at a time, I tucked them in with a kiss. My guided meditation had worked magic on the children.

Bad Dreams and Nighttime Fears

Jonathan, aged five, was allowed to watch a movie each night before bed, and each night he would ask for his favorite, *The Wizard of Oz*. His parents knew their son really loved watching this classic movie.

But Jonathan suddenly began to have recurring nightmares. When his parents went into his room to comfort him, he would repeat, "The monkeys are coming to get me." By the third night, Jonathan's parents realized he was referring to the monkeys in the movie. It took no wizardry to decide to pay closer attention to the movies Jonathan watched before sleep.

The monsters conjured out of children's imaginations are very frightening and, to the children, very real. There's no sense in trying to convince a child that "it's all in your imagination." Instead, calm the child with a hug and reassure him that there is nothing to worry about and that "Mommy and Daddy are right here." You may even need to stay with him until he falls asleep, and the next night, for additional reassurance, you may want to leave a lamp on and the door open.

But if nightmares become a regular occurrence, it's important to try to identify what is causing the anxiety. Was there an off-the-cuff comment about money or health problems—a comment that might have been blown out of proportion by an uncomprehending child? Is the family undergoing change of some sort? Is the child?

While you are trying to determine the cause of your child's anxiety, be sure to give him extra one-on-one time and a calm, structured day. Say no to scary or action-packed TV shows or computer games. Encourage your child to have relaxed, happy thoughts before bedtime by making sure there

When Sickness Challenges Sleep

When a child is feeling unwell with a cold or flu, he can have a hard time getting to sleep and staying asleep. Try massaging a little VapoRub onto the soles of his feet after he gets into bed. Or rub a few drops of eucalyptus or tea tree oil into the wood of his crib. Or set up a humidifier or vaporizer in his room. These remedies ease breathing, clear a blocked nose, and help a sick child get some sleep.

is no conflict in the house at that time. It is never advisable to argue with your partner or other family members in front of your children, but it is to be particularly avoided before bedtime. Even harsh words with an older sibling can be stressful to a small child.

We've found that a creative approach is helpful in calming a child before sleep and putting an end to nighttime fears and bad dreams. Happy bedtime stories, or guided meditation, or even a few drops of lavender oil on a child's pillow help to relax him for a peaceful night's sleep. A "dream catcher" hung above a child's bed, accompanied by a story about how it will "catch" the bad dreams and bring happy ones, often does the trick with young children. If you have a portable tape or CD player, a children's story on tape can distract your child from her fears as she falls asleep— and may help turn children's nightmares into the sweet dreams all parents wish for.

The Well-Rested Child

★ Your child needs anywhere from twelve to fourteen hours of sleep every day.

★ Sleep can be taught, and parents are the best teachers of the sleep basics.

★ Sleep basics:
  • a calm environment
  • an early bedtime
  • an end-of-day routine—a "nanny classic"
  • a bedtime ritual—a "nanny classic"
  • a one-callback rule

★ Bad sleep habits can be reversed at any age.

★ Sleep disturbances are inevitable; to nip them in the bud, just go back to sleep basics right away.

Chapter Five

Secrets from the Nannies' Kitchen

Giving Your Children a Healthy, Balanced Diet

F ive-year-old Tilley's formidably sophisticated grandmother, just back from a month in Paris, is stunned to see pesto dribbling down her granddaughter's chin, strands of linguini being slurped up through her lips, and a floret of broccoli on her spoon.

"Tilley! What are you eating?" Grandma asks in disbelief.

"Green s'getti," Tilley replies.

"But I thought you only liked French fries and ketchup."

Tilley's mother steps in to answer. "Well, that was before Nanny came to work for us. Now Tilley likes all kinds of yummy food, don't you, Tilley?"

Tilley nods in agreement as she chews the broccoli.

"What do you like?" asks her still dumbfounded grandmother.

"She loves broccoli and orange beef stir-fry, chicken and noodles, and shepherd's pie," her mother says. Tilley nods vigorously.

Tilley, who has finished chewing and swallowing her food, finishes off the list with a flourish. "But green s'getti is my favorite, Grandma."

Grandma turns to me. "How did you manage such a transformation in only one month?"

"With a bit of persistence," I answer. "I just kept offering her new foods to try—again and again—until slowly but steadily, she began to accept a wide variety of food; now she really enjoys all kinds of meals." I give Tilley a big smile.

Grandma sits down. Her stunned look is turning into one of pleasure. "Well, Tilley," she says, "now that you eat more than just French fries, how would you like to come with Grandpa and me to our favorite Italian restaurant on Friday night?"

"Yes, please!" Tilley exclaims, thrilled at the promise of such a grown-up treat.

One of the definitive ways we nannies show our love for the children we care for is with healthy, home-cooked food shared at regular mealtimes in a peaceful and nurturing environment. We know how important nutrition is in building a strong foundation for healthy growth, and we know too how important all the varied pleasures of fresh food this world has to offer are. We also believe that mealtimes shouldn't be TV-watching, every-one-for-himself affairs, and with menus consisting of highly processed junk food.

It concerns us to see so many children missing out on the pleasures of fresh and flavorful food—pleasures of both taste and health. It's upsetting, too, to see the experience of shared meals falling by the wayside. What has happened to the family meal where kids might be exposed to the natural sweetness of butternut squash, the crunchy texture of green beans, the creaminess of mashed potatoes, or the tenderness of a roast chicken—varied tastes and textures and nutritionally balanced meals? Along with good table manners, such mealtimes are becoming a thing of the past, replaced by TV dinners, fast food, and nutritionally empty snacks eaten on the run. If kids are given only highly processed junk, they will naturally reject fresh meals. But how can it be acceptable for a growing child to eat hot dogs and fries exclusively?

Yet keeping children away from a diet consisting mainly of fast food and processed food is no easy task. In fact, it may be one of the toughest challenges parents face today. Fast-food outlets are everywhere, enticing children with the promise of a toy with their fries. Supermarket shelves overflow with candy cereals, sodas, high-sugar imitation yogurts, and prepackaged convenience foods that are marketed in nonstop commercials during children's favorite television shows. These foods are full of additives, fillers, genetically modified ingredients, unhealthy fats, sugar, and salt; they do not offer the essential vitamins and nutrients that children's growing bodies need. It's no surprise to us, seeing what kids are taking into their bodies, that more and more children are becoming overweight, that many are having trouble concentrating at school, and that behavioral issues are so common.

Adding to the challenge are mealtime battles, and we have witnessed just about every variation on the struggle—from a child who eats five foods (and five only) to one who needs to be begged and bribed to eat, to another who hasn't learned how to behave at the dinner table, to another who expects multiple choices of meals.

But imagine this: the entire family gathered around the table, and your child tucks into a homemade tomato soup, dipping chunks of bread into the bowl to catch every last mouthful. Finally, he looks up from his soup bowl and asks, "Is there any more, Mommy?"

Sound unrealistic? Not at all. It really is possible for a child to enjoy fresh homemade food while seated at the table, making an effort toward good table manners—at a family mealtime all can share and enjoy. This chapter tells you how to make it happen.

First, we talk about a healthy, balanced diet. Everyone knows that providing a variety of nutrients is essential for a child's growth and development, but we tell you exactly what a healthy diet should consist of—and we set out ten steps for ensuring one, even if your kid is currently living on fast food.

Then we discuss the importance of regular, shared mealtimes and of good manners—and we tell you how to achieve them.

We also address the various phases kids go through when it comes to eating, and we talk about how to deal with some common eating issues: getting kids to the table, dealing with fussy eaters, avoiding bribery or begging antics, and more.

Finally, we talk about the process of meal preparation, and, since we both love to cook, we offer some of our all-time favorite recipes for easy, tasty, healthy, balanced meals. These recipes are all kid-tested and kid-proven— and in demand with parents and other nannies. They include such classic English nursery food as shepherd's pie and rice pudding, old-fashioned childhood favorites like macaroni and cheese, and internationally inspired dishes like stir-fries and Asian soup. In addition to the recipes, we show you our tricks and tips on how to fit cooking into your busy life, to encourage you to make the commitment to cooking for your children. When you do, you will be giving them an important and wonderful gift for life.

A Healthy, Balanced Diet

Three-year-old Orion and I were sitting in the shade in the park alongside New York's Hudson River, enjoying a picnic lunch. Swallowing a bite of banana, Orion asked me, "What's in my sandwich today?"

"Cheese and tomato, sweetie."

Orion smiled. "That's my favorite!" he exclaimed.

As I handed him the sandwich, I noticed a mother staring at us from the opposite bench.

"Wow," she said, "how do you do that?"

"What do you mean?"

"My two-year-old son refuses to eat anything healthy. He only eats McDonald's Happy Meals." She paused. "What can I do?"

"Well," I said, "I don't mean to be harsh, but the truth is, he doesn't take himself to McDonald's."

Expose your kids to a diet of fast food, and that's what they will learn to like and accept. Expose them to a variety of fresh, flavorful foods, and they will be comfortable with different tastes and textures and will be open to trying new foods. It's as simple as that.

The choice is up to parents. They're the ones in charge of what their children eat while they are young. It is parents who shop for food, make the food choices, and cook the meals. It is parents who are responsible for making sure their children eat a healthy, well-balanced diet. If children are given only such premade, processed foods as candy cereal for breakfast, frozen chicken nuggets for lunch, and hot dogs with French fries for dinner, they will have a limited palate and will want only those types of foods. If they are introduced to the taste of fresh strawberries on morning cereal, the crispness of a cheese, tomato, and lettuce sandwich for lunch, and the rich flavor of homemade beef stew for dinner, they will learn to enjoy such tastes and experiences.

As illustrated by the story of Tilley at the beginning of this chapter, a bit of persistence in introducing your child to a healthy, balanced diet will eventually make such a diet second nature to her. In return, she'll reap health benefits and the gift of being able to enjoy the numerous diverse pleasures of fresh food.

The Kids' Food Myth

It's a myth that children cannot tolerate strong flavors and prefer bland-tasting food. The fact is that children will quite happily eat flavorful food—if they have been exposed to it from a young age. We routinely offer children pesto, Asian noodle soups, fish dishes, stir-fries, and mild curries, with great success.

Everyone knows that growing kids *need* fresh food, but what do we really *mean* by fresh food? We mean real food, not food that has been processed to the point that all its nutrients are gone and all that remains is an artificial concoction. Real meats, fish, fresh vegetables and fruit, dairy products, bread, rice, and pasta: that's fresh food. It's food that contains no additives or hidden ingredients. And giving up the processed and packaged choices doesn't mean you have to put together fancy, time-consuming extravaganzas; rather, we're talking about simple, homemade food that is both nutritious and tasty.

Growing children also need a balanced diet. Every day, they need protein like red meat, poultry, fish, beans, or tofu; and carbohydrates like bread, pasta, potatoes, rice, or whole grains. They need the calcium found in cheese, milk, eggs, and yogurt, and they need vegetables and/or fruit at every meal for healthy growth and development. This doesn't mean you can get away with giving your child a slice of toast for breakfast, a sole piece of chicken for lunch, and a bowl of plain pasta for dinner. Those are not balanced meals; they don't even add up to a balanced day. And without the nutrition from all the different food groups, your child is missing out on the health benefits he needs.

An Early Start on Healthy, Balanced Eating

The best way to ensure that your child grows up with the habit of eating a healthy, balanced diet is to start early. How early? As soon as you begin to wean your baby onto solid foods. As we said in Chapter Two, it really is crucial to start early to offer a variety of balanced meals daily. A child under the age of two is usually very keen to try new foods, and the moment she sees others eating something new she will be eager to taste it. Once a child turns two, however, she may become fussy and insist on only a small selection of foods. But if you have already introduced her to a varied diet, you should be able to continue serving the foods she already knows and likes, gradually expanding her diet at the same time.

On page 176, we present a sample one-week menu for a child's healthy, balanced diet—meals and snacks for seven days. It's just a sample, but it gives you an idea of the kinds of foods we're talking about.

Another essential for ensuring that your child eats a variety of healthy foods in a balanced diet is to model that behavior yourself. Kids are natural imitators. They learn by example. So if your child sees you eating fruits and vegetables, proteins and carbohydrates, and calcium-rich dairy products, he will assume that is the right way to eat. By contrast, if he sees you

Common Diet Misconceptions

"Are you sure John should have carbohydrates with every meal?"

"Why are you giving Jane whole milk?"

"Potatoes are fattening, I don't think Melissa should be having them . . ."

Some parents have misguided beliefs about what their children should be eating. We've even seen kids—lots of them—who are on their parents' latest fad diet and are fed only low-fat or low-carbohydrate foods. It's a mistake. Kids need to eat whole-milk dairy products—not low-fat or skim. They also require some form of carbohydrate with every meal to maintain healthy growth and development, to fuel their busy days, and to help them function well. If you are concerned about your child's weight, consult your doctor, not your diet guru.

eating a bowl of cereal for dinner, or he hears you muttering how you hate vegetables, he will do the same. And if he sees you eating the bowl of cereal while standing up and reading the newspaper, just before heading for the TV, he'll think that's an acceptable way to have a meal, and he'll reject the whole idea of sitting at a table at mealtimes.

Parents can also encourage a healthy, balanced diet by telling their toddlers and preschoolers how big their muscles will get if they eat their dinner up, and how fruit and vegetables will prevent them from catching lots of colds, so that they won't miss their playtime with friends.

Just presenting kids with varied foods—over and over—encourages them to accept variety. If you give your child a sandwich for lunch each day, always include something else with it—raw vegetables, for example, or fresh fruit, or a piece of cheese. Try offering baby carrots, cherry tomatoes, peeled cucumbers, fresh blueberries, and slices of juicy watermelon—kids tend to love these foods. If your child eats plain pasta for lunch, add a marinara sauce as a dip with some cheese and a salad. If he eats a piece of chicken for dinner, serve vegetables, a salad, and rice or potatoes with it. Keep on offering additional foods, and keep varying what you offer, and your child will not only be used to a variety of foods at each mealtime, he will come to expect it.

Another good suggestion is to present your child's favorite foods in many different ways. For example, if he loves eggs, serve them in a variety of styles—scrambled, poached, fried—so that he will be open to eating eggs any way they come. If chicken is his favorite food, roast it, grill it, and put it in soups and stir-fries, and he will be less likely to be fussy about how it is served. And when he goes to a restaurant or has dinner at a friend's house, where chicken is served in a new way, he will be open to trying it. As much as children like the safety of eating foods they know, if they are exposed to many foods with different tastes and textures, they are less likely to be fussy when faced with a new food at any age.

Copying Siblings' Habits

Younger children look up to their older brothers and sisters and love to do what they do—in matters of food and diet as in everything else. Peter, aged two, tried to copy his older brother Mike, aged eight, in all things. Peter had always been a good eater, but when he noticed Mike's preference for only a handful of foods, he began to mimic both the limited diet and his brother's cries of "I don't like that!"

To nip this in the bud, I emphasized variety in the meals I served to Peter while Mike was at school. After a while, even though he liked to shout "I don't like this," he actually did like it—and he ate it. I was satisfied that Peter had avoided picky eating habits—and I was also delighted that I still got to cook fun meals.

Of course, there are always days when convenience food or take-out meals seem like the only option, and when a healthy, balanced diet has been established, the occasional fast-food meal is of no consequence. It is fine to give your child some frozen tater tots, chicken nuggets, or a quick slice of pizza once in a while. Do try to limit these occasions to just once or twice a week, though, and be sure to serve some fresh vegetables or fruit with these meals. If kids eat processed foods and junk food on a regular basis, they may begin to reject healthy, balanced meals and can quickly turn into fussy eaters. Balance is the key to setting up and maintaining good, healthy eating habits, and both rigid restriction and overindulgence should be avoided.

Turning Diets Around

Here are some actual comments we've heard from parents:

"Linda only eats plain pasta or chicken nuggets for dinner."

"Liam likes hot dogs, white rice, or pizza. "

"There are only four meals that my child will eat."

Poor eating habits like these *can* be changed—whatever your child's age. We have turned around children's diets many times, taking kids from limited, unhealthy diets to a preference for fresh foods in a healthy, balanced, highly varied way of eating—with complete success. Change may come gradually, but with commitment and a positive attitude, you can literally transform your child's diet.

How? Here's our plan.

The Nannies' Ten Strategies for Turning Diets Around
1. Don't stock junk food.

If it isn't there, your kids can't eat it. So start by going through your cabinets, freezer, and fridge for high-sugar cereals, fat-soaked frozen TV dinners, packets of artificial foods, or any other junk food in your home. Now throw it all out. Once that's done, just do not regularly buy such foods again. The reason is simple: when these foods are just not available, it will be much easier to encourage your child to eat nutritious food. When Jenny asks for the packet of mac and cheese she is used to instead of the fresh meal you've just prepared, you won't need to come up with a lengthy explanation: simply show her that there are no more mac and cheese packets in the house.

2. Substitute fresh food for fast-food favorites.

Children are more open to trying fresh food when it is similar to the food they already know. That's why we suggest substituting fresh food for your child's fast-food favorites. If your child lives on processed chicken nuggets, begin to make homemade nuggets using chicken breast strips and fresh bread crumbs. If he eats frozen French fries, make fresh ones with tasty

Idaho potatoes cooked in olive oil or baked in the oven. It is crucial not to give up if your child rejects the fresh food substitute the first time—even the first few times. Keep offering fresh food, and keep in mind that it takes more than two or three attempts to change habits.

3. Expand the range gradually.

Once your child has begun to accept fresh food instead of processed foods, continue to slowly build on this base. If your child is used to eating frozen pizza, plain rice, and plain pasta, offering him a radically different meal— say, poached salmon or a vegetable curry—will be met with confusion, disbelief, and a likely uproar, and that will only turn him off these new foods. Instead, start expanding his diet with simple fresh meals—spaghetti and meatballs, stir-fries, homemade burgers, roast chicken, breaded chicken or fish, noodle soups, or sausages and mashed potatoes. Once these simple meals have been accepted, slowly begin to extend the range of offerings to more distinctive flavors. That way, you'll progress to the salmon and even to the curry in due course. Little steps are the key to turning diets around.

4. Alternate the new food with familiar food.

It is important to offer kids a variety of foods, as this is the only way to expand a child's diet, but it's equally important to avoid introducing a steady diet of new foods all at once. Don't shy away from offering kids new meals they are likely to reject; just make sure the next meal is something they like and will eat well. For example, offer your child a new meal—say, shepherd's pie—for lunch, and in the evening for dinner offer him his favorite pasta dish. This allows you to introduce new foods your child may eventually like, but if he rejects the new food at first, you can still be assured that he will eat well at the next meal.

5. Be inventive.

We know that's easy to say, but inventiveness really does help when it comes to devising healthy, balanced kids' meals. For a snack, try giving your child some fresh strawberries or a yogurt instead of chips, or homemade milk shakes and fruit smoothies instead of sugar cereals. A child who is used to drinking soda can be given juice diluted with water or with seltzer, and eventually he will be open to accepting plain water. If your child refuses to eat vegetables, you can easily disguise them in his meal by chopping them up into small pieces, or even shredding or grating them, and adding them to sauces, one-pot dinners like stews, or baked lasagna. Those kids who eat only plain pasta can be given a little marinara sauce or pesto on the side and encouraged to dip their pasta in it. Think about serving food your child isn't keen on in a different way; we have had great success in getting kids who "hate" fish to eat it by offering fish cakes or by cooking it in bread crumbs.

6. Try finger foods.

Finger foods are a fabulous way to introduce varied foods into a child's diet. A platter of finger foods on the table—with choices like cheese, bread, cold cuts, chicken drumsticks, raw vegetables, crackers, dips, and fruit—encourages kids to help themselves. Toddlers especially like to choose food from platters; they may refuse a piece of steak or a chicken cutlet but will quite happily tuck into mini-meatballs or small chicken sausages. Similarly, kids who refuse whole fruits may readily accept a few bite-size pieces of apple, orange, banana, tangerine, melon, or blueberries.

7. Make an impact with shared meals.

You'll probably be surprised at the impact shared meals can have on your child's diet. Kids are natural imitators, and they will copy the behavior of their parents, siblings, or friends. This can make an enormous difference; even the fussiest eaters will be inclined to try something new if everyone else is eating it.

In fact, a child who is used to sharing meals with her family is far less likely to be fussy; she will be accustomed to eating the same meal as everyone else—the meal that's being served. That means you get to cook one meal for your whole family. And here's a tip: when you serve the meal, put the broccoli your child normally rejects on her plate anyhow, just as you serve it to the rest of the family. One day she might surprise both you and herself by trying it and discovering she loves it.

8. Make food and meals interesting and fun.

When children are interested in the food they are offered, they are more likely to eat well. The fussy eater who normally pushes away a bowl of stir-fried noodles with vegetables might be intrigued by your story about eating this dish in an exotic country called Thailand or in a basement restaurant in Chinatown. He will probably be very impressed if you tell him that stir-fried noodles with vegetables is his father's favorite meal; in fact, it's practically guaranteed he'll try it.

Of course, not every food can be a parent's favorite, but try serving up stories about your own childhood experiences with eating. We tell our own personal stories, including one that's handy when serving a chicken potpie, about the dog knocking into little Nanny just as the pie was coming out of the oven; the chicken potpie flew into the air and landed on the floor. Another story describes making pancakes as a kid and tossing one of them so high it stuck to the ceiling. This story is requested every time pancakes are on the menu.

9. Get your kids involved.

Little children love to help out in the kitchen, and a child who helps prepare his meal is going to be excited about eating it. Involve your child in shelling peas or putting cheese on the sandwich bread or shucking corn, and he will be far more likely to eat those foods when they are served at the table. Moreover, assigning a child the task of setting the dinner table or calling other family members to dinner will incline him to think that being at the table is important—which it is.

The Nannies' One-Bite Rule

Children must take at least one decent-sized bite of every new food.

10. Introduce the one-bite rule.

It's all too easy to offer kids only the foods you know they will eat—especially if they're suddenly being fussy. But giving in to this limited diet only entrenches the fussy eating habits and the restricted diet, and that, as we've established, isn't good for your child's health or growth. How will a child learn to like new foods if he is offered the same few things over and over?

To break the pattern and to give your child the opportunity to expand his diet, we recommend the nannies' "one-bite rule." The rule asks children to take at least one decent-sized bite of every new food. With the one-bite rule, you are not forcing kids to eat something they don't want, but you are getting them to at least try something new. Many children we have cared for have admitted to learning to like potatoes, cheese, fish—you name it—after being exposed to a food with our one-bite rule.

Breakfast!

It shocks us to see how many young children start their day without breakfast. Children need a good breakfast to give them a healthy start and to keep them going, through all their busy activities. Without the fuel and nutrition of the morning meal, most kids are not able to manage very well. They tend to have difficulty concentrating, to lose patience easily, and to become grouchy.

It is important to offer kids a breakfast with high nutritional value. Avoid high-sugar cereals, super-sweet pastries, or breakfast bars. Make the effort to give your child a good breakfast of eggs, toast, oatmeal, a fruit-and-yogurt smoothie, fresh fruit, or organic cereal.

If mornings are a rush in your household, we suggest setting the table for breakfast the night before. Set out a good-quality cereal along with peanut butter and jelly for toast. Cut up some fruit and put it in the refrigerator so all you have to do is take it out in the morning. We have worked for a lot of busy families—like yours—and we've found that these few breakfast preparations quickly become an easy habit—and really do make all the difference in ensuring both a smooth morning and a healthy breakfast.

And remember: even if a child rejects the food after one bite, do not assume he will never like it. Keep offering the new food; children's likes and dislikes are unfixed and change daily.

Regular Mealtimes

Young children are busy little people and often seem too occupied with other pursuits to sit down and eat a meal. They also have a short attention span, as is well known, and they often have a small appetite. So it may feel like a waste of time to ask them to sit down, on a regular basis, to eat a meal. Nothing could be farther from the truth.

In fact, we strongly believe that regular mealtimes may be the defining factor in encouraging a child to eat well. Most young children are not able to recognize their own hunger; it can creep up on them really fast, and before you know it, they are overhungry, upset, and cranky. Overhungry children may refuse food completely, may require special attention, and may still not eat their meal. By establishing regular mealtimes, you ensure that your kids are getting the food they need—and you avoid many mealtime dramas.

Ideally, children should eat three small meals and two snacks at regular times each day. (See the charts on page 94 for more information on meal and snack scheduling.) When a child is used to a routine like this, she will be happy to sit down at the table at the usual time, and she will be ready to eat her meal.

Shared Mealtimes

Four-year-old Linda, her seven-year-old brother Luke, and his friend Joe ran into the kitchen as I was placing the napkins on the table.

"What's for dinner?" asked Joe, who was dining with us that evening.

"Macaroni and cheese with corn on the cob and salad," I replied, handing the children their glasses to put on the table.

"Yum," said Luke. "When's it ready?"

"As soon as Mommy and Daddy get home," I said. "Remember? It's family dinner night."

Just at that moment, the kids' parents came through the door, setting off a flurry of noisy activity as children and parents greeted one another, dogs ran about in excitement, briefcases and coats were set down or hung up. A few minutes later, we all sat down at the table to share dinner.

"Thanks, Nanny," Mom said. "This is a wonderful meal on such a chilly night." Then she turned to the kids. "Luke, please eat with your mouth closed. Joe, let me pour you some water. Linda, let Daddy cut your food into smaller pieces."

As Dad did so, he asked his daughter if she had a good time at pre-school.

"I suppose so," Linda answered a bit uncertainly. "I played with Tom and Mel today."

"And Samantha?" asked her Mom. Samantha was Linda's very best friend.

Linda shook her head. "No, I can't play with Samantha anymore."

"Why not?" asked Dad, a bit surprised, as he buttered Linda's corn.

"Tom said Samantha is yucky and no one can play with her anymore," Linda explained.

Across the table her parents and I exchanged glances; Tom had a reputation for being a bit of a bully at school.

"That's silly," Luke piped up. "If someone told me not to play with Joe, I wouldn't listen." Joe, his mouth full, nodded in agreement.

"Darling," Mom said to Linda, "Samantha is your special friend. You need to make up your own mind about her."

"Do you think she's yucky?" Joe asked Linda in a serious voice.

"No." Linda shook her head.

"Then Tom can't tell you what to do," Luke told his sister, "and you shouldn't listen to him."

I could see that Linda was considering her brother's advice as she munched on her corn. Her little mind kept considering it even as the dinner conversation turned to Luke's day.

Later, as Mom and Dad and I were clearing the table, I overheard Joe telling Luke, "I like having dinner at your house. At my house, we just have family dinner on Thanksgiving and Christmas."

Communication, conversation, the sharing of ideas—and good, healthy food as well: it's an example of how the shared meal can enrich your family life and help ensure that your kids eat a healthy, balanced diet.

Family meals are one of the most powerful tools parents have for connecting family members to one another and cementing family bonds. When families share meals on a regular basis, kids are more likely to share their experiences and look to their parents for help and advice. The communication skills learned at the family dinner table can become a habit kids maintain for the rest of their lives.

Creating Traditions

You can make the shared family mealtime even more special by giving particular meaning to certain mealtimes. You might start a tradition in your family by designating a special day on the weekend for family breakfast or lunch. Or, you might declare a "theme" for a particular family meal. We once worked for a family that had "multicultural night" once a week, where we ate food typical of a particular country and talked about that country. The children loved their multicultural nights, and the parents enjoyed exposing them to a range of new foods and to a broadened understanding of the world's cultures and cuisines.

To sit at a table with people we love—to share food and conversation—is such a simple thing, yet its impact on a child can be tremendous. The excitement and anticipation of the meal as the aromas fill the house, the ritual of setting the table, being called to dinner, sitting in a place reserved just for you, eating the same meal, talking about the day and sharing stories: these are the comforts of home life that mean the most to children, giving them a sense of stability, confidence, and well-being. Sharing family meals is one of life's greatest experiences, and it teaches children a love of good food and a powerful appreciation of family.

It's at the dinner table that a child learns to interact with the people in his life—and, by extension, with others. It's there that he discovers the pleasure of good eating. It's there that he learns good table manners—the foundation of courtesy and of getting along with others. Over a shared meal, family culture, history, and tradition are passed down to a child—a legacy that he in turn can pass on to the next generation. Special memories are created at the family dinner table that will stay with a child throughout his life.

You can share family meals with a baby in a high chair, a toddler in a booster chair, a preschooler in a big chair, or all three at once. The food served doesn't have to be fancy; a bowl of soup or a simple dish of spaghetti works as well as a time-consuming roast. The aim is not to be elaborate but to serve good, healthy food and to serve it to the whole family together. And, if you can't do the shared meal every night, then aim for a couple of nights a week.

But do be sure that the atmosphere of the shared mealtime is calm and enjoyable. Children will neither eat well nor gain the benefits of family sharing if mealtimes are filled with chaos or stress. If the phone is constantly ringing, or if bribing or begging has become a necessity for getting kids to eat, then you and your children will not be able to enjoy sharing meals together. To make sure your shared family mealtime is peaceful, do not bring stress to the table, do not use the shared mealtime as a place for criticism, and do not indulge in emotional mealtime battles with your kids. Just enjoy the good food and each other's company.

Teaching Table Manners

It may be very British of us, but what could be nicer than a young child with good table manners? It makes mealtimes far more pleasant, and it means that you can take your children out to other people's houses or to restaurants for meals without fear of embarrassment or worry.

What do we mean by good table manners? Here are the basics we teach children at every meal:

- Sit down at the table: no climbing or sprawling on the chair or the table.
- Make a real effort to use silverware.
- Don't talk with your mouth full.
- Say "please," "thank you," and "may I be excused" (after a reasonable time), and say "thank you" to the person who cooked the meal, especially if you're at someone else's house.

Our guess is that right about now, you are saying to yourself that there is as much chance that your child will do any of these things as there is that pigs will fly. Well, we don't know about pigs flying, but we do know that your child can learn table manners. Young children are quite capable of doing all the things we just mentioned. They can sit at the dinner table without running around, watching TV, or playing games while they eat; they can feed themselves independently; and they can interact with others in courteous ways. They can do it all—if someone shows them how and encourages them to.

The trick is to teach good table manners to children daily and to reinforce the teaching constantly—with gentle reminders at just about every meal. Expect your children to have good table manners, and keep encouraging them to be well mannered, and it will happen.

Of course, parents are the best and most appropriate teachers of good table manners, and the best way they can teach manners is by demonstrating them. Remember that children will mimic the table manners they see around them, so if you sit down calmly, eat slowly and with enjoyment, listen to and participate in the conversation, your child will do the same.

Setting boundaries is another absolute necessity if mealtimes aren't going to be chaos, and it's especially helpful with fussy eating or just plain old bad behavior. If your child knows that throwing food or climbing around during meals is unacceptable, he will be far less likely to carry on this way.

Common Mealtime Battles

Many parents dread mealtimes with their children. They worry about what their child is eating and about whether she is eating enough. In their worry, some parents will do just about anything to get their child to eat. We have seen parents running around the house chasing after their child with spoonfuls of food and begging her to eat. We have seen children being fed in the most unusual places—in the bathtub and even in bed—by parents hoping that the novelty of the location will encourage better eating. And we have frequently seen television used to distract a child while her parent sneaks a few morsels into her unsuspecting mouth.

We've also seen worried parents confront a picky eating phase in their child's development by drawing back from a well-established foundation of healthy, balanced eating and moving to a diet of junk food, nutritionally empty snacks, and excessive amounts of drinks. "At least Simon is eating something," they tell themselves for reassurance, "and juice is nutritious, isn't it?" Well, it's not nutritious enough to replace food.

It's all too easy to slide out of the routine of a healthy, balanced diet served at regular mealtimes and shared with the family. You tell yourself that your kid is going through a fussy phase and you promise that when it's over, you'll go back to the good habits. Or you say to yourself "Just this once" when your child asks to watch TV while he eats his dinner. Or you resort to feeding your son in the bathtub one night, and now he wants a meal in the tub every night.

But these occasional lapses can be the first step on a slippery slope to bad habits that will be hard to break. So what do you do when your kid refuses to eat? Or throws a tantrum at the table? Or won't come to the table at all? Or suddenly turns into a picky eater who demands to eat anything but what is on his plate? Desperate tactics and extreme measures aren't necessary. Instead, here are our tried-and-true suggestions for what to do when you come up against mealtime battles or eating issues. No matter how challenging the issue or how stubborn the battle, these suggestions work. But do keep in mind that it is always best to continue bringing your child to the table or high chair for meals, best to continue making sure mealtimes are calm, and best to feed your kids healthy, balanced meals at regular times.

"My child won't eat!"

When it comes to feeding kids, it is pretty much guaranteed that there will be days when they cannot stop eating and days when they won't seem hungry at all. This is normal for young children—especially toddlers.

Young children commonly eat poorly when they are teething, sick, tired, distracted, or just having a bad day. Of course, if a child doesn't eat well, he may simply not be very hungry. It's important to remember that a healthy child will not starve if he refuses to eat a meal; your child will eat when he is hungry.

Some children just get too tired or distracted to eat well at night, although they do fine at breakfast and lunch. If that is the case with your child, the best solution is to give him a good, hearty breakfast, feed him his main meal at lunchtime, and make dinner a lighter meal—serving something you know he loves to eat.

If you are concerned about your child's reluctant eating, however, the place to start is with a food diary. Jot down what your child is eating and drinking over a period of seven days—like this:

FOOD DIARY

	BREAKFAST	LUNCH	DINNER	SNACKS	DRINKS
DAY 1					
DAY 2					
DAY 3					
DAY 4					
DAY 5					
DAY 6					
DAY 7					

Seeing your child's diet over the course of a week—the big picture, so to speak—may reveal the pleasant surprise that she is actually eating a well-balanced diet after all. Or, the diary may show that your child is not eating well at all. But look more closely: the diary will also help you understand why she isn't eating well. You'll be able to see just what she's eating—and you'll easily be able to ascertain if she is filling up on snacks and/or drinking too much juice, soda, or milk.

Fifteen-month-old Michael was never interested in eating meals. Instead, from the minute he woke up to the minute he went to bed, he drank endless bottles of milk. His mother came to me for advice, and I had a ready nanny solution. It was clear to me that Michael was too full to eat meals, so I advised his mother first to cut back on the amount of milk and on the frequency of his bottles, then switch from bottles to sippy cups—as Michael was clearly using the bottles as a comfort aid rather

than out of thirst. I urged Michael's mother to make these changes immediately so that Michael would have a chance to get used to balanced meals
before he hit the fussy toddler years, when his picky eating habits would

Nanny Wisdom

Too Many Snacks, Too Much to Drink

In our experience, the number one reason young children do not eat well at mealtimes is because they are eating too many snacks between meals and drinking milk, juice, or soda all day long. Certainly, snacking is essential: young children have small tummies and are very active, so they do need snacks in between meals to fuel their day. But too many snacks make kids too full to eat at mealtimes, and that may mean that they miss out on the essential vitamins and minerals that balanced meals provide. The same is true of all those sodas, juices, and milk: they suppress a young child's appetite. And if he's not hungry at mealtimes, he certainly won't be willing to eat his food. So here are our special "nanny snacking rules" for between-meal eating and drinking:

Nanny Snacking Rules

- Make sure all snacks are healthy and nutritious. Offer a healthy variety of yogurt, cheese, finger sandwiches, nuts (only to kids three years and older), or fruit instead of chips and candy.
- Limit the frequency and portions of the snacks. Young children shouldn't be able to access snacks on their own and should not be going into the fridge or cupboard to help themselves to snacks all day long.
- Establish a cut-off time for snacks. For example, if dinner is at six, snacks should stop after four in the afternoon.
- If your child shows more enthusiasm for snacks than for meals, offer finger foods and platters of varied foods at mealtimes. Toddlers especially like to eat finger foods.
- Instead of sodas and juices, give children water: it's better for them. If they still insist on juice, dilute the juice with water. And here's a tip for encouraging your child to drink more water: present the water in a new cup—maybe a character cup with Sleeping Beauty or Scooby Doo on it—add an ice cube and a straw, and we promise that your child will be won over from juice to water.

become more firmly in place. She did so, and within three weeks, Michael was hungry enough to eat at mealtimes. From that point on, his mother was easily able to expand his diet.

But what if your child's lack of eating is not the result of filling up on snacks or drinks? And what if it is a regular occurrence and not just a passing phase? Then it's time to look for other possible causes:

- Does your child have a regular mealtime schedule?
- Does he eat alone?
- Is he overhungry or overtired at mealtimes?

We've talked about the importance of a regular mealtime schedule for ensuring a healthy, balanced diet. The flip side is what happens when mealtimes are irregular and not on a schedule. It's simple: kids become hungry at erratic times, and the result can be meltdowns and/or the rejection of food. Moreover, if your child is eating erratically—not on a schedule—you'll never be able to judge how hungry he is, and neither will he.

If your child has his meals all by himself, mealtimes won't be much fun for him, and he won't learn to appreciate and understand the importance of good food and shared mealtimes. Result? He'll be less likely to eat well. If your child does eat at a different time than you and your spouse or partner, we suggest that at least one parent sit with him while he eats—and eat a small plate of the same food. Don't make mealtimes all about him and how much he eats; if you share your child's mealtime with him, he will be more likely to pick up his spoon independently and eat with enthusiasm.

Without a regular mealtime schedule, your child may simply be overhungry by the time he has his lunch or dinner—whether you're sitting with him or not. Again, by setting a regular mealtime schedule and sticking to it, you can be pretty sure your child is getting the food he needs when he needs it. An overtired child can also be reluctant to eat: too tired to know if he is hungry, too cranky to approach food well. In a sense, this child's eating problem is a sleeping problem, so see Chapter Four.

When a child who "won't eat" does eat his meal well, be sure to praise him for his good efforts. (Eating well doesn't mean clearing the plate; as long as he has made an effort to eat a good serving of each food on his plate, that is just fine.) The praise should not include a treat after every meal; after all, eating well should be a normal, everyday occurrence.

If your child does not eat well, don't scold him or make a big deal out of it. Giving a child attention for not eating is counterproductive; it shows him that he can use food and mealtimes as powerful tools for getting attention.

 Small Portions

Plates piled high with food can be overwhelming for some children and can lead to a rejection of the entire meal. Offer children small portions; they can always have a second helping if they want.

Emotional Mealtimes

Liz Jones lifted her twenty-month-old daughter, Rebecca, into her booster seat. "I have made you a lovely lunch today, Rebecca," she said, "and I want you to eat it all up for Mommy. I know you didn't eat your breakfast this morning, but you are going to eat now, aren't you, sweetie?" Standing beside the booster seat, a look of real determination on her face, Liz picked up a piece of chicken and offered it to her daughter.

Rebecca closed her mouth tightly, shook her head, and said, "No."

"Darling, eat for Mommy, please," her mother begged.

Rebecca shook her head again, tightened her mouth even more, and turned her head away. Liz hovered, her determination fading into anxiety. "Why won't you eat for Mommy?" she pleaded.

"No!" Rebecca said again, and she threw her sippy cup onto the floor. In mid-toss, Rebecca spotted a package of pretzels on the kitchen counter. She pointed at the package excitedly. "Me have it!" she demanded.

Uh oh, Liz thought; she's seen the pretzels. She sighed. "Okay, you can have one."

Rebecca munched the pretzel quite happily, but when her mother tried to feed her again, she again refused the food. This time, she began to climb out of her booster seat.

"Darling," Liz begged, "please don't get up. I spent half an hour cooking this meal for you." Liz's voice was heavy with disappointment.

Rebecca ignored her mother. She simply continued to struggle against the booster chair. Hoping now just to distract her, Liz turned on the kitchen television. It worked. Rebecca sat down again and began to watch *Teletubbies*. Liz seized the opportunity to sneak a bite into her daughter's mouth, but Rebecca, looking her mother right in the eye, immediately spat it out.

Now Liz resorted to bribery: "You can have some ice cream if you eat just a couple of bites."

Rebecca was unmoved. "No."

Totally exasperated, Liz decided to give up on lunch altogether. Rebecca watched as her mother tossed her carefully prepared lunch of chicken and pasta into the garbage can.

"Darling," Liz said to her with a sigh, "you will eat your dinner tonight, won't you?"

Rebecca's reply was not a surprise. "No," she said firmly.

The emotions running wild in this scenario are not just the child's. After all, behavior like that can be expected from a twenty-month-old. It's the way Rebecca's mother reacted to her behavior that really turned the mealtime into an emotional battleground.

Kids understand early on that mealtimes are the perfect occasion to assert their independence and get some attention from their parents. If they refuse to eat, take too long to eat, chew with their mouths open, or climb around at the table, parents are bound to react, guaranteeing attention. It's not uncommon to see a child who refuses to eat well for Mom or

 **Nanny Wisdom**

"I'm not hungry, but can I have dessert?"
A promise of dessert at every meal soon makes dessert the main focus for a child and takes away from the enjoyment of the whole meal. When that happens, a child may refuse to eat a well-balanced meal until he is bribed with dessert, and mealtimes will quickly become burdensome.

Dad quite happily eat the same meal for Nanny, Grandma, or Aunt Susie. This is usually because Nanny, Grandma, and Aunt Susie are more detached from the mealtimes and less likely to react emotionally. But Mom and Dad can pretty much be counted on to respond instantly to acting up at mealtimes.

Messy Mealtimes

Nanny Wisdom

When a child begins to feed himself, he is going to make a mess. You may not like the feel of spaghetti sauce smeared from one ear to the other, but your fourteen-month-old certainly does. Here's how to deal with it: just lay a plastic sheet on the floor under the high chair, put a huge plastic bib on your child, and hand him the spoon. It is the only way he will learn. He will be so delighted to master a new skill and gain some independence that soon your attempts to help him will be greeted with shouts of "I can do it!"

In short, the mess is not only inevitable, it's a sign of progress.

Some kids act *out* at mealtimes. Maybe the arrival of a new baby brother or sister sets them off, or perhaps a friend has come over for supper, or maybe they're going through a fussy stage, or maybe they're just testing your boundaries and their limits. Acting out in any of these situations is perfectly normal. It is your reaction to the acting out that will determine whether it escalates and becomes a regular occurrence or simply fades away. If you react in an emotional way, showing your own anger, frustration, or anxiety, your child will know instantly that she has succeeded in getting a rise out of you. It would only be logical for her to repeat the behavior meal after meal until you come to dread mealtimes with your child.

If your child starts acting out at mealtimes, keep your emotions in check. Sit down with your child and share the meal with her instead of hovering over her and verbalizing about what she is or is not eating. Give her the independence she craves by letting her feed herself, and do not worry or make a fuss about the mess she makes; it is all part of the process. If your child refuses to eat, even if it's a meal you know she likes, tell her calmly that dinnertime is going to be over very soon. Then wait until you or the other children have finished, and if she is still refusing to eat, take her down from the dinner table or high chair and end the meal. Your child will quickly learn that her non-eating is no longer an attention-getting tactic, and it won't be long before she begins to eat well at mealtimes.

Begging, tricking, or bribing a child to eat is not a good idea; it sets a bad precedent and encourages mealtime antics. "If you eat all your dinner, you can have an ice cream or some candy" may certainly work at first, but used too frequently, it can quickly become a draining tactic you'll have to rely on at every mealtime. Once you start down that path, it soon spirals out of control, and there is no easy way out. A child really is perfectly capable of eating his meal without being bribed, tricked, or begged to do so, so it is best not to entertain such tactics at all.

Dealing with a Fussy Eater

Children can become fussy eaters as early as sixteen months, and their food likes and dislikes can change daily. Your child may suddenly reject the chicken soup that has long been his favorite meal. He may want to eat the same meal for breakfast, lunch, and dinner, or the sight of carrots on his plate may cause tears and hysterics. Don't worry: the fussiness is not permanent; it is probably just a phase that will soon pass—if it is handled the right way.

It's How You Say It That Counts

Multiple choices at mealtimes encourage fussiness and confuse children. Children need limits—a choice between one thing or another, not a long menu of options. "Would you like a cheese sandwich or a ham sandwich?" offers a clear choice. "What would you like for lunch?" opens an abyss. Similarly, when it's time for a meal, make a statement—"It's breakfast time now"—rather than asking a question such as "When do you want your breakfast?" or "Do you want your breakfast now?" Multiple choice works well in school tests; where kids and meals are concerned, it's best to be straightforward.

The wrong way to handle it is the easy way—by indulging it. It is a sure path to a limited and unbalanced diet. On the other hand, you can't force food down a child, so if he rejects a particular food, either withdraw it temporarily from his diet—say, for a couple of weeks—or serve the same thing in a different way. Above all, don't assume that he will never eat the rejected food again.

Victoria had always been an easy child to feed, and she loved trying new foods. But when she hit her second birthday, her eating habits began to change rapidly, and there were many fussy moments at the dinner table. Victoria had loved chicken. Now she wouldn't eat it anymore. She began to push away cheese and to turn up her nose at the vegetables she once loved. After a few days of watching Victoria continually reject her favorite foods, I realized I would have to change her diet a little to keep her eating in a healthy, balanced way. I also knew I would have to be inventive with her food preparation and presentation.

One of the first things I did was disguise the foods she was rejecting by combining them in soups, sauces, and baked dishes. Instead of serving her grilled chicken, for instance, I made chicken rissoles and served them with a dipping sauce. Instead of giving her pieces of cheese, I cooked up a dish of macaroni and cheese. And as for the vegetables she had rejected, I put them in sauces. I also prepared meals of finger foods and laid them out on the table at mealtimes so she could choose what she wanted. She would quite happily pick up finger sandwiches, mini-quesadillas, chicken drumsticks, raw beans and cucumber, cherry tomatoes, and sliced fruit to munch on. So with a bit of subterfuge and some imagination using finger foods, I transformed Victoria's sudden fussiness into the perfect opportunity to expand her diet and keep it balanced with a variety of foods.

I also made sure, after a few weeks, to reintroduce the foods and meals that she used to like. Like the rest of us, kids sometimes just get bored with the food they are eating.

"But I'm busy playing!"

Sometimes the fun they are having will be more important and interesting to children than coming to the table to eat dinner. They may refuse to budge when you call them to the table, and they can become upset at the suggestion that they end their playtime.

Once again, a regular mealtime schedule is the best solution to this struggle between playtime and mealtime. If your child knows that afternoon play will be followed by dinner, he won't be surprised when you ask him to wash his hands and get ready to eat.

Divider Plate

While toddlers in general like one-bowl meals—pasta with vegetables, or casseroles, for example—there are always exceptions, and the exception in this case is the child going through a phase of not wanting different foods to touch each other. Should the chicken even touch the peas, this child will refuse to eat his entire meal. A good solution we've found to get him through this phase is a divider plate, with separate, walled-off sections for individual foods.

When it does become a fight to get kids to the dinner table, it's probably because they need a transition from playtime to mealtime—a little preparation for the end of play, and some signals about what is coming next. Small rituals work well to create this transition: ask your child to place his cup or napkin on the table, or get him to tell his big sister that dinner will be ready in five minutes, or assign him to turn off the television because "we're going to have dinner now." But whatever you do, do the same thing in the same way at the same time each day; then it will become a well-loved ritual and an effective bridge between playtime and mealtime.

"Why can't I have that?"

You've been committed to providing your child with a variety of fresh food from an early age. You have made it a point to steer clear of the nutritionally empty processed food that is marketed toward children. And you have raised a child who eats a healthy, balanced diet, enjoys a variety of tastes, and is open to trying new foods. But now he's in school and—inevitably—he has begun asking you for the candy, soda, artificial yogurt, and high-sugar cereals he sees his new schoolmates eating. What should you do?

This was exactly what happened with four-year-old Adeline, a good eater who had grown up on a well-balanced diet. Each morning, she would leave the house proudly holding her Cinderella lunch box. Each afternoon, when she returned home, I would take a look inside it to see what she had eaten, and would usually find only a few crusts of bread left over from her sandwich.

Nanny Wisdom

The Nannies' Terrific Timer

Three-year-old Scott would become so wrapped up playing with his toy dinosaurs that he wouldn't want to come to the table for dinner. Even when I gave him ten minutes' notice, there were still cries of protest. I knew that the only solution to this nightly struggle was my Terrific Timer—which was nothing more than a simple kitchen timer for helping kids having a hard time adjusting to everyday transitions. Here's how it worked with Scott:

I would set the timer for ten minutes, place it near where Scott was playing, and tell him that when the bell rang, it would be time to finish playing and come to the table for dinner. Scott was clearly intrigued; even on that first night, I could sense him listening for the timer to go off. After a few days with the timer, Scott no longer refused to come to the table. Instead, he would jump up when it went off, because he understood clearly that the buzzer meant it was time to come to the table for dinner.

But after a few months of preschool, I noticed that most of Adeline's lunch was going uneaten. She was only taking a few bites of her favorite cheese sandwich, and although she was drinking her milk, she was leaving her apple and carrots. When I asked her why she hadn't eaten her lunch, she replied that she didn't like cheese.

"And what about your apple and carrots, sweetie? Why didn't you eat them?"

"Jenny doesn't like apples and carrots," Adeline said, referring to her new best friend at school. Then she added, "Jenny has pink Cinderella drink yogurts, and chips and soda in her lunch box. Why can't I have those things in my lunch box?"

I tried to frame a convincing answer. I told Adeline that those foods were just snacks, not the kind of foods you should eat every day, and I explained that it was important to eat a good lunch for thinking power at school and for growing up healthy and strong. But to a four-year-old, this was a less than convincing argument.

So we compromised. We agreed that I would include a packet of chips or a Cinderella yogurt in Adeline's lunch box twice a week if she would eat her sandwich and fruit on the other days. I wasn't happy giving her food that I knew was nutritionally empty, but I determined that it was better to let her have these foods occasionally than to restrict her from having them at all. Denying children certain foods—specifically junk food or candy—only makes them fixate on the junk and candy until fresh, nutritious food loses its appeal altogether.

So when the healthy, balanced diet meets the realities of furiously marketed children's food products, the healthy, balanced diet must yield a little—but not too much.

Mom, the Caterer

Five-year-old Jimmy and three-year-old Lily looked unimpressed when their mother served them their favorite meal of pot roast for dinner. "I don't want that tonight," Jimmy piped up, "I want pasta."

"I want a grilled cheese sandwich," said Lily.

"Can't you just eat what I've made you?" pleaded their mother.

"No," said Jimmy. "Then we won't have anything."

"All right," said their mother with a sigh. "I will make you something new, but it has to be just one thing. Can't you both have the same thing if I make something new?"

"I only want pasta," said Jimmy.

"I just want my sandwich," said Lily.

Their mother heaved a sigh of frustration and went back to the kitchen to cook two more meals.

It's natural for parents to worry that their child will go hungry when she refuses to eat a meal. To make sure she doesn't go hungry, some parents will readily offer other choices. To a child, this action and reaction quickly becomes a game, and she will soon learn she doesn't have to eat the first choice of food served if she doesn't want to. But when this becomes a regular occurrence, the kitchen soon turns into a catering service—with Mom or Dad as the short-order cook.

There's only one way to close down this catering service, and that's by making a conscious effort to offer your child only one meal at mealtimes. Cook a meal you know she likes, and if it is refused, do not offer her any other choices. As soon as she realizes you won't play the catering game anymore, she will eat what's offered, and you'll be back to cooking just one meal at each mealtime.

"Dinner was over an hour ago, but I'm hungry now"

It is a very common occurrence: your child eats poorly at dinnertime, then claims he's ready to eat an hour later—usually close to bedtime. Precisely because this is so common, before you offer your child something to eat, make it clear that he can have something to eat just this once. Otherwise, not eating at dinner and demanding a meal before bed will become a nightly habit that delays bedtime.

If you do feed him something to eat before bed, make sure it is simple and nutritious. Offer leftovers from dinner, a piece of cheese, or perhaps some fruit. Do not begin cooking again: dinner is over, and dinnertime is past. Besides, there is a good chance he may not even eat what you make, and you will have wasted your time and grown more frustrated. Your child, meanwhile, might latch onto this new "game" of getting you to cook for him and expect the same thing tomorrow night.

Cooking for Kids: Preparing a Healthy, Balanced Diet

Cooking for children doesn't have to be difficult or time-consuming. Chances are it can't be, anyway, since those people doing the cooking are strapped for time, and confronting tired and hungry kids. But can health-ful, nutritious, balanced meals really be prepared quickly and easily? The answer is an emphatic yes, because fresh ingredients, healthfully prepared, make the quintessential fast food—especially once you know our three se-crets to cooking healthy, balanced meals fast and without stress:

- Plan ahead.
- Keep a well-stocked kitchen.
- Use our "nanny shortcuts."

Plan ahead.

Try to make it an early morning habit to think about dinner that evening. If you can, plan lunch and dinner at breakfast. That way, you have time to check that you have all the needed ingredients, or to take something out of the freezer to defrost, or to prep some of the meal during your child's nap time. If it's going to be a busy day, plan a simple meal; save the more in-volved recipes for when you have more time. On days when you do have more time, wash and cut up vegetables and fruit to stockpile in the fridge for snacks, side dishes, or main dishes.

Keep a well-stocked kitchen.

This is a must. If you always keep such basics as pasta, rice, couscous, canned tomatoes, beans, eggs, vegetables, and cheese on hand, then find-ing something delicious to cook for dinner will be easy. For example, if you have eggs and cheese in the fridge, you can whip up an omelet in less than ten minutes. Or, if you have a can of tomatoes, some olive oil, and some garlic, you can make a simple tomato sauce for pasta in just fifteen minutes. Or, you can put a few potatoes in a hot oven to bake while you bathe the children or help them with their homework; by the time the potatoes are ready to eat, all you will need to do is top them with a little cheese, sour cream, tuna, or beans and serve them with a salad or some vegetables.

Use our "nanny shortcuts."

Since we love to cook, there are days when there is nothing we would rather do than putter about the kitchen, lingering over slow-cooking food.

Attention: Allergies!

On a trip to the British Virgin Islands, I noticed my six-year-old charge, David, taking a bite of a friend's chicken satay dinner. I ran to his side instantly and used my fingers to scoop what he had just eaten right out of his mouth. Why did I react so dramatically? Because David had a serious allergy to peanuts that would have sent him to the hospital if he had swallowed the satay sauce—an Indonesian classic with a peanut base.

The most common kids' allergies are to dairy foods, wheat-based foods, nuts, eggs, and citrus. Allergy symptoms can include a rash or hives on the body, swelling, respiratory problems, nausea, and vomiting. If any of these symptoms occur after eating, call the doctor immediately.

Nuts in particular can cause a very serious reaction, one that can move with lightning speed. For this reason, it is a good idea simply not to give nuts to children under the age of three.

When a child has a food allergy, it is essential to take extra care to check all the ingredients in all the food he eats; sometimes the most innocent item—a muffin, for example—is actually made with nuts. Or a birthday cake has strawberries in the center. In those cases, the food must be avoided. It is equally crucial to make certain that everyone who is in contact with the child is aware of the allergy and knows what to do in case of an allergy emergency.

FOODS TO AVOID

UNDER THE AGE OF . . .	DO NOT GIVE KIDS . . .
ONE YEAR	honey—risk of infant botulism berries—allergy risk citrus fruit—allergy risk
TWO YEARS	shellfish—allergy risk popcorn—choking risk hot dogs—choking risk small candies—choking risk
THREE YEARS	nuts—allergy and choking risks

Most days, however, we need to get meals on the table in a flash. After years in the nanny profession, we know every shortcut there is to achieving a fresh, nutritious, balanced, speedy meal, and here they are.

Batch cooking and freezing is one of the most useful time-savers there is when you're cooking for kids. It is easy to cook double the quantity of a meat sauce for spaghetti, chili, soup, stew, or a casserole and then freeze the extra—be sure to label the food with both date and contents. Most food will keep well in the freezer for two or three months, so on a night when you're pressed for time or are too exhausted to cook, just reach into the freezer for an easy dinner option.

To defrost food safely, place frozen food on a plate in the refrigerator (for a slow defrost), or submerge the container of frozen food in a bowl or sink full of cold water (for a faster defrost). Alternatively, you can defrost in the microwave. Always make sure food is heated through evenly when reheating.

When you are really pressed for time, choose a recipe that is *simple and quick*. Dinner need not be a nightly extravaganza of meat and three vegetables; eggs, soups and toasted sandwiches, quesadillas, and one-bowl dinners like ravioli, beans and rice, pasta dishes, couscous and vegetables with chicken, and stir-fries make superb and entirely satisfying meals.

Cooking one meal for children and another for adults is not only time-consuming, it's also unnecessary. With a few slight *adjustments*, you can cook just one meal that suits both grown-ups' and kids' tastes. For example, serve everybody the same chicken and vegetable stir-fry, but add some simple herbs and spices or some chili sauce to the adults' plates.

Using *leftover foods to create new meals* is not only a time-saver, it is also a practical use of food that would otherwise be wasted. For example, left-over mashed potatoes can be used to make salmon cakes; leftover rice can be combined with eggs, bacon, and vegetables to create quick fried rice; and leftover marinara sauce can be used for pizzas.

Fortunately, there are some high-quality *convenience foods* available; by all means, make use of these foods to cut down significantly on prepa-ration and cooking time. For example, a rotisserie chicken from the mar-ket can be used to make chicken quesadillas or can be added to a vegetable soup, pasta sauce, or risotto. A good pesto from the specialty shop, some ready-made potato gnocchi, and a few pieces of broccoli make a terrific standby meal for busy nights. You can get dinner started with a pizza base, top it with a pasta sauce and a few pieces of packaged salami, pop it into a hot oven, and dinner will be on the table in fifteen minutes. Or you can assemble a yummy quiche with a premade pastry shell and a

A CHILD'S HEALTHY, BALANCED DIET:
A ONE-WEEK SAMPLE

	BREAKFAST	SNACK	LUNCH	SNACK	DINNER
MONDAY	Boiled eggs and toast	Fruit	Pita Pizzas with salad	Yogurt	Nanny's Shepherd's Pie with vegetables
TUESDAY	Oatmeal with fresh fruit	Glass of milk	Sandwich with raw vegetables	Yogurt and blueberries	Orange Beef and Broccoli Stir-fry
WEDNESDAY	Toast and Sunshine Smoothie	Glass of milk and cookies	Teddy Bears' Picnic platter	Pear and slice of cheese	Aussie Fish-and-chips or take-out meal
THURSDAY	Cereal with fruit	Cheese and crackers	My Best Spaghetti with salad	Fresh fruit	Mini-quesadillas with rice and beans
FRIDAY	Muffin with fruit	Raw vegetables and hummus	Asian Soup	Fruit with yogurt	Miller Family Salmon Cakes with vegetables or salad
SATURDAY	Pancakes with fruit (brunch out with family)	Carrot sticks and guacamole	Sandwich with fruit	Glass of juice, piece of cheese	Chopstick Chicken and Noodles, Glorious Fruit Crumble or Perfect Rice Pudding
SUNDAY	Scrambled eggs with bagel	Fresh fruit	Fabulous Finger Foods	Yogurt/treat	Old-fashioned Macaroni and Cheese with vegetables

mixture of eggs, cheese, and bacon; in the twenty minutes it takes to bake, you can catch up on a chore—or just put your feet up.

It's important, however, to check the ingredients of convenience or premade foods. Try to avoid any product with ingredients you don't recognize or with such items as high-fructose corn syrup or hydrogenated oils—the former is highly genetically modified, and the latter contain trans fats, which are extremely unhealthy. In addition, many convenience foods contain fillers and other unknown ingredients which have no nutritional or health value.

Precut fruit and vegetables, prewashed salad leaves, and precut meat can certainly help speed up meal preparation, but they tend to be quite expensive. For some families, however, the additional expense is worth the time saved and the convenience.

Keeping Kids Busy While You Are Cooking

Trying to cook a meal around young children who are unoccupied and demanding of your attention can be difficult. That's why your cooking time can be a great opportunity for the kids to play on their own—of course, in a safe play area with age-appropriate toys. Such playtime is an important part of your child's development: it encourages independence and teaches him to enjoy his own company.

Kitchen Safety

When kids are in the kitchen, it's essential that you always know exactly where they are and what they are doing. Never turn your back on a child who is near an oven or an electric appliance. Never let children run with utensils or walk around with silverware in their mouths. Always turn the handles of pans inward, toward the back of the stove, so that children can't reach them. Wet floors can be slippery; keep kids out of the kitchen if you've washed the floor.

So put on some music and set the child up with a toy or game in a place in or close to the kitchen where you can see him and he can see you. Or sit him at the kitchen table or in his high chair with crayons and paper so he can draw and talk to you while you cook. Many of the children we have cared for have drawn their first circle or learned the names of colors while we were making their dinner. Play-Doh is also a great entertainment for slightly older children while you are busy in the kitchen.

But one of the best activities to occupy older kids while you are cooking is to have them help out in the kitchen. We love to assign our charges with washing vegetables, stirring batters, or setting the table—and they love it, too. They find it a highly enjoyable and interesting activity; it is also an excellent way to encourage a healthy interest in food, mealtimes, and cooking.

A Healthy, Balanced Diet

★ Kids need fresh food and healthy, balanced meals.

★ Turning kids' diets around is possible at any time: use the Nannies' Ten Strategies.

★ Family mealtimes have a powerful and positive impact on kids.

★ If mealtimes have turned into a battleground, check the following:
  • Do you have regular mealtimes?
  • Do you share meals with your children?
  • Do you reward fussiness with attention, by bribing, begging, or similar tactics?
  • Are you offering multiple choices at mealtimes?
  • Is your child snacking and drinking excessively in between meals?
  • Could your child be going through a fussy stage?

★ Good table manners need to be taught to kids daily and reinforced consistently.

Nanny Recipes

Here is a selection of our best-loved recipes. Each one has been tried and tested by kids and their families on three continents.

We've divided the recipe offerings into two categories. "Meals in minutes" are literally that—entire meals you can prepare in well under thirty minutes, in most cases. Dishes that are "worth the wait" take a bit longer to prepare and cook, but on those days when you have the time, we promise you'll be glad you made the extra effort.

We've also noted "time-savers"—ways to make preparing a recipe even faster, or ways to use the recipe to make life easier later on.

We hope you'll make these recipes the foundation of a healthy, balanced diet for your children. Let the recipes be the starting point for your own creativity as you give your kids the gift of health and pleasure that is good eating.

Meals in Minutes

SUNSHINE SMOOTHIES

2 adult servings

Fruit-and-yogurt smoothies are the perfect quick breakfast for busy mornings or for a child who doesn't eat breakfast very well; they also make an ideal snack during the day. These Sunshine Smoothies are full of vitamins and nutrients, and kids just love them. For added fun and enjoyment, give your child a straw to drink them with.

> 1 cup orange juice
> 1½ cups frozen or fresh berries: strawberries, raspberries, blackberries,
>   or blueberries are ideal
> 1 large banana
> Optional: ½ cup plain, full-fat yogurt
> NOTE: If fresh berries are used, you will also need 4 ice cubes.

Put all the ingredients in a blender and puree until smooth.

MINI-QUESADILLAS

1–2 adult servings

A few years ago, I went on a trip to Mexico with a family I was working for. We stayed in a small, very cozy hotel and became fast friends with the owners; my three-year-old charge, Julie, spent a lot of time playing with the owners' children. The owners were Mexican and Italian, and they had introduced their kids to a variety of foods from both cultures in shared meals, with the children eating the same food as the parents. The result was two very adventurous eaters. Julie, whom I had known only a month, was not an adventurous eater; rather, she always stuck with the same foods and was not open to trying anything new—until she became friends with the hotel kids and began to try all the foods her new friends were eating. These mini-quesadillas were her all-time favorite.

> *1–2 tablespoons olive oil*
> *Choices of fillings: spinach, mushrooms, peppers, chicken*
> *¾ cup grated cheese*
> *2 tortillas*
> *Optional: guacamole, salsa, sour cream*

Over medium heat, heat olive oil in a large frying pan or griddle and sauté your chosen fillings until cooked.

Sprinkle some cheese and then your fillings on top of one tortilla, sprinkle with more cheese, and stack the second tortilla on top.

Place the tortillas back in the pan, cover, and cook over medium heat until the cheese has melted and the tortilla is slightly browned (you can press the tortilla together with a heavy spatula). Let the tortilla cool a little, then cut into triangles and serve with optional extras: guacamole, salsa, or sour cream.

Serve with rice and beans, salad, or vegetables.

TEDDY BEARS' PICNIC

This picnic food always reminds me of cool summer afternoons in London with James and Hannah. They became very excited whenever I told them it was time for a teddy bears' picnic, and they knew exactly what to do. They would help me lay out plastic plates, cups, and napkins on a blanket in the garden, and then they would collect all their teddy bears together and invite them to our picnic, where we would dig into the picnic-style finger foods. This picnic is a wonderful way to introduce young children to a variety of unique foods: olives, hummus, guacamole, and salsa. All of the dips can be purchased at the supermarket, or you can make them fresh at home.

> Small servings of hummus, salsa, and guacamole
> Selection of cheeses: cheddar, goat, cream, cottage, baked ricotta
> Selection of cold cuts: turkey, ham, salami, roast chicken, roast beef
> Crackers, pita bread, baguette, rolls
> Pitted olives, pickles
> Carrot sticks
> Celery sticks
> Cucumber, sliced and peeled
> Cherry tomatoes
> Boiled eggs

Arrange small portions of each ingredient on a large platter. Dig in.

PITA PIZZAS

2 adult servings

Having always liked cheese, James, at two and a half, suddenly declared it "icky." He would refuse even a mouthful of anything that smelled or looked like it was made with cheese, so you can imagine my astonishment when, at his friend Jack's house, he began to share the pizza Jack was eating. What amazed me was how much he enjoyed the pizza, which of course was covered with melted cheese. From that day on, whenever we went to Jack's house for a playdate, James would ask to have pizza for dinner, his dislike of cheese disappearing for those few moments while he was eating the same meal as his friend.

> *4 small pita breads*
> *4 tablespoons tomato paste or marinara sauce*
> *Optional toppings: salami slices, slices of tomato, mushrooms, red or green*
>   *peppers, ham, baby spinach, turkey, pineapple pieces*
> *¼ cup fresh mozzarella, cut into thin slices, or cheddar cheese, grated*

Place pita breads under hot broiler and toast for 1–2 minutes or until just browned; turn and toast other side very lightly.

Spread the lightly toasted side of each pita with 1 tablespoon tomato paste or marinara sauce; arrange optional toppings on pitas and cover with cheese.

Broil until cheese is melted (2–4 minutes).

Allow to cool a little (cheese will be very hot), then cut into pieces small enough for toddlers to handle.

Serve with salad.

ASIAN SOUP

4 adult servings

When two-and-a-half-year-old Jenny told me she'd like "noodle soup" for dinner, I knew she was not thinking of a traditional noodle soup but of an Asian broth she and I both loved. Jenny lived in Sydney, Australia, where Asian fusion-style cuisine is everywhere. In fact, it is not unusual to see Aussie kids tucking into a pad Thai or a mild shrimp curry. Since caring for Jenny, I have taken this simple soup recipe across the world to all my nanny jobs, and it has consistently been a great success.

6 cups chicken stock
¼ cup soy sauce or tamari
1 clove garlic, crushed
1 teaspoon fresh cilantro leaves or stalks, finely sliced
1 carrot, sliced into thin long strips
½ zucchini, sliced into long strips
½ cup broccoli, sliced into small pieces
2 chicken cutlets (with skin and bone removed), sliced very finely into long strips
Optional: fresh lime juice, sweet chili sauce (to taste)
8 ounces rice noodles

> ★ **TIME-SAVER** ★
>
> Use leftover cooked chicken breast or leftover roast chicken in place of chicken cutlets, or buy a rotisserie-style chicken, remove the skin, shred, and add to the broth at the end of cooking time just to heat it through.

In a medium-sized pot, add the chicken stock, soy sauce, garlic, cilantro, and carrot; stir to combine and bring to a fast simmer.

When the liquid is simmering, add the zucchini, broccoli, and chicken. The chicken will cook quickly in this liquid, turning white in 3–5 minutes—depending on how thinly it is sliced. You do not want to overcook the chicken. It should be cooked through, but still moist and tender, not rubbery. Add a good squeeze of lime juice, if using. Remove from heat and cover to keep warm.

Meanwhile, cook the rice noodles as directed on the package; they should take anywhere from 1–8 minutes to cook depending on the type of noodle.

Fill four bowls halfway with the cooked rice noodles. Ladle the chicken, vegetables, and broth over the noodles. Adults and older children may want to add extra cilantro, lime, or sweet chili sauce to their serving.

MY BEST SPAGHETTI

4 adult servings

This spaghetti sauce is famous in the West London neighborhood where the family I worked for lived. Children who would eat only plain pasta without sauce would gobble it down as soon as it was placed in front of them. Parents and nannies routinely asked me my "secret," but the truth is there is no secret to this recipe; it's just a very simple homemade sauce. It is also a perfect recipe for disguising vegetables for kids' fussy stages, which can be accomplished by pureeing the sauce. And here's a tip to make spaghetti easier for young children to manage if they can't be persuaded that half the fun of eating spaghetti is to suck up the "worms": just chop it up with scissors.

16 ounces spaghetti

1–2 tablespoons extra-virgin olive oil

1 small red onion, chopped very finely

2 cloves garlic, crushed

One 28-ounce can whole crushed tomatoes

*Optional vegetables: finely sliced
    mushrooms, carrots, or zucchini*

*Optional: 2 tablespoons finely chopped
    fresh basil*

Parmesan cheese to serve

Cook spaghetti as directed on package.

In a medium-sized saucepan, sauté the onion and garlic in olive oil over medium heat for 3–5 minutes, or until onion is soft; stir to prevent the garlic from burning.

> ★ TIME-SAVER ★
>
> This sauce is fantastic for freezing, so make double the quantity and freeze half. Measure individual portions of the *cooled* sauce and pour into plastic Ziploc bags or containers to freeze. When I am in a hurry, I just pull out the individual portions from the freezer and defrost them by holding the bags or containers under a stream of hot tap water. The sauce will then pour easily into a saucepan to reheat while the spaghetti is cooking.

Add the can of tomatoes to the saucepan and stir to combine; cook the sauce over medium-high heat for 15–20 minutes, uncovered, stirring occasionally; add the optional vegetables and cook for another 5 minutes.

When sauce is thick, remove from heat; stir in basil if desired; add salt and pepper to taste.

Serve over spaghetti, and sprinkle some grated Parmesan cheese on top.

Serve with a side salad.

CHOPSTICK CHICKEN AND NOODLES

2 adult servings

This particular recipe brings back memories of teaching toddlers to use chopsticks. On a visit to Chinatown, I discovered training chopsticks for kids—small wooden tongs that were joined together at one end, perfect tools for little fingers. I used this recipe for Mark's first chopstick experience; many giggles and much flying food accompanied the meal. He had so much fun that Chopstick Chicken became a regular request. Soon enough, Mark's chopstick skills were perfected, and within two weeks, he was teaching his friend Jonathan to use them.

8 ounces fresh fettuccine or egg/rice noodles
3 tablespoons sesame oil
2 cloves garlic, crushed
1 teaspoon fresh ginger, sliced
1 small onion, chopped finely
2 chicken breast cutlets (skin and bone removed), cut into very thin slices
1½ cups green beans, sliced
¼ cup red pepper, sliced into strips
1 carrot, peeled and cut into very thin strips
¼ cup water
¼ cup soy sauce or tamari
Optional: ¼ cup chopped fresh basil or fresh cilantro

Cook the noodles as directed on the package and drain well.

Meanwhile, heat the oil in a wok or large frying pan over high heat. Add the garlic, ginger, and onion; sauté for 3 minutes.

Add the chicken and sauté for 5–8 minutes, until slightly browned and cooked through. Remove chicken from pan and set aside.

Add the green beans, pepper, carrot, water, and soy sauce; if more liquid is needed, add a few extra tablespoons of water, then cover with a lid and allow the vegetables to cook on high heat for 3–4 minutes, or until cooked through.

Remove the lid, and add the cooked chicken and fresh herbs. Stir and cook for another 1–2 minutes.

Serve with the noodles.

EASY PEASY RICE

4 adult servings

Here's a recipe I would often turn to after rushing into the house from a busy afternoon of after-school ballet or swimming lessons. It's quick and simple so you can get dinner on the table really fast, and it is perfect for tired and hungry little children who need something satisfying before bath and bedtime. Kids call this dish Easy Peasy Rice. It can be whipped up in under twenty minutes using basic ingredients from a well-stocked kitchen.

> 1 red onion, roughly chopped
>
> 2 cloves garlic, crushed
>
> 2 tablespoons olive oil
>
> 1 cup white rice
>
> One 28-ounce can Italian whole or plum tomatoes
>
> 1 cup water
>
> 1 cup peas, frozen or cooked fresh
>
> 1 cup corn kernels, frozen or cooked fresh
>
> 1 zucchini, sliced finely
>
> Optional: 1 small can butter beans, slices of rotisserie chicken,
> small can of tuna (drained)
>
> Salt and pepper
>
> ½ cup fresh basil
>
> Freshly grated Parmesan or cheddar cheese to serve

In a medium-sized saucepan over medium heat, sauté the onion and garlic in olive oil for 2 minutes.

Add the rice, stir vigorously to coat in oil mixture for 1 minute.

Add the tomatoes and water.

When the liquid is bubbling, turn heat to medium-low and add the vegetables. Cover and allow to cook for 10 minutes, stirring occasionally. Add optional ingredients, if using.

Remove lid and cook for a few minutes more, until the vegetables are done and the rice is tender, with a risotto-like consistency, adding water if needed.

Season with salt and pepper to taste.

Top with grated cheese and serve.

CHICKEN FINGERS

2 adult servings

We love to hear a child claim "That's my favorite" as he rushes eagerly to the dinner table. With the kindergarten set, this is the recipe most likely to bring on that kind of response. Children really love these chicken strips; expect that you will be asked to make them at least once a week.

> *1 cup flour*
> *1 egg, lightly beaten—and a splash of milk*
> *1 cup bread crumbs (homemade, fresh from bakery,*
> *   or good-quality packaged brand)*
> *Generous amount of olive, vegetable, or sunflower oil (approximately 1 cup)*
> *2 boneless chicken breast cutlets, pounded and cut into 2-inch strips*

Place the flour in one medium-sized bowl, the egg in another, and the bread crumbs in another.

Dip the chicken strips in the flour, then in the eggs; then roll and cover the chicken in the bread crumbs.

Heat the oil in a medium-sized frying pan over medium heat; then add the chicken strips and fry until golden brown and cooked through, about 4–5 minutes on each side.

Remove the chicken strips and drain them on a paper towel.

Serve with salad or vegetables. Homemade fries, or baked or mashed potatoes, are delicious with this dish.

FABULOUS FINGER FOODS

2 adult servings

This combination of tempting finger foods is the ideal solution for toddlers in a fussy eating stage. Being able to pick and choose small things to nibble on is exactly how many toddlers like to eat their meals, and if you let your toddler help himself, you may be surprised at just how well he eats.

TASTY 'TATOES
2 medium red-skinned potatoes, washed and sliced into quarters
2 tablespoons olive oil
A sprinkle of salt

Preheat oven to 500°F.

Toss the potato quarters in olive oil and salt and place on a baking tray.

Place the tray in the oven and bake for 25–30 minutes, or until potatoes are crispy and brown on the outside and the inside is soft and cooked through.

BITE-SIZE TURKEY BURGERS
½ pound ground turkey
Salt and pepper to taste
Generous amount of olive or vegetable oil
Optional: small rolls and a dash of ketchup

Combine the turkey with salt and pepper in a bowl. Form heaping tea-spoon–sized portions of the turkey mixture into balls.

Heat the oil in a frying pan over medium heat. Cook the turkey burgers for a few minutes on each side, until browned and cooked through completely. Take care not to crowd the pan or the burgers will not brown well. Remove from the pan and allow to sit for a minute before serving.

Serve the burgers on rolls, with ketchup, if desired.

VEGETABLE OPTIONS
Raw carrot sticks
Steamed broccoli florets
Cooked corn on the cob, cut into 2-inch pieces
Cherry tomatoes

Serve the turkey burgers on a platter with the potatoes and the vegetables.

ORANGE BEEF AND BROCCOLI STIR-FRY

4 adult servings

We have both lived in the same Brooklyn neighborhood since coming to New York. Much to our delight, there is an abundance of Asian restaurants that are both affordable and delicious. When working the occasional weekend, we have taken our charges to these fabulous restaurants, which are always a huge success with the toddlers and preschoolers we care for. This recipe, to be served with rice noodles, spaghetti, egg fettuccini, jasmine or white or brown rice, was inspired by these outings.

2 tablespoons hoisin sauce

2 tablespoons water

3 tablespoons orange juice

1 pound lean beef, sliced very thinly into long strips

2 tablespoons sesame oil

1 clove garlic, crushed

½ red onion, cut finely

2 medium carrots, peeled and cut into thin matchsticks

1 cup broccoli, cut into very small pieces

Optional: 1 cup baby corn

2 tablespoons soy sauce

> ★ TIME-SAVER ★
>
> Purchase thinly sliced meat and/or precut vegetables. These prepared foods tend to be more expensive, but for the super-busy person, the time-saving can prove invaluable. I have heard from some parents that just having vegetables and meat cut and ready to use at the end of the day can make the difference between dialing for pizza and finding the energy to prepare a homemade meal.

Mix hoisin sauce, water, and orange juice in a medium-sized bowl. Add the beef to the liquid and allow to marinate 10 minutes to 1 hour—however long you can wait.

Heat the oil in a wok or large frying pan over high heat, add the onions and garlic, and cook for 1–2 minutes.

Add the beef and carrots; stir-fry over high heat for 8–10 minutes, or until cooked. Remove from pan and set aside.

Add the broccoli and optional baby corn to the pan with the soy sauce and ¼ cup water, cover, and allow to cook over high heat for 3–5 minutes, or until the vegetables are cooked but still crispy.

Add the beef and carrots back to the pan and cook for 1–2 minutes. Serve immediately.

Worth the Wait

NANNY'S SHEPHERD'S PIE (Good enough for the Nanny Club)
4 adult servings

As I sprinkled the last bit of cheese on top of my shepherd's pie and popped it into the waiting oven, I made a little wish that it would turn out just right. I had to admit I was feeling a bit of pressure to make a good impression on the "Nanny Club"—as my boss had secretly nicknamed a group of local nannies and their charges—due to arrive for lunch any minute. Anne, my boss, liked to compare the Nanny Club to a popular British soap opera, *Coronation St.*, because of the high drama with which the nannies discussed neighborhood gossip at their regular get-togethers—but I was new to the area and keen to be included in this well-established group.

The London nanny scene was a community unto itself. With its frequent playdates, regular meetings in the park, and nanny social life, it had its own unwritten rules and standards. Top nannies had the highest standards; the Nanny Club was far tougher than any employer could be, and pleasing the club members would be no easy task.

Nor was competitiveness unknown. The previous week we had gathered at Monica's for an afternoon tea of hot scones, homemade plum jam, and clotted Devonshire cream—a treat for all of us, nannies and kids as well. And yesterday, Vanessa had won everyone's admiration when she involved the kids in making their own individual pizzas for lunch. I told myself I was not getting caught up in the competition, but I also knew that my shepherd's pie lunch was my bid to join the Nanny Club, and I fully expected my meal to be judged rigorously on the following criteria: it had to be a hit with the kids and the nannies; it had to be ready on time; and it had to be nutritious as well as tasty.

Nanny's Shepherd's Pie was my charge's favorite meal. It also just happened to be the dish I was famous for in this family and in all the other families I had worked for. There was a secret to it, which grown-ups told me made my dish better than the usual—a dash of Worcestershire sauce, some fresh herbs, and a tomato sauce instead of the traditional gravy.

Did this shepherd's pie get me into the Nanny Club? It did.

PIE BASE

2 tablespoons olive oil

1 onion, chopped

2 cloves garlic, sliced or crushed

Optional: 1 leek, washed and finely chopped

1½ pounds ground lamb, beef, or turkey

1 cup green peas, frozen or cooked fresh

2 large carrots, washed and finely sliced

One 28-ounce can whole tomatoes

Generous dash of Worcestershire sauce

2 tablespoons fresh rosemary or thyme

Salt and pepper

1 bay leaf

> ★ TIME-SAVER ★
>
> I always cook double the quantity of the meat mixture and freeze half. The next time I want to cook shepherd's pie, all I need to do is defrost and heat the meat while cooking the mashed-potato topping. Another great time-saver is to cook this dish when you have leftover mashed potatoes.

MASHED POTATO TOPPING

4 or 5 large potatoes, peeled and chopped

½ cup milk or heavy cream

2–3 tablespoons butter

¼ cup grated cheddar cheese

Optional: Fresh chives, chopped

Preheat oven to 400°F.

Add the olive oil to a large saucepan and sauté the onion, garlic, and optional leeks over medium-high heat for 3–5 minutes, or until soft. Add the meat to the pan and cook until browned, stirring occasionally.

Add the peas, carrots, tomatoes, Worcestershire sauce, and herbs to the pan. Reduce heat to medium and cook for 20–30 minutes, stirring occasionally, until carrots are soft and liquid is reduced. Add salt and pepper to taste.

Meanwhile, add the potatoes to a large pot of salted water, cover, and cook over medium-high heat until they are soft, about 20 minutes. Drain the potatoes and return them to the pan. While the potatoes are still steaming, add the milk or cream and butter, mashing until smooth and creamy. Add salt and pepper to taste.

Pour the meat mixture into an ovenproof dish, evenly spoon the mashed potatoes over the meat, and cover the mashed potatoes with the grated cheese and optional chives. Bake for 40 minutes, until topping is brown and crisp.

AUSSIE FISH-AND-CHIPS

4 adult servings

The most common sight on the beach at the end of a long, hot Australian summer day is kids still in their wet cossies (Australian for "swimsuits"), their skin greasy with thick sunscreen, munching away on fish-and-chips wrapped in paper. The tender fish with its crispy coating and the hot fried potatoes satisfies the hunger worked up by hours of swimming in the surf.

One evening in New York, homesick for the bright Australian sun, I decided to make my own version of fish-and-chips for Nicky and Charlie, who had until this point rejected every attempt I had made to convince them to try fish. It worked. Accompanied by my tales of home that I served up with the meal, the dish was an instant hit with these New York boys—and a breakthrough for fish in their diet.

> *1 cup all-purpose flour*
> *2 eggs, lightly beaten*
> *1 cup bread crumbs*
> *4 fillets of thin white fish (cod or flounder, for example),*
> *   skinned and de-boned*
> *Generous amount of olive or vegetable oil (you will need enough oil to just*
> *   cover the potatoes and fish when they are in the pan)*
> *3 Idaho potatoes, peeled and cut into one-inch-thick strips*

Put the flour in one medium-sized bowl, the eggs in another, and the bread crumbs in another. Coat the fish in the flour, then dip into the eggs, then coat well in the bread crumbs.

Heat the oil in a deep, large frying pan until it is very hot but not smoking and place the potatoes in the pan. Do not leave unattended. The key is to use very hot oil and not to move or turn the chips until the side that is browning is crisp. Too much turning, or oil that is not hot enough, will result in a mushy potato pancake. When browned and cooked through, remove the chips with a slotted spoon and set on a plate covered with a paper towel to drain excess oil; sprinkle with salt.

Meanwhile, in another large frying pan, heat the oil and panfry the fish until the outside is browned and crispy—usually just a few minutes on each side.

Serve with lemon wedges and a salad.

OLD-FASHIONED MACARONI AND CHEESE

2 adult servings

Macaroni and cheese is one of those classic dishes many adults long for when thinking of childhood—the quintessential comfort food. On bitter midwinter evenings in New York, when I made this meal for Joseph, I would always make an extra amount for his parents to welcome them when they came inside from the cold. It goes particularly well with buttered beans and peas. Other classic kids' meals can be made with this cheese sauce, or it can be mixed with steamed cauliflower or broccoli to make a vegetable bake; or added to tuna and sweet corn to create a tuna casserole.

> *8–10 ounces macaroni pasta*
> *2 tablespoons butter*
> *2 tablespoons all-purpose flour*
> *2 cups milk*
> *1 heaping teaspoon Dijon mustard*
> *1 cup grated cheddar cheese, plus 2 tablespoons extra cheese*
> *Salt and pepper to taste*
> *¼ cup bread crumbs*

Preheat oven to 450°F.

Cook the macaroni as directed on package and drain well.

Meanwhile, make the cheese sauce. The key to this sauce is constant stirring to prevent lumps. Place the butter in a medium-sized saucepan and stir with a wooden spoon over medium heat until it is melted. Add the flour and stir quickly to combine. Cook for a few minutes but do not let the mixture brown. Bit by bit, slowly add the milk, mixing to prevent lumps. Keep stirring until the sauce starts to bubble (this may take 5–10 minutes), mix in the mustard, and allow to cook until the sauce has thickened a little—5–8 minutes more.

Remove the sauce from the heat and stir in the cheese, stirring until the cheese has melted; season with salt and pepper.

Combine the sauce with the macaroni and pour into a buttered ovenproof dish. Sprinkle with bread crumbs and top with the remaining cheese.

Bake for 15 minutes or until top is golden.

MILLER FAMILY SALMON CAKES

4 adult servings

One of my first nanny positions was for the Miller family. On Rosh Hashanah, the Jewish New Year, Grandma Miller taught me how to make their family's traditional salmon cakes. They were a huge hit with the children, and since then this recipe has been part of my nanny recipe repertoire. Kids enjoy the crunchy texture of the salmon cake with its soft potato filling and subtle fish flavor.

3 large potatoes, peeled and cubed
1 tablespoon lemon juice
12–14-ounce can red salmon
*2 tablespoons matzo meal or bread
    crumbs for patty mixture*
1 teaspoon fresh parsley, chopped
1 teaspoon fresh chives, chopped
1 egg, lightly beaten
Salt and pepper
¼ cup matzo meal for coating
*Generous amount of olive or vegetable oil
    for frying*

> ★ **TIME-SAVER** ★
>
> This is a great recipe for using up leftover mashed potatoes or leftover pieces of cooked fresh salmon, and using leftovers substantially cuts preparation time. These salmon cakes freeze well for one month. Place pieces of waxed paper or foil between cakes before freezing. When you are ready to use them, place the salmon cakes on a baking tray and reheat in a preheated 450°F oven for 20–30 minutes, or until cooked through.

Place the potatoes in a pot of water, bring to a boil, and cook on medium heat for 15–20 minutes, or until soft. When the potatoes are soft, drain the water thoroughly and mash them with the lemon juice.

Check the salmon for fine bones and remove any remaining skin. Combine the salmon, parsley, chives, egg, matzo meal or bread crumbs, salt and pepper to taste, and mashed potato in a bowl. Form the mixture into round patties.

Pour the matzo meal onto a plate and roll the patties in the meal to coat them. Refrigerate the patties for 15–20 minutes or overnight.

Remove salmon patties from the refrigerator. Heat the oil in a large frying pan over medium-high heat. Panfry the salmon in the oil for 4–5 minutes on each side, turning only once. When the patties are brown, remove from the pan and blot excess oil with a paper towel.

Serve with vegetables or salad.

GLORIOUS FRUIT CRUMBLE

4 adult servings

Holly and I would often cook together while her baby sister was napping; it was our special time together when we could chat uninterrupted. Holly's mom, a professional chef, taught us this recipe. Holly and I would work side by side, each taking a task; for example, I would slice the fruit while Holly mixed the crumble topping. We would chat about school, our favorite things, and the places we wanted to visit. On gray midwinter afternoons in London, the kitchen was always brightened by our flowing conversation and the cozy smell of cinnamon and sugar as the crumble baked.

FRUIT MIXTURE

½ stick butter

2 tablespoons white sugar

1 cinnamon stick

2 pears, peeled, cored, and cut
   into thick slices

6 red apples, peeled, cored, and
   cut into thick slices

2 teaspoons ground nutmeg

2 teaspoons ground cinnamon

2 teaspoons water

CRUMBLE TOPPING

2 cups all-purpose flour

¾ cup white sugar

1½ sticks butter, cut into cubes

1 teaspoon powdered ginger

1 teaspoon grated or powdered
   nutmeg

2 teaspoons powdered cinnamon

Preheat oven to 350°F.

In a large, deep frying pan, melt the butter over medium-high heat, add the sugar and cinnamon stick, and stir. Add the fruit and spices, and fry for 2–3 minutes. Add the water and cook, covered, until the fruit is soft but not mushy.

Meanwhile, place all the topping ingredients in a medium-sized bowl and mix well with hands, rubbing the butter into the flour until the topping resembles bread crumbs and all the butter is worked through.

Place the fruit in a buttered ovenproof dish, sprinkle the topping over it, and place a few dabs of butter on top. Bake for 20–30 minutes, until top is golden.

Serve with ice cream or whipped cream.

Variations: In summer you can use berries, peaches, or plums instead of apples and pears.

PERFECT RICE PUDDING

4 adult servings

There is something very comforting about homemade baked rice pudding with its simple flavor and creamy texture; it was always a favorite dessert at my family table. My English mother was taught this classic British recipe by her mother, and she then passed it on to me. When I worked as a nanny in London, my charges adored this recipe and would ask me to make it often. Their parents reminisced with me about the rice pudding they had at school; they claimed it was the one thing they looked forward to—British school lunches were notoriously inedible!

> 1 pat butter for buttering dish
> 1 cup cooked white rice
> 2 eggs
> 3 tablespoons superfine sugar
> ¼ cup heavy cream
> 2 cups whole milk
> 2 teaspoons vanilla extract
> Optional: ½ teaspoon freshly grated or powdered nutmeg

Preheat oven to 400°F.

Generously butter a medium-sized ovenproof dish, and place rice evenly in the buttered dish.

In a medium-sized bowl, whisk together the eggs, sugar, cream, milk, vanilla, and nutmeg (if using) until just combined.

Pour the milk mixture into the buttered dish over the rice.

Place the dish in the oven and bake until set and golden, about 1 hour. Take care not to overcook; the pudding will be slightly wobbly when ready.

Can be eaten warm or chilled with a splash of heavy cream.

Optional: Serve with a teaspoon of jam—it's heavenly!

Chapter Six

Loving Discipline

How to Be Firm and Fair with Your Children

It's eleven-thirty on a Saturday morning in the Harris household. Tom Harris has gone to pick up his mother so she can enjoy Saturday lunch with her granddaughters, three-year-old Louise and six-year-old Ashley, now glued to the tube in the Harris living room. "Girls," their mother calls out, "would you turn off the TV? Daddy will be home soon with Grandma."

The request is blithely ignored. Ashley and Louise remain mesmerized by the cartoons flitting across the screen.

Katie Harris repeats her request twice more from the kitchen, where she has begun to prepare lunch, then comes into the living room and sits down. "Girls," she begins, "Mommy would really like you to turn the TV off. Please, girls, Mommy really means it. You have been in front of this television for three hours already, and Daddy will be very annoyed if it is still on when he gets home."

"No, Mommy, we don't want to," Ashley replies straightforwardly.

"I know you don't, darlings, and I am sorry, but will you let me turn it off?" Katie waits a moment, then hesitantly hits the off button. Both girls immediately start screaming with outrage. Louise throws herself at her mother and tries to drag her away from the set. As Katie pleads with her younger daughter, her older daughter rushes to the TV and switches it on again.

Defeated, Katie sinks back down onto the sofa. "Ashley, please don't do this to me today. Oh, I suppose you can watch a little more, but when Daddy and Grandma come home, you have to turn the TV off. Okay?"

Her announcement has an instantaneous effect: the girls stop screaming and once again plunk themselves down in front of the television.

Soon after, Tom and his mother walk in. "Grandma is here, girls," says Katie in a forced cheerful tone. "Can you turn the TV off now, so you can say hello?"

"No!" the girls shout in unison, and Ashley adds, as she always does, "This is my favorite show."

Tom now enters the fray. "I am going to count to three," Tom announces, "and I want you to listen to your mother and turn this television off." He pauses. "One." Another pause. "Two."

Engrossed in the cartoons, the girls pay no attention to their father. Sensing a battle brewing, he takes a deep breath. "Two and a quarter," he goes on. "Two and a half. Two and three quarters . . ." The suspense builds. Will the girls move?

"Three," shouts Tom, marching over to the TV and switching it off.

Ashley immediately runs over to her mother. "Mommy," she whines, "can we just have ten more minutes?"

Louise, trying a different tactic, throws herself on the floor and commences a tantrum of spectacular proportions, screaming at the top of her lungs, "I want more."

Katie rushes to Louise's side to cuddle her. "Please don't cry, honey," she pleads. "Mommy and Daddy are sorry we made you cry." She looks up at her husband. "Why are you always so tough on the girls? They only want to watch TV for ten more minutes."

Tom raises his voice above the sounds of whining and crying. "My mother is here. It is time for lunch. And you know it won't be ten minutes, and we will have to go through this all over again."

The crying and whining grow louder.

"You've really upset them now, Tom," says Katie. "Come on, girls. Let's get a treat in the kitchen, and you'll both feel better." She turns to her mother-in-law. "The girls are really very tired today," Katie explains.

"You told me that last time I was here," says Grandma.

Clearly, the Harrises are lost when it comes to imposing discipline or instilling responsibility. Together, Katie and Tom's attempts at discipline were ineffective and even counterproductive. Their approach to discipline was inconsistent, and, lacking clear boundaries, the girls didn't pay attention to their parents' requests. Katie and Tom's methods of pleading, shouting and long, drawn-out countdowns were pointless. The girls ignored their father, as they knew their mother was an easier target. Katie and Tom disagreed with one another, in front of the kids, about their daughters' behavior. Katie rewarded her daughters for their unacceptable behavior with a treat, and then she made an excuse for their behavior to their grandmother, who was not persuaded. Perhaps Grandma knew what her son and daughter-in-law had yet to learn: that they weren't doing their children any favors by not imposing discipline consistently, effectively, and—of course—lovingly.

Without a doubt, discipline is the hardest part of a parent's role. And without a doubt, it is at the very core of parenting. Of course, you love your children with all your heart. You want them to be happy, and you want to give them everything you can. Your natural inclination is to say yes to every request. Besides, when every answer is yes, you avoid most conflict, tears, and tantrums. When every answer is yes, you don't have to be the bad guy—you can be the friend instead of the parent.

But the reality is that you are the parent, and, as we are sure you know, it is up to you to prepare your kids for the world outside your immediate family. They'll also get preparation for life from school, peers, religious institutions, sports, and the like, but the core values, knowledge, and skills they need for life will come from you.

These essential life skills are taught through loving discipline. What do we mean by "loving discipline"? We mean teaching, not punishing. We mean nurturing self-esteem by setting age-appropriate boundaries and limits. We mean being firm and fair, communicating clearly and acting consistently. We mean offering praise and encouragement when deserved and imposing consequences when needed. Loving discipline is not about controlling children, and it is certainly never about withholding affection or speaking harshly; it is about guiding your children and giving them the skills to find discipline within themselves. By imposing discipline lovingly, you ultimately instill in your children responsibility for their own actions and their own behavior.

Parents are their children's first teachers, and the most formative years of life are the early ones, so what you teach your kids early on will set them on the path to becoming well-adjusted, happy, functioning adults. The reverse is also true: what you don't teach your kids can leave them unprepared for dealing with others and for getting on well in the world.

To get on well in the world, children need to be taught fairness, kindness, and consideration for others. They need to be encouraged to take responsibility, to act independently, and to develop social skills and confidence. They need practice dealing constructively with frustration, anger, and disappointment. They need to know that life is not all yeses.

Without this knowledge, your child will not only be at a disadvantage; he could well be at a loss. If he won't share his toys at age three, or can't follow simple instructions in preschool at age five, or has trouble managing his frustrations and anger in class at age twelve, or cannot take responsibility for his actions and make healthy choices when faced with peer pressure at age sixteen, he will face many difficulties—maybe throughout his lifetime.

Some parents may be able to overlook shouting, tantrums, hitting, and kicking, but you can be sure that a child's playmates, teachers, and society at large will not overlook such behavior. The truth is that excusing or overlooking behavioral problems early on will only become magnified as the child grows older.

It can be hard for parents to say no to their children; parents who work long hours may find it particularly challenging. Many are struggling with guilt over going to work, long hours away from home, family schisms, or other upheavals, and may overcompensate by indulging their children in many different ways. Each indulgence seems minor at the time—saying yes to candy just before dinner, letting a child set her own bedtime, overlooking shouting and hitting, or giving in to a demand for the latest toy. Parents who feel guilty often refrain from saying no to their child. It's easy to understand why parents who have been at work all day don't want to spend the little time they have with their child being the disciplinarian. No parent wants to be the bad guy, and all parents want their children to love them. And sometimes, discipline falls by the wayside.

The truth is that your children will not love you any less if you discipline them and set appropriate boundaries. They will not become permanently unhappy, and your relationship with them will not be damaged. On the contrary. Imposing discipline lovingly shows your kids that you really care, and letting them know clearly what their boundaries are helps them feel secure. What's more, family life is more pleasant when simple things like brushing teeth, bedtime, bath, and getting dressed proceed without a fight or fuss, and when children communicate without screaming, hitting, or tantrums.

In a way, imposing loving discipline is simple. You just establish boundaries, set limits, and articulate rules. Then, if and when your child crosses a boundary, goes outside the limits, or breaks the rule—and every child does; it's a necessary part of growing up—you follow through with appropriate consequences. In time, your child will learn what constitutes acceptable behavior and what does not. But of course, it isn't simple at all.

Every step of it, from setting the standards and communicating them, to carrying out the consequences, is hard work. It is also very, very important. And it must all be done with love.

This chapter shows you how to make loving discipline an effective part of your parenting. First, we help you assess your own approach to behavior and discipline. Then we talk about how to set and enforce boundaries, limits, and rules while building independence. We also give you the tools for turning around a situation that's off on the wrong foot, and we provide tips on how to deal with some of the more common behavioral issues and for instilling the sense of responsibility that builds confidence in your children and nourishes their self-esteem.

Imposing Discipline, Instilling Responsibility: A Parent's Quiz

To start with, it makes sense for you to have an idea of your current approach to your kids' behavior. Sometimes, as we well know, it gets hard to see the forest for the trees. You're doing the best you can but it's difficult, in the midst of the day-to-day, to judge what the long-term effects of your discipline approach may be. In fact, it's not unusual for parents to make things a lot harder for themselves—and their kids—than necessary. So here are a few questions that will help give you an idea of your approach—and of how that approach can directly affect your child's behavior and your interactions with each other. This is not a test; it's a way of helping you find the potential soft spots in your approach to discipline.

1. Do you regularly make excuses for your children's behavior? For example, if your child is behaving badly, do you dismiss or "explain" the behavior by telling yourself and others that "he's tired" or "he's not feeling well"—even when that is not the case at all?

2. Do you have to beg or bribe your children to get them to pay attention to your requests? For example, do you ever tell them you will give them candy or a treat if they get dressed and ready quickly?

3. Do you hear yourself making empty threats—that is, threats you don't really intend to carry out? Let's say your older son hits your younger one. "If you hit your brother again you will go to your room," you declare, but he does, and you give him a second chance, then a third, and, in fact, he never goes to his room. That's an example of an empty threat.

4. Do your kids listen to you—or do you have to repeat instructions over and over again to get them moving?

5. Do you find yourself constantly shouting at your kids? And do your kids only listen to you when you raise your voice?

6. Do your kids run the household? Do they decide when they go to bed? Are they watching endless TV, telling you what to do, telling you what they will have for dinner each night, and shouting their demands?

7. Do you ignore your children's bad behavior in the hope that it will go away all by itself? For example, have you decided that whining, rudeness, or shouting is just a way for your kids to express themselves or it's a phase they will outgrow?

8. Do your rules change—monthly, weekly, daily? Do you find yourself allowing candy before dinner one day, then deciding the next day that "we don't have candy before dinner"? Did the jumping on the sofa you found funny yesterday suddenly become grounds for your kids to be sent to their room?

9. Do you ever reward bad behavior? For example, you tell your daughter no, and it prompts a tantrum that breaks your heart and/or that you just don't have time for, so you change your mind and say yes.

10. Do your kids eat and sleep at regular times? Or do they frequently miss naps, go to bed at different times each night, eat junk food on the run, and in general live an erratic life?

11. Do all the members of your household follow the same approach to discipline? Do you find that your mother-in-law is very strict, your husband lets the kids do what they like, and you struggle to find a middle ground?

Answering yes to any of these questions should help you identify those areas where your approach to discipline has been less than effective. Chances are you already knew your soft spots, and the quiz has simply shown you the direction you want to go. The rest of this chapter will help get you there.

Boundaries

It's really all about defining boundaries, setting limits, and establishing rules. Clearly communicated and consistently applied, boundaries, limits, and rules spell out for children which behaviors are acceptable and which are not. Without knowing what constitutes good behavior, kids can't practice it. So boundaries are essential guidelines for everyday interactions; they are the standards on which your children will base their idea of good judgment.

But they are much more than that. Kids crave boundaries. To a small child, a world without boundaries is an unclear world. Children feel safe when they know the perimeters of their world and what the rules are; they don't like gray areas or question marks. That is why defining boundaries, setting limits, and establishing rules are so important.

Boundaries, limits, and rules are your way of protecting your children. You let them know from an early age that a hot oven is off-limits because it can burn them. You make a rule that they must not run on the stairs because you don't want them to fall and hurt themselves.

But boundaries, limits, and rules are also your way of preparing your children for life with other people in a wider world. That's why your children may not touch your crystal glass set on display—so they learn to take care of what is precious to others. It's why they need to be taught early that it is not okay to snatch toys from a friend or hit a sibling. When kids learn those boundaries early and consistently, they come to accept and respect the whole idea of boundaries. It will make life a whole lot easier later, when you decide to set a curfew for your teenager, or when you insist that he has to take responsibility for mowing the lawn.

Kids can't find their boundaries without guidance, without somebody telling them where the boundaries are, why they're there, and how to meet them. A child learning to walk will walk away from you but will keep looking back. He's questioning you to see if he can keep going; he is feeling out his boundaries. A one-year-old pulling your hair will keep pulling it until you say stop; he is asking you what his limits are. In every case, you, the parent, are the key. Your children look to you in order to make sense of their world. Children want you to tell them what they can and cannot do, what is safe and what is unsafe. They want your permission, and they yearn for your approval.

Simply put, setting boundaries and enforcing them consistently are essential aspects of loving discipline.

No Boundaries

To get her mother's attention, eighteen-month-old Jocelyn would pinch her mother. She tried to do the same to me when we first met, and when I told her no, she was so shocked and outraged by my response that she began to cry. It was clear to me that Jocelyn simply didn't know that pinching was unacceptable.

In fact, as I learned, pinching had been Jocelyn's way of communicating ever since she was ten months old. Her mother had never told her to stop it because she thought it was more important to respond to Jocelyn's wants than to set up appropriate boundaries.

Jocelyn's mother failed to see not just that pinching someone was unacceptable, but also that she was setting her daughter up for problems later on. I explained that if Jocelyn didn't learn how to communicate in a more appropriate way, she would begin to do the same to other people as well—other children, other adults. The parents of those other children would not want their kids playing with Jocelyn.

So together, we determined to put a stop to the pinching and teach Jocelyn other ways to communicate. From then on, when she pinched her mother—or me—she was first told no in a firm voice and with a serious expression, and then she found she was not given what she wanted. Instead, we demonstrated what kind of communication we would like— saying "please" and asking for what she wanted. With consistent effort, in time Jocelyn stopped pinching and began to use her words to express her desires.

Setting Boundaries: The Nanny Absolute Rules

We set basic boundaries with basic rules. There aren't many of them, and they are pretty simple, and there is no budging on them, ever. We call them our "nanny absolute rules," and we teach them to all the kids in our care. They represent what we feel to be the most important behavior—important for keeping kids safe, for teaching them how to interact positively with others, and for nurturing their own personal development.

The "nanny absolutes" are non-negotiable. Other rules—things like "no TV in the morning"—might be relaxed when a child is sick or when it's a snow day, but a "nanny absolute"—like wearing a seatbelt in the car—is never, ever relaxed. Here they are:

Safety
- Kids must be strapped into their car seats or seatbelts in the car.
- Kids must be strapped into their strollers.
- Young kids must hold hands with us when out on the street, and always when crossing the street.
- No playing with matches, scissors, knives, electrical outlets, sharp tools, power tools, or other dangerous objects.
- Sunblock and a sun hat must be worn outdoors in summer, and a hat and gloves in winter (when appropriate).
- No running in the kitchen.
- No running on stairs or running with objects in your mouth.

Respect for Others
- No hitting or biting.
- No throwing objects.
- No screaming or whining.
- "I wants" don't get: ask nicely.
- Share with others.
- Pack up toys after playing.
- Meanness, rudeness, or deliberate cruelty are not allowed.
- No little-prince behavior—in other words, your parents, your nanny, and your friends are not your slaves.

Self-Esteem
- Think well of yourself: you *can* do it, you *are* good at it.
- Try your hardest, do your best.
- Feel good about yourself and all the things that make you *you*— freckles, long legs, green eyes, or whatever. Don't make negative comments about yourself.
- Respect yourself.

Changing Your Kids' Behavior for the Better

The "nanny absolutes" are the bedrock of discipline and responsibility for kids, but how do parents turn around bad behavior once it has started?

Put another way, what would we nannies do if we were suddenly hired by the Harrises you met at the beginning of this chapter?

We've boiled it down to ten essentials for turning around a pattern of difficult behavior. Kids respond very well to the kind of loving discipline these essentials demonstrate. One reminder: When confronted by poor behavior on your child's part, it's important to consider why he is acting in this way. Is he trying to get your attention? Is he having trouble dealing with some upheaval in his life? It might be a major upheaval—a move, a parent going back to work, starting school—or something that seems minor on the outside but is actually troubling him a lot. Whatever it is, it's important to talk with your child to get to the root of the problem. It will make the ten essentials go much more smoothly and much more effectively.

1. Start from a solid foundation.

It will be hard to make positive changes to your child's behavior without the solid foundation provided by a regular schedule that ensures that your child is sleeping and eating well. A child who is tired or hungry or who doesn't know what to expect in his day will be more likely to be uncooperative, impatient, and moody. He won't listen well if he is unable to function well. So establishing a consistent routine, as well as ensuring that your child is well rested and eating a healthy, balanced diet, are essential for turning around behavior. (See Chapters Three, Four, and Five for more on these essentials.)

Respect Yourself

Nanny Wisdom

Six-year-old Joe asked me for some Pokémon cards that he wanted to give to his friend Philip. It sounded like a generous gesture—till Joe explained that Philip had promised to be Joe's friend in exchange for the cards.

"A real friend doesn't need toys in exchange for friendship," I said to Joe. "Philip should like you without the Pokémon cards. Would you expect Philip to give you Pokémon cards for your friendship?"

Joe shook his head "no." He decided against giving Philip the Pokémon cards.

2. Set boundaries, define limits, articulate the rules.

The first thing you need to do is determine what is and is not acceptable behavior in your household. The "nanny absolutes" are a good place to start, and they're appropriate for all children of all ages. But every family has its own values, so you must define what's important for your family, then put it into practice with boundaries, limits, and rules.

How to Set a Boundary

One-year-old Jason was crawling around in his mother's garden when he discovered a row of plants she was just getting ready to pot. Intrigued, he began pulling the leaves off the waiting plants. As soon as Mom noticed, she rushed over to stop him. She tried to pick him up, but he wriggled out of her arms and began to cry. A few minutes later, he was back pulling the leaves off the plants again.

His mother understood that Jason was asserting himself and testing his limits. She wasn't quite sure how to handle the situation. After all, it is hard to explain to a one-year-old why he must not rip up plants. But she also knew he must learn not to do it. Once again, she took the plants away from him. "No," she told him firmly as she picked him up and removed him from the immediate vicinity of the plants. Jason's reaction was the same as before: he screamed. But Mom held firm. "You may not destroy the plants," she told him. When he crawled back to make a third try at the plants, she again told him no—and this time she removed him from the situation altogether and took him inside the house.

Set a clear boundary, establish a consequence for crossing it, and be consistent in carrying out the consequences: it works.

Make sure your boundaries, limits, and rules are both age appropriate and realistic. It is neither age appropriate for nor is it realistic to expect a two-year-old to keep her room tidy all on her own. It is unrealistic not to expect a three-year-old to throw a tantrum if it's ten o'clock at night and he hasn't had dinner yet—and it's inappropriate to discipline him if he does. It is age appropriate to tell a two-year-old not to throw things at people, and it is realistic to expect a five-year-old to be able to dress himself.

Everyone who cares for your children—Dad, Mom, Granny, Nanny—must know what the boundaries, limits, and rules are and must consistently follow them. If your two-year-old throws his lunch across the room and gets a time-out from you, a mild reproach from Granny—"Please don't do that, sweetie"—and an amused chuckle from Dad, he is obviously getting mixed messages about where his boundaries are, what limits you will stand for, and what the rule is. The truth is that until he gets a consistent message consistently applied, he will continue to throw his lunch across the room—consistently.

3. Take one thing at a time.

Always tackle one thing at a time when attempting to change behavior. Kids are wary of change, and because they need to feel safe and secure while changes are being made, make them slowly. If you are trying to get your child to sleep in her own bed, for example, it is too much to start this at the same time she is having difficulties at preschool. If you've just had a baby, it's not the time to address your two-year-old's bottle or pacifier fixation. By the same token, the middle of toilet training is no time to start enforcing boundaries and rules for the first time.

One thing at a time.

4. Communicate clearly.

The key to getting kids to behave well is to be clear about what you want them to do. To communicate clearly with children, it's essential to do the following:

Be specific. "I don't want you watching too many DVDs tonight" is one of those vague and open-ended statements that really say very little. How many are "too many"? When does "tonight" start? And just how firm is your rather wishy-washy "I don't want"? Much better is a specific "You may watch only one DVD after dinner tonight." The child hearing that statement knows exactly where you stand. It's a statement that leaves little room for confusion, delay, or discussion.

Don't plead or beg. Begging and pleading are not effective ways to communicate with your child. They send the message that you are not in control; instead, your child is. "Please darling, can you listen to Mommy and put on your shoes this time?" is a perfect setup for your child to think it is entirely up to him whether he puts on his shoes or not, and even if he chooses to put them on this time, he needn't next time. It also tells your child that he really doesn't have to take you all that seriously.

Give real choices, never false ones. Pretending that kids have a choice when they don't is not only unfair, it also leads to uncooperative behavior and avoidable conflict. Asking a child "would you like to have a bath" or "do you want to put on your coat" gives him an opportunity to say no—an opportunity that most kids will seize. And that puts you in a fairly weak position, as you must now deal with a child who needs to be convinced to have a bath or put on his coat.

Real choices, on the other hand, are a wonderful way to foster independence: "Would you like to go to the park or play at home this morning?" "Would you like a glass of milk or a glass of water?" Questions like this let young kids be assertive in a safe and productive way, and give them practice in making decisions for themselves.

Make sure they're listening. Some kids listen well, while others get distracted by their own daydreams or plans. When five-year-old Teddy was in my care, I would have to make eye contact with him, tell him what I wanted him to do, and then ask him to repeat it back to me before I could be certain he had heard me. Even then, it sometimes took two repetitions before he actually listened. Teddy is a teenager now, and sometimes he still doesn't hear me unless I communicate important information to him in the same way.

Focus on the behavior, not the child—and be positive. It's not the child who's "naughty," it's the behavior—and it's essential to keep that distinction when you communicate your displeasure to a child. He's not a bad boy because he drew on the wall. Rather, drawing on the walls is not allowed; it is unacceptable behavior, and he shouldn't do it. Personally negative comments are even worse, and they never lead to good behavior. Being told "you act like a baby" or being adversely compared to a sibling or other model of good behavior is humiliating, not helpful, and can be very damaging to self-esteem.

5. Be consistent.

Only through consistency will discipline be understandable to a child; only through consistency can it be fair. If the rule is "no ball playing in the house," and if each time your child throws a ball in the house you take the ball away from him, then the consistency of the consequence will eventually teach him not to play ball in the house. In fact, it is the consistency, not so much the consequence, that brings the lesson home, reinforcing it time after time so that your child knows what to expect and so that the consequence makes sense to him; it hasn't just come from nowhere.

Consistency is also about teamwork; everyone who cares for the child must work together to enforce the boundaries, limits, and rules you have established. Kids must feel you are a united team, so it's important that you settle any misunderstandings among yourselves up front, so you can always support each other in front of the children. That way, there's little room for negotiation or maneuver.

The tough thing about consistency is that it takes real commitment. There are no two ways about it; at the end of a long day it would be very easy to turn a blind eye to your son snatching a toy from his brother, or your daughter bending the "one hour of television" rule by another hour. But if you always make an effort to be consistent about your rules, you will be one step closer to this behavior becoming less frequent and eventually disappearing.

6. Help them deal with their emotions.

Learning to understand and deal with emotions is an important part of a child's development. Children need to know that while it's okay to feel emotions like anger and jealousy, it is not okay to hit someone they are angry at, or to scream at someone they are jealous of. Helping your children learn how to manage their frustration and develop their patience is essential to good behavior and to interacting with others.

So what should you do if your child's behavior is driven by his emotions and he loses his temper or acts out in unacceptable ways?

First, acknowledge how he feels and explain to him why his behavior is unacceptable. Here's an example. We'll assume that your child, whom we'll call Larry, is so frustrated at losing a game to his friend Jim that he has hit Jim. What do you say? Try this: "It is unacceptable to hit. I know you wish you were the winner of the Chutes and Ladders game, Larry, but Jim won fair and square. If you hit again, you will have to go to your room and Larry will go home. Now please say you're sorry to Jim."

Or suppose Tony throws his Play-Doh across the room in frustration because he can't make a shape the way he wants to. Try this: "I know you feel frustrated with the Play-Doh, but you must not throw things, so take it slowly this time and try again."

Once your child is old enough, give him space to feel his emotions. If you send your child to his room for a time-out and he cries or becomes angry, go ahead and let him get it out of his system. If he feels like crying, then let him cry. We disagree with parents who tell their children to "stop that crying, or you will be in even more trouble." Other parents, sensing tears on the horizon, will do anything they can to stop those tears from falling. Let your child express what he is feeling.

Giving your child space and time when he is frustrated or upset allows him a chance to feel his emotions and to think about why he feels that way. After a few minutes, you can go to him and suggest, "Let's talk about it." If he says no, give him some more time and go back again a few minutes later; again ask if he has finished or suggest talking it through. This technique doesn't just give you and your child space from each other, it's also an opportunity for your child to express himself and communicate with you when he is calmer.

7. Give praise and encouragement.

Teaching good behavior is not simply about discouraging difficult behavior; of equal importance is recognizing and encouraging good behavior. Children crave approval from their parents; telling them they've done well, or thanking them for their help, or saying how much you appreciate their having listened to your request, can really work wonders.

Star charts, as described in previous chapters, are also a great way to praise and encourage your kids. By reinforcing good behavior, star charts motivate kids to want to change their bad behavior. But use them mainly to get through a difficult phase or as an incentive for a particular behavior. Be careful not to overuse them; good behavior should be something that is expected, not something that deserves a reward every time.

Praise and encouragement for good behavior can also be an effective tool for turning around potential misbehavior before it happens. If you see that Edward is about to throw a block at his brother, intervene quickly:

"Edward, you have been playing so well today. Can you build a tower with those blocks? You build such great towers." Chances are good Edward would rather bask in the pleasure of your praise than enjoy the momentary satisfaction—to be followed by certain consequences—of hurting his brother.

8. Pick your battles, work around problems, and keep a sense of humor.

A certain perspective about your children's behavior is advisable. There really is no point pulling your hair out over every little thing, especially since you can usually find a way to work around most issues. If you tell your daughter to put on her sweater, and she refuses because she says that wearing wool is itchy, let it go. She can wear fleece instead; there are lots of ways to stay warm. If you are wearing a crisp white T-shirt and your baby smears banana all over it, it's best to retain a sense of humor and keep things in perspective. There is no point in letting something like this upset you.

Two-year-old Tom offered a classic example of how to avoid a battle by finding a creative solution. When friends came over for playdates, it upset Tom if the friends picked up his special teddy bear. Yes, we could have made an issue out of it and turned it into a lesson about sharing. But Tom was actually very good about sharing his toys; it was just this toy he wanted to keep for himself. So to save anxiety, I suggested to him that he keep his special teddy bear in his room when other kids came over. It soon became a well-loved ritual for Tom and me; each morning we would tuck his teddy into bed, the bear's special place, where he was available only to Tom.

Diversion can also be a creative solution. You've told your four-year-old to get dressed, and he has not yet begun to do it. "Okay," you suggest, "I'm going to time you to see how fast you can get dressed. Ready?" We'll wager he'll be dressed in no time.

A tactic of opposites is another work-around for contrary toddlers. Just tell your uncooperative child with a smile, "Don't get out of the bath," and he will soon want to scramble out of the tub and into a waiting towel—which is what you wanted him to do in the first place.

Solutions like these help get you and your kids through tricky and uncooperative stages. Once the phases have ended, the need for the solutions will end as well.

If you don't pick your battles, every day will become a long list of criticisms and you will soon find yourself constantly in a battle with your children—which will not be pleasant for anyone. Keep a perspective on things, remember that not everything is a crisis and that most problems have a solution, and by all means keep a sense of humor.

9. Mean business.

Kids must know you mean what you say. They have to understand that *no* means *no*, that warnings are followed by consequences, and that no amount of pleading, negotiation, screaming, or tantrums will change a *no* into a *yes* or lessen the promised consequences.

Many kids over the age of three tend to challenge requests, negotiate demands, debate instructions. Obviously, the sooner you make it clear that you mean business when you say no, the easier the challenges, negotiations, and debates will be. It is perfectly all right to say to your child "because I say so" as a rationale for your having said no to a request. End of discussion. Otherwise, quite frankly, the discussion can last till your child is in his teens.

As to warning of consequences, it only works if you follow through. One warning with follow-through will show you mean business, but ten warnings with no follow-through are pointless. The one with follow-through can be incredibly effective; there will be less need for consequences in the future.

To make sure your warning is seriously understood, it is important to deliver it in a firm voice and with a serious face. We've found that an absolutely unsmiling expression and saying either "that's it" or "right, that's enough" usually gets across the fact that we are serious. Eventually, kids simply recognize "the look," and know that a consequence will follow if they continue. Three-year-old Elizabeth got so used to Kim's serious look she gave it a name—"Kim's cross face"—and quite often it stopped her naughty behavior in its tracks.

The countdown can also be an effective way to deliver a warning; it certainly helps in gaining a child's attention. "I will count to five," you say, "and by the time I get to five, if you haven't gotten dressed/picked up your toys/stopped screaming, then you will not go outdoors to play/be allowed to watch TV/get to make cookies later on." The countdown gives the child an opportunity to listen and do what you have asked. It becomes less effective, however, if you drag it out by adding in halves and quarters as Tom Harris did in the story at the beginning of this chapter.

The other way to show you mean business, of course, is not to back down. This can be the hard part. Your child may get upset when she is in trouble for ignoring your warning, and you may be tempted to back down, but you really mustn't. If you are fair, firm, and consistent, and if you communicate clearly, the upset will be short-lived and will have no negative effects. If you back down and give in when your child begins to cry, you are sending her mixed messages; that's not fair to her and will lead to further problems down the road.

In short, if you say it, mean it. Since you mean it, act on it.

10. Follow through on consequences—firmly and lovingly.

Okay, you've established your boundaries, limits, and rules, and you've given a clear warning that a particular behavior will not be tolerated. You've let it be known, firmly and precisely, that if the behavior does occur, there will be consequences. Spell out the consequences. Then, when the behavior does occur again, follow through. We find that time-outs, removal from a situation, and confiscation can be effective consequences.

It sounds simple, but it is absolutely basic to imposing loving discipline and instilling a sense of responsibility in your children. Consequences reinforce your boundaries, limits, and rules. They get the message across loud and clear so there is no need ever to shout at a child—and certainly there is no need ever to spank a child, which we consider unnecessary, counterproductive, and damaging.

Consequences need to make sense to a child, be used consistently, and, of course, be age appropriate. If your two-year-old refuses to put on sunblock on a hot summer's day, keep him indoors—no going outside to play. If your three-year-old refuses to put his hat or gloves on when the weather is cold, do not let him play in the snow. These consequences are logical to children in that age group; they make sense and they have a powerful meaning. Given all that, it won't take more than a few times using these consequences for your kids to listen.

The time-out. The purpose of the time-out is to highlight behavior that is not acceptable. We find that time-outs really help get the point across to children.

Time-outs can be used for any child over the age of two—when she has done something seriously unacceptable, like hitting—or if warnings have been ignored. To give a time-out, remove the child from the situation for a short period of time. Put her someplace where she can be by herself, and where she has time and space to think about what she has done. Many British nannies sit children on a naughty step for time-outs.

Here's a sample time-out:

Meg hits Jo. Meg is then taken away from Jo and is told she is having a time-out because she mustn't hit anyone, ever. Meg is taken to a different part of the room, or is seated on a chair, or is brought to her room. Whichever place it is, it is the same one Meg is taken to each time she has a time-out. She is told to stay there until she is calm and ready to play nicely and apologize to her friend. But Meg tries shouting, screaming, negotiating the time-out, and arguing. So she is simply ignored. The whole point of the time-out is to give Meg a clear message that hitting is not acceptable; any negotiation will distract from that clear purpose.

After a while, Meg is calm. Soon, she is ready to talk to her parent. After a little chat together, Meg is ready to apologize to Jo and play again.

A good time-out.

Removal from a situation. Your two-year-old is having a bad day at a friend's playdate, throwing one tantrum after another. Instead of putting everyone through torture, just take her home.

Your five-year-old repeatedly pushed a younger child off the swing at the park. After he has apologized, take him home immediately. He really doesn't deserve the pleasure of remaining in the park when he has behaved like a bully. Sometimes, the very best option is to remove your child. Scoop him up and announce: "We're going home!"

Confiscation. Confiscation can be an extremely effective way to end bad behavior involving a plaything. When your child starts using an outside toy inside the house—a skateboard across your parquet living room, for example—give him one warning and if he doesn't stop, take the skateboard away for the rest of the day.

Illogical Discipline

Example one: Ryan's mother reprimands him for shouting at his sister, but she shouts her reprimand at him. Example two: Rebecca hits her brother, and her father spanks her as a punishment. What is a child to make of such contradictions? What is the message being sent to the child?

Discipline should not be a matter of devising a "punishment to fit the crime," but of teaching good behavior, and you can't teach good behavior by practicing bad behavior—especially if it's the very behavior you're trying to discipline. In both these cases, the parents are only setting an example of exactly the behavior they are supposedly trying to stop.

It may be creative for your child to use the broom as a sword, but it isn't much fun for the person on the receiving end who gets poked in the eye. Explain that the "sword" is dangerous, and tell your child you will take it away if he continues with his behavior. If he does continue, do not discuss it further; do as you said you would and take it away from him.

Confiscation is also a good idea if two kids are fighting over one toy and, even after a warning, they will not share. If that happens, confiscating the toy for the rest of the day will put a quick end to the squabble.

Dealing with Common Behavior Issues

A child goes through a lot of physical and mental development in the first few years of life; he becomes more independent each day, while exploring his personality, his world, and his relationships with others. This growing independence, fueled by the child's developing sense of self, is expressed in various ways—not all of them easy to deal with. Here are our tips for coping with some of the most common behavior issues.

Tantrums

These outbursts of crying and screaming—perfect expressions of frustration—can be as distressing as they are dramatic. It is important to keep in mind, however, that tantrums are a normal part of a child's development, integral to the child's learning to deal with his newfound assertiveness, and with emotions such as anger, impatience, and frustration.

Tantrums can start as early as the age of fourteen months but are most common between the ages of eighteen months and three years; by the age of three or four, they should be infrequent. Most commonly, they erupt when a child is refused permission to do something or when he is having trouble doing something on his own. Maybe you've given your child a red cup when he wanted a green one, or maybe he can't get a toy to work—both fairly common grounds for a tantrum. As fast as a tantrum comes on, it disappears, and the child forgets all about it within minutes of its being over.

To be sure, tantrums are more frequent when a child is tired or hungry. That is why they tend to occur at dinnertime or when a child has missed a nap or gone to bed late for the past few nights.

As your child goes through his second year, the duration and intensity of tantrums can increase. Be prepared for your child to throw himself on the floor, stiffen his body, and turn red in the face as he screams with all his might. After three years of age, a child should be able to communicate his needs and express his emotions and frustrations without having a tantrum. If tantrums still play a large role past the age of three, it is time to look at your approach to your child's behavior. Could you in any way be giving your child a reason to keep throwing tantrums? Are you giving in to his tantrums? Failure to deal effectively with tantrums now can be the path to later problems: a four-year-old who is still throwing himself on the floor in a fit, a six-year-old who screams and cries when he doesn't get his own way, and an eight-year-old who knows that having a tantrum is the best way to get exactly what he wants.

So how do you deal effectively with a tantrum? Rule number one is never give in. If you do, you are teaching your child that tantrums are an effective way to behave. You are sending your child a clear signal that he will get what he wants by screaming. And it goes without saying that this pattern of behavior is never helpful to parent or child, now or in the future.

So you say no to your child, and he reacts with a tantrum. What do you do? Stay calm, and try not to respond while the tantrum is in full swing. Listening to a child scream for ten minutes or so can be difficult, but as

Nanny Tales

The Terrible Twos

TWO-AND-A-HALF-YEAR-OLD Jessica was curled up in her cozy bed next to her faithful teddy bear Fred, with her pink Barbie quilt pulled up to her chin. Watching her sleep, my heart warmed to this picture of sweetness. It had been no trouble at all to convince Jessica that she needed a nap after our busy morning in the park. She had ridden her new red tricycle all the way there and all the way home, proudly showing me how fast she could ride all by herself. She had hopped off the bike only to feed the ducks, one of her all-time favorite activities. She would break off bits of the stale bread, then lift her arm high over her head and hurl the bread into the water, shouting excitedly as the ducks swam toward it. She would call encouragement to the littlest duck: "Hurry, hurry, come on little baby ducky, you can do it."

That day, while she was napping, I decided to cook her favorite meal, lasagna. It was not a meal I made very often, as the preparation was fairly time-consuming, but I thought it would be a nice surprise.

"I made your favorite, Jess," I said at dinner later, as I put her plate on the table. Jessica eyed the plate of food, pulled a face, and shouted, "I don't want the Sleeping Beauty plate; I want my Cinderella one!"

I was a bit stunned, but I replied very firmly, "Jessica, you need to ask me nicely. You know that 'I wants' don't get."

At this, Jessica pushed her plate away and sent it hurtling across the table and onto the floor. I stood there watching as the little girl who had sweetly fed the ducks that morning, the same little girl who had tranquilly napped that afternoon, turned into a different child. Throwing a tantrum, she hurled herself onto the floor sobbing hysterically and screaming "I want it! I want it!" between the wailing and tears.

As I watched her, tantrum in full swing, I contemplated the erratic ways of a two-year-old—how my giggling, delightful Jessica had gone from smiles to tears in seconds—all because I had given her what she suddenly decided was the "wrong" plate.

long as the child is in a safe place, you are much better off letting him get it out of his system—so leave him to it. If you need to leave the room to cool off yourself for a minute, do so.

If your child is having a tantrum in a public place, it is much harder to ignore, so it is usually best to remove the child from the situation if you can. Take him to the restroom, or outside, or even home. It will be easier to deal with a screaming child away from the judgmental looks that other people may give you.

Nanny Wisdom

Pushing Buttons

If you find yourself snapping every time your kids misbehave, it won't be long before your children learn how to push your buttons. It goes like this: your kids act out, you react, your kids respond with more misbehavior, and you lose your temper. You are in a common self-perpetuating cycle that is very hard to break. If this is the case, try to become aware of the cycle you are in, change your patterns by staying calm, try not to react emotionally, and look for opportunities to praise instead of criticize.

Once your child has calmed down, comfort him with a cuddle. You can sit him on your lap and briefly explain to him why you said no in the first place. And then put it behind you. Do not give your child a treat to eat or a new toy to make him feel better because you now feel sorry for him. The cuddle and explanation are all that is needed. But do avoid punishing your child for having a tantrum. (If he is older than four and frequently throws tantrums, though, a time-out would certainly reinforce that you consider his behavior completely unacceptable.)

Make sure the tantrum is not due to hunger or tiredness. Regular meals and adequate sleep—at night and in daytime naps—can make a huge difference to the frequency and intensity of tantrums. With a consistent approach, it won't take long for your child's tantrums to lessen; just keep repeating to yourself that the key to success is to send a clear message to your child that tantrums will not get him what he wants.

Uncooperative Behavior

Each morning, six-year-old Jamie's father would face the same battles. He would ask Jamie to come to the table for breakfast only to be completely ignored. He would repeat the request again and again—and again and again Jamie would disregard it. Finally, by about the fifth time, Dad would shout the request, and then and only then would Jamie come to the table.

During the meal, Dad would ask Jamie not to swing on his chair. No response. "Don't swing on your chair," he would say again. Again, no response. Eventually, as before, Dad would shout the instruction—and Jamie would stop swinging. The same thing would happen when Jamie was asked to eat his cereal, or put on his coat, or pick up his schoolbag. Every single action required repeated requests until finally a shout got through to Jamie. By the time father and son left the house in the morning, Dad was so wound up he once found himself yelling, "Why don't you ever listen to me? Why are you always so difficult, Jamie?"

Clearly, Jamie was "so difficult" as a result of a long-term communication pattern that was ineffective. Unproductive requests followed by an eventual resort to shouting had now become a habit. His father had, in effect, taught Jamie that he didn't mean business until he raised his voice. So naturally Jamie waited for the shouting before he would pay attention.

If a child is uncooperative, first check to make sure that you have established a solid household routine so that the child knows what is expected of him during the day. Then take a look at your own means of communicating what you expect of the child. If there has been habitual lack of cooperation, as in the case of Jamie, talk to your child about the situation and the changes you would like to see. The next time you have a request for your child, look him in the eye, state the request clearly, and then ask your child to repeat it back to you. If your child does not do as he is asked, it's time to give a warning and, if necessary, to follow through with consequences.

What doesn't help, of course, is to raise your voice or to make the kind of negative comments Jamie's dad did. On the contrary. To break a pattern of uncooperative behavior, you need to offer praise and encouragement each time there is good behavior. A star chart can be very useful here. In Jamie's case, for example, a star chart could encourage Jamie to want to listen, thus reinforcing the behavior his father wants to see.

Screaming

Eighteen-month-old Brittany squealed every time she wanted something, and every time she squealed, her parents would give her what she wanted. If she wanted a toy she couldn't reach, Brittany would squeal and her parents would jump. If she wasn't picked up fast enough, she would squeal, and they would come running. After a few months, the squealing turned into a high-pitched screeching, and Brittany's parents couldn't figure out why she was screaming for everything instead of trying to use words. But they assured themselves that she was too young to understand their instructing her not to scream—and anyway, they thought, all children her age scream, don't they?

"A proper voice, please!"

Whining can quickly turn into a habit for some kids, and it needs to be nipped in the bud before it becomes a way of communication. Make it clear that you will not respond to any whining requests—and make sure you don't. The minute you do, your child will think it is okay to communicate in this way, and the whining will soon become a permanent fixture. Insist on being spoken to in what we nannies like to call "a proper voice, please."

Well, yes—up to a point. It is not unusual for an eighteen-month-old to go through a screaming phase. That's around the age when children are discovering the volume that their lungs can produce and are learning to express what they want. But if you indulge it, screaming will become a permanent way for a child to communicate her desires, wants, and needs.

To make sure that doesn't happen, start by telling your child in a firm voice to stop screaming. With older babies you can put your fingers to your lips and gently say, "Sssh," then demonstrate a quieter way to ask for something. At the same time, simply do not respond to the request made through screaming—do not get the drink, toy, or book the child was screaming for.

To let older children know that screaming is not acceptable—that it is not the way to communicate—ask them to use words to ask for things in a

The La-La Incident

EIGHTEEN-MONTH-OLD CHLOE was obsessed with the children's television program *Teletubbies*. Her yellow La-La doll was her best friend. Chloe slept with La-La by her side, sat next to La-La at meals, and included La-La in every trip to the park. The only times Chloe didn't have La-La with her were when we went to friends' houses for playdates. This became a house rule after a few near disasters when La-La had been picked up by another child or accidentally left behind. Chloe was happy to accept this rule and understood that La-La needed to stay home whenever we went out on playdates.

One afternoon, we went to Isabelle's house for a nanny and child playgroup. We were all enjoying the pleasant late-afternoon sun in Isabelle's backyard—the children playing happily together, the nannies watching over them while drinking tea and chatting. Chloe was enjoying sharing building blocks with Rebecca, a little girl new to our playgroup.

Rebecca was carrying a small pink bag, and after a while, she opened it up to reveal a yellow La-La doll identical to Chloe's. I saw Chloe's expression turn from disbelief to horror as she stared at the familiar doll in Rebecca's hands. I knew exactly what was going to happen next, but before I could prevent it, Chloe lunged at Rebecca, reaching for the doll and screaming, "My La-La!"

In an instant, chaos had broken out. Rebecca hugged her doll to her chest, crying hysterically, while Chloe tried desperately to rip the doll from her new friend's grip. Before I could separate them, Chloe opened her mouth and sank her teeth into Rebecca's arm. I was stunned.

I pulled Chloe away from Rebecca, but she was so upset that she was beyond the point of listening; it was useless to discuss her unacceptable behavior now or to explain that she was not the only one with a La-La doll. I picked up Chloe and took her home. I knew that given her hysterical state, only removing her from the situation would make an impression on her that biting was never allowed. As soon as Chloe was calm, I told her that biting was not allowed and that she had hurt Rebecca. I could only hope that this was an isolated incident.

regular voice. Tell your child, "You need to speak to me in a pleasant voice, and please use your words." Let her know that "I will not listen to you when you are screaming," and remind her that "I don't scream at you, and you will not scream at me." And make sure you follow through by not responding to the screaming and by not shouting. With consistency, the screaming will soon disappear.

Biting

Biting is not uncommon among children between the ages of one and two years, but you can end it quickly if you make it clear that it is an unaccept-

Siblings

Siblings fight. If it is any consolation, it's how they learn to interact with others and to share. It can be very hard for parents—and nannies—to listen to their children arguing nonstop. We recommend confiscation of the disputed object and/or separation as solutions to most sibling fights. If your children are fighting over their dolls, tell them you will count to five and they must decide who is playing with which doll, or all the dolls are going away for the rest of the day. Remind them that it is important to be kind to one another, that brothers and sisters need each other and are special to one another. If they still can't get along, separating them will be helpful; it will give them some space from each other—and you will get a rest from the arguing.

Siblings can become competitive, with each trying to outdo the other; they can also become jealous of one another. That can be a signal that one sibling feels you show favoritism to the others. Consider carefully whether you do or not, as favoritism is a sure path to trouble. You must take care to treat all your children the same, especially when it comes to discipline. If you punish one child for a particular behavior, make sure the others face the same exact consequences if they behave in the same way.

In addition, kids often act out when they are not getting to spend enough time with their parents on their own. If you have more than one child, try to arrange special times with each one. Ask your family or friends for help and support so you can spend one-on-one time with each child regularly.

able way to behave. Some parents laugh and think it's cute. Well, it's not cute when your two-year-old has bitten another child and drawn blood. So here's how to stop it:

If your child is biting you, pull her off and show her a stern face to make it very clear that it is not allowed. If you are holding her, put her down immediately to communicate that you are unhappy about what she is doing.

If she bites another child, tell her no sternly. Then make a big fuss over the child who was bitten, comfort her, maybe even show her an exciting toy. The biter will now feel left out and will regret her behavior. If she does it again, simply remove her from the situation.

Hitting and Kicking

Here's another behavior that must be addressed immediately. The idea that "she's just a kid; she doesn't know any better" is wrong: parents need to teach their children to know better, and this kind of behavior should never be excused or accepted.

Talk to your child about why this kind of behavior is not allowed. And keep in mind that roughhouse or pretend fighting that you do with your child may seem to him a model of play he may then do with his friends— perhaps too vigorously.

If your child hits or kicks another person, just remove him from the situation—by taking him home or by giving him a time-out. Communicate clearly to him that the behavior is unacceptable. Do this consistently, and he will soon learn that hitting and kicking have consequences that are unpleasant for him.

Problems with Sharing

Some children have a hard time sharing their toys or belongings with others. Problems with sharing are not uncommon—shouts of "mine!" are heard as soon as a child learns to speak—and we have cared for children who scream when another child touches their toys (as well as for others who are happy to share).

Sharing is, of course, an important life skill children need to learn. If your child is never willing to share her toys with anyone, other kids will simply not want to play with her. So if sharing is an issue for your child, your job will be to reinforce the importance of sharing with others.

With toddlers, we recommend staging a "pretend" teddy bears' tea party, at which you and the toddler share the cups and "snacks" with each other and with the teddy bears. Ask your child to pass you her cup and pass her yours: you're showing her how to relinquish an object to someone else. A ball game also works well with young children; each person takes a turn rolling the ball to the next person—again, a model of giving up something to another person.

If your child is two years or older and is not sharing during a playdate, for example, ask her to share a toy with her friend; if she doesn't, it is best to remove her from the situation with the simple statement, "When you are ready to share, you can go back and play." Or take the problem toy away from her, explaining why. Wait a few minutes, then ask her if she is now ready to share.

Don't stay away from a playdate because you are embarrassed about your child's non-sharing behavior. It is a normal phase that should be addressed, not avoided; otherwise, it will happen again and again.

There is one exception to the sharing rule: if there is one special toy your child deems his and his only, put it away when kids come over and don't take it with you when you go out. Keep it special.

Cheekiness

Granted, it's a very British word: "cheeky." We use it to describe kids who answer back and "give attitude," kids who are rude or smart-mouthed,

 "I'm your mother, not your maid . . ."

Let your kids know that you are not there to pick up after them when they drop their candy wrappers, sweaters, or toys in the middle of the floor. A four-year-old can find the garbage can, laundry basket, and toy box by himself, so make sure you teach kids basic cleanup early so it becomes second nature to your children—now and in the future.

kids who are ill-mannered. Whatever the specific aspect of the behavior, cheekiness needs to be addressed right away.

Let's face it: kids can learn cheekiness from television and movies—or from other kids. It is up to you to make it clear that what is cool for Bart Simpson or Pokémon, even if it's considered okay in other people's homes, is not cool in your household—ever.

Knowing How to Say You're Sorry

Taking responsibility for your actions means acknowledging you've done wrong and being able to offer a genuine apology. That's a lesson children need to learn. Suppose your four-year-old throws sand at another child in the playground. Certainly, you must explain to him why it was wrong—that it hurts to have sand thrown in your eyes—and why he needs to say sorry. If he refuses to say sorry, insist; failure to acknowledge doing wrong and failure to apologize let a child pretend it didn't happen; if he can pretend it didn't happen, he can also escape his responsibility.

As always, the way to deal with cheekiness is to make sure your child knows that it won't get results. We also recommend the kind of manners blitz we discussed in Chapter One. The blitz is a way to encourage good behavior and manners for a week—or some other period of time—using a star chart to track the behavior. It's an intensive incentive to good manners, and it's a very good way to encourage children to be aware of their behavior.

I Want It / I Need It

Most children go through phases of wanting everything they see: the latest DVD, action figure, or doll, or anything they clap their eyes on—just for the sake of wanting it. You pass a toy store and your child demands a present. You're in the supermarket and the appealing kids' balloons and candies, deliberately placed at their eye level, prove as tempting as they were intended to be. But of course, if you indulge your child's every want and need, you will be setting yourself up for a whole series of problems.

The Golden Shoelace Club

"**W**HAT ARE YOU UP TO?" I asked five-and-a-half-year-old Max. For about the tenth time in a row, he was trying to knot his shoelaces, but without any luck.

"Nothing," he replied, hunched over his sneakers in a state of intense concentration.

"Are you trying to tie your shoelaces by yourself?"

Max looked up in surprise. "Yes, but I can't do it," he said, miserably.

"Don't worry, sweetie," I said, as reassuringly as I could. "It's very tricky. You'll work it out when you are ready."

"I have to know how to do it *now*!" Max blurted out. "I want to be in the Golden Shoelace Club in my class. If I can show Miss Potter I can tie my own shoelaces, she'll write my name in the Golden Shoelace Club book and I'll get a certificate. Melissa and George and Michael all got their names in the book today, and I want to do it too."

"Oh, I see," I said. "Well, then, I'll show you how to tie your shoelaces. Let's get cracking."

The next couple of days were a blur of shoelaces and knots. Max's determination astounded both his parents and myself, but even after a week of practicing we were still no closer to the Golden Shoelace Club than when we started.

Then one morning, when I was playing with Max's baby brother, I heard a shout from the next room. "I did it!" Max cried.

I picked up the baby and walked into Max's room where I found him giggling hysterically—and with one shoe tied. There it was—the first shoelace Max had tied himself. "Hooray!" I cried, engulfing Max in a huge hug and laughing with delight.

If ever there was an example of a kid wanting to do something on his own, working to do something on his own, and succeeding in doing something on his own, this was it. I only prayed he would be able to do it again in front of his class tomorrow so that he could bring home his much longed for certificate. The truth was, however, that certificate or no certificate, he had achieved something important for himself by himself—and his burgeoning confidence and growing self-esteem were evident.

For one thing, the whole "I want/I need" syndrome will only grow in intensity. As you get tired of saying yes, your child will turn more and more to nagging and maybe even to tantrums to get what she wants. But there's another problem with indulging the "I want/I need" syndrome. Children who get everything they want and expect end up appreciating nothing. They aren't overjoyed with birthday or holiday gifts because they get treats all the time. They don't know how to look forward to presents, and they almost can't feel the heartwarming joy of receiving a treasure and cherishing it.

That's why the English nanny's classic expression is that "'I wants' don't get." In other words, demanding something is not the way to get it. And getting things should be a pleasure.

Growing Up Independent—and Confident

Nathan was often called "the little prince." At the age of six, he carried on like he expected everyone to do everything for him. Maybe that's because his mother more or less did do everything for him and gave him everything he wanted. Nathan's mother brought him a glass of warm milk in bed in the morning, warmed his clothes in the dryer before he put them on in the winter, dressed him, brushed his teeth for him, fed him breakfast while he was watching TV. Naturally, he learned to expect everything to be done for him at all times.

For her part, Nathan's mother congratulated herself on taking such good care of her son. If his soccer team lost a game, she told Nathan that the referee had made a mistake and that his team "should have won." When she and Nathan bought a birthday present for a friend, she would buy Nathan one too, so he wouldn't feel left out. And even though Nathan's teacher had told her he was lacking in independent skills and maturity, Mom was able to dismiss this by telling herself the teacher obviously didn't like her son.

Although she thought she was doing the best for her son, the exact opposite was true: Nathan's mother was actually depriving her boy of opportunity after opportunity to learn to do things on his own. By doing so much for him, she was keeping him from acquiring important skills he would one day need to face life and the world independently.

It is not uncommon to find a six-year-old who cannot dress himself, a ten-year-old incapable of packing his own schoolbag, and a sixteen-year-old who cannot make her own breakfast. These children haven't been "well cared for," as Nathan's mother assumed; they have been mollycoddled, and they have missed out on learning essential life skills.

But of course, a child needs a sense of responsibility and independence if he is to be well prepared for life. Babying a child does him no favor. On the contrary, it denies him opportunities to develop independence and confidence through self-discovery. It also goes against children's natural eagerness to learn and their natural developmental urge to do things on their own.

You can help by starting early to encourage your child to take off his own socks, to feed himself, even to try brushing his own teeth or packing up his toys. Whenever your child says, "I can do it by myself"—as children typically do—encourage this desire for independence. Each time you do—safely, of course—your child will become more capable and more responsible, better prepared for school, adolescence, and the rest of his life.

Instead of doing everything for your child, as Nathan's mother did, show him how to do things for himself. Give him age-appropriate tasks or chores to encourage responsibility. Demonstrate to your one-year-old how to scoop mashed potato onto a spoon, then give him the spoon and let him try. Show your three-year-old how to hang up her coat, and make it her daily task. Show your five-year-old how to set the table, and assign it as his chore.

Then give your child time and space to do what you've demonstrated—and to make mistakes. Mistakes are an essential part of learning, but they require patience on your part. It is all too easy to rush over and prevent the mistake from occurring, but unless your child is in danger, let him make the mistake because that is how he will learn. A two-year-old working on a new puzzle and trying to fit the round piece into the square hole needs to discover for himself that it won't fit—and where it will fit, no matter how many attempts it takes. Similarly, when you play a game of memory with a four-year-old, play fair; don't let him win without his making an effort. If he makes mistakes and loses the game, he will still have learned the lessons of trying hard, of striving toward a goal, of knowing that you can't win everything.

With your support, your child will learn from his mistakes and will also learn to keep trying. And one thing is certain: without ever being given a chance to try, like Nathan, he'll never learn how to do anything by himself or for himself.

The very sense of independence that learning how to do things inspires is also essential for confidence building and self-esteem, for giving children a positive attitude about themselves. That's why assigning children age-appropriate chores and tasks is so important; it demonstrates that they play an important role in the household and makes them feel good about themselves—and it gives them a sense of family unity and belonging.

The perfect starter tasks are the simple ones—putting toys away, wiping down the counter after using Play-Doh, or pouring cereal into their own bowls. The next step up might be chores like putting shoes away, helping to feed the pets, and setting the table. Keep adding tasks and chores as children get older; more responsibility means more self-confidence.

Yes, you will have to remind children of their tasks and chores, but that's part of their learning process, too. And here's a tip: try a star chart to encourage older children to remember for themselves.

Loving Discipline

★ Discipline is love; it teaches kids essential life skills.

★ Appropriate boundaries, limits, and rules must be set—and followed.

★ It is okay to say *no*, but *no* really does mean *no*.

★ Consistency is essential.

★ Praise and encouragement for good behavior also help end difficult behavior.

★ Children need opportunities to develop independence and a sense of responsibility, which foster confidence and good self-esteem.

Chapter Seven

Fun, Play, and Parties

Making Every Day Magical

Jane, Sophie, and Walter are celebrating Jane's birthday—again. Her actual birthday—and her actual birthday party—was the week before, and Jane now uses the silver birthday hats left over from the party for the celebration with Sophie and Walter, carefully placing the hats on everyone's head.

"I am so glad you could both come to my party," she tells Sophie and Walter. "I'm the birthday girl, and I'm five now. Are those presents for me?"

She helps Walter hand her a parcel wrapped in a child's paper drawing.

"Oh, Walter," Jane exclaims as she opens the parcel, "this book is my favorite! How did you know?" The gift is one of her old storybooks.

She imitates a grown-up's voice when she opens Sophie's very small gift box containing a plastic bracelet. "This is just what I always wanted," she says. "Thank you, Sophie."

With the gift-giving portion of the party now complete, Jane moves on to the food. She places pink plastic teacups and saucers before Walter and Sophie, and grows a bit bossy upon observing Sophie's behavior. "Sophie," she chides, "please don't snatch from Walter. You have your own cup." But she has nothing but praise for Walter. "You are a good boy," she tells him as she pours his tea. "What did you say, Walter? You would like some sugar?" She duly adds two cubes and gives the tea a stir.

"Now it's time for some birthday cake," Jane says excitedly, "and let's all sing the birthday song together." She begins to sing: "Happy birthday to me, happy birthday to me . . ."

Of course, Jane's tea party is a pretend tea party, and her guests, Sophie and Walter, are, respectively, her favorite doll and her preferred teddy bear. It is safe to say that all three party participants are enjoying themselves immensely.

Fun and play are what being a child is all about. The magic, laughter, silliness, fantasy, and creativity a child naturally finds in the world, through play, are a fundamental part of childhood. In play, anything is possible: a child can be a king, fairy princess, warrior, mermaid, firefighter, cowboy, space alien, hero. In play, a child's teddy bear can talk, just as Walter did, and can serve as friend and companion. In play, children can construct the world they want: pretending makes it possible to eat chocolate cake all day, or stay up all night, or become whatever they want to be. All children have a natural inclination for the imaginative and for play; they have a natural urge to explore and learn through discovery. Yielding to that inclination and following that natural urge through fun and play make children very, very happy.

But fun and play are more than just amusement. They unleash creativity and teach kids valuable life skills. Through play, a child can express himself, explore his emotions, gain confidence and self-esteem. Play is how kids learn about the world and their place in it, as they imitate and act out a range of scenarios and situations. Kids hone their skills through play:

language and motor skills are developed, social skills are practiced, and the intricacies of friendship are explored.

For all these reasons, children need fun and play every day—on their own, with other kids, with you. This chapter tells you how to make sure that they get what they need, that you nurture the very special spark of creative imagination in your children, and that they reap all the developmental benefits of fun and play—at home, outside, on playdates, through organized activities, and by throwing the very best birthday party. In doing so, you may even recapture the sense of wonder from your own childhood.

Fun and Play at Home

Home is usually a child's favorite place to play. He feels most comfortable at home. He is familiar with the environment and with the playthings: toys, pencils, crayons, puzzles, books. Creative and educational fun and play at home require only a safe space, appropriate playthings, and opportunities for structured and unstructured play in interaction with others and by himself.

There are definitely benefits to be gained from having a special room just for play, and if you have a spare room of some sort, you might want to consider converting it into a playroom. That's where your child can keep all his toys; it's where he knows he is free to go play at any time. In a separate playroom, a child can create a driving course for cars and trucks, establish a farmyard, or throw tea parties without intruding on other family members' need for space. When things get messy in the playroom, you can always close the door. Your child can decorate her playroom in fun ways, and larger toys like tents or playhouses can be left set up; the kids won't have to take them down because it's dinnertime, or because Dad needs the table for his work, or because company is coming.

But while playrooms are great, they are certainly not necessary for play. If your child has his own room, that will do just as well. If not, think about dedicating a corner of the living room as his area for play. If space is very limited, even a toy box stored under your child's bed will give him the benefits of a special play space. Children are very adaptable and have huge imaginations, so they will find plenty of places to play in whatever space is available.

What should kids play with? Playthings can be anything from figures, cars, dolls, and blocks to books, games, or everyday household items.

Children do not need every expensive toy in the store; basic toys are enough to keep them happy. In fact, children with a lot of toys typically end up playing with only about half of them and quickly lose interest in the other half. What's more, overindulging a child by giving him every new toy on the market only teaches him to expect everything, and eventually he will appreciate very little. Soon simple toys and even old favorites will lose their value in the child's eyes. So when it comes to toys, keep it simple, and keep the number of toys moderate.

A toy collection should be a mixture of creative toys, educational toys, and toys that are sheer fun. Good basic toys for babies six months to eighteen months old include the following:

- toys with sounds
- pushing and pulling toys
- stuffed animals
- peekaboo toys

- toys that hide things
- books with large illustrations
- stacking toys
- bright, colorful toys

Good basic toys for toddlers and preschoolers include the following:

- tea sets
- kitchen sets
- cars and trucks
- miniature farm and house sets with people, animals, and vehicles
- building blocks
- age-appropriate LEGO, Duplo, and Playmobil
- puzzles

- books
- teddy bears, dolls, and dinosaurs
- musical toys
- sports toys
- hand puppets
- age-appropriate card games and board games
- craft items: crayons, coloring books, Play-Doh, and paints

Toys like these teach children numerous valuable skills and concepts: motor skills; problem-solving; creative thinking; a sense of color; distance and space relationships; role-play; teamwork; patience; interaction; manipulation of small objects; coordination; cause and effect. Toys should be age appropriate: remember that children under the age of three love to put things in their mouths, so toys with small pieces should be assiduously avoided until children are well past that stage.

Sometimes the best toys are the simplest and cheapest ones. We have often seen a toddler reject an expensive toy in favor of the box it came in, which turns out to be far more enthralling. With a bit of imagination, many everyday items can become fun toys.

Kids over two years of age really love the dress-up box: just a big chest or box filled with old handbags, bracelets, dresses, jackets, scarves, and briefcases. Watch your child's excitement grow as she rummages through endless possibilities for dress-up and games of "let's pretend."

Kids over three love to play "shop" with empty cereal boxes, egg cartons, and plastic bottles; or to take used envelopes to a pretend post office. Plastic containers, bowls, spoons, some clean dishcloths, and an apron can be useful for pretend cooks or bakers. Old boxes can be painted and decorated with glitter to become cradles for teddy bears or dolls—with clean dishcloths as blankets. With imagination, a packing box can become a firehouse or even a farmyard.

Time for Play

Make sure your kids have enough time for play in their day. This may sound obvious, but too many activities and too much television can encroach on kids' playtime.

Cleaning Up the Mess

Kids eighteen months or older can help pack up their toys. Make a game out of putting things away in the toy basket or toy cupboard. Get children into the habit of packing up one game before they start the next. Or you can make it a house rule that toys must be put away at certain times of the day, like before a meal or bath.

We recommend a big sorting-out of toys, the playroom, or the bedroom at least once a month. This provides the perfect opportunity to organize everything, put crayons back in pencil cases, sharpen pencils, find "lost" game pieces. It's also a good time to discreetly throw out broken toys and give away the toys your child has grown out of. Kids love these clean-out days, too; they find toys they had forgotten about and are thrilled to have all the pieces of their games back again.

Toys

Nanny Seal of Approval

- Brio tracks and trains by Imaginarium
- Cars, trucks, diggers by Little Tikes
- Clifford Nesting Blocks by Scholastic Inc.
- Crayons and craft/construction paper by Crayola
- Duplo
- LEGO
- Lincoln Logs by K'Nex
- Little People by Fisher-Price
- Magnetic Geomag set by Plastwood
- Picnic Play Pack by Learning Resources
- Play-Doh by Hasbro
- Playmobil
- Pop-Onz Building System by Fisher-Price
- Puzzles by Melissa and Doug (LCI)
- Squeaky Eggs by Tomy
- Thomas the Tank Engine Trains and Tracks by Learning Curve
- Wooden toys, shape sorters, building block sets, alphabet blocks by Melissa and Doug (LCI)

A few scheduled activities can be a wonderful experience for a child (see Organized Activities, page 248), but a child who is attending activity after activity will miss out on unstructured playtime with his own toys at home. And that means he will miss out on the opportunity to amuse himself with his own thoughts, ideas, and daydreams.

Similarly, television can be a double-edged sword. Appropriate and interesting television programs or movies can be a wonderful part of childhood. Children adore simple shows like *Thomas the Tank Engine, Clifford the Big Red Dog, Harold and the Purple Crayon,* and *George Shrinks,* not to mention Disney movies and other classics. The characters from these movies or shows often become central figures of children's play.

But too much television simply gets in the way of play. A child sitting in front of a television for hours on end does not need to explore other ways to entertain himself. He's not using his own imagination, and he will soon simply get out of the habit of directing his own amusement. Pretty soon, play won't come as easily to him as to the child who is playing all day long.

ARTS AND CRAFTS FOR KIDS TWO AND UP

BUTTERFLY PICTURES	Put a few dabs of colored paint into the center of a piece of white paper, fold the paper in half so the two sides press together, then open the paper to reveal the beautiful butterfly.
COLLAGES	Cut pictures of animals and kids from magazines, or cut colored paper into interesting shapes. Then show your child how to glue the pictures onto a piece of paper or card to make a collage. To add to the collage, your child can color, paint, or glue glitter around the pictures.
FIGURES, SNAKES, POTS, ETC.	Have kids use Play-Doh molds or cookie cutters to make shapes out of plasticine or Play-Doh (see the recipe on page 262). Snakes, worms, houses, and pots are particularly fun to make.
FINGER PAINTING	Cover a few dinner plates or large plastic lids with foil (for easy cleanup), or use a paper plate. Squeeze a generous amount of paint onto the foil or plate. Let kids dip their fingers in the paint and then paint onto paper.
HOLIDAY CARDS	Make cards with your child that she can give to friends or relatives for Valentine's Day (heart-shaped), Christmas (snowman or Christmas tree), birthdays, and the like. Fold a thin piece of posterboard or paper in half. Draw half the shape, using the seam as the dividing point, then cut out the shape. Open the paper to reveal the whole symmetrical shape. Decorate the card with glitter, glue, paint, and stickers.

In short, the kid who is glued to the tube is a kid who is missing out on opportunities to grow and learn through the experience of play—opportunities to exercise, experience nature, and use up the abundant energy that kids naturally have. When it comes to television for children, a balanced approach is necessary.

Playing Together

It is important and rewarding to spend time playing with your child, a way of saying to a child loud and clear: "I love you and I want to spend

LEAF RUBBINGS	Use leaves you have collected from a walk in the park in fall to make leaf rubbings. Place a leaf under a piece of paper and rub over the paper with wax crayons.
PASTA OR BUTTON NECKLACES/ BRACELETS	Paint large rigatoni pasta, allow to dry, then string together with yarn to make a necklace or bracelet. Or string large buttons to make a necklace or bracelet. Make necklaces loose, and do not let young kids wear them unsupervised.
RAINBOW PICTURES	Color a white piece of posterboard over with different colored wax crayons, then paint over the crayon color with black paint. Next, use a pencil, the end of a paintbrush, or a coin to scratch shapes into the black paint. The paint will be removed to reveal the bright colors underneath.
SPONGE PAINTING	Cut shapes like squares, triangles, and hearts from clean kitchen sponges, or buy precut sponges from a craft or toy store. Dip them into paint and press onto paper to make shaped pictures. Teach your child to recognize shapes and colors as you go.
STRAW PICTURES	Put dabs of paint about the size of a quarter onto a piece of posterboard. Give your child a drinking straw, with one end positioned an inch above the paint, and have her blow through it. Her breath will force the paint in different directions to make a picture. (Make sure she doesn't *inhale* the paint through the straw, and see to it that the straw is always above the paint and not in it.)
WIZARD HATS AND PRINCESS CROWNS	Cut a large triangle out of posterboard and tape the straight sides together to make a cone shape. Staple some long ribbon or wool from the pointed end of the cone so that it dangles down. Decorate the hat with glitter, or draw stars, moons, or hearts on it.

time with you." A wonderful idea—especially for working parents or very busy parents—is to schedule regular playtime into your day or week. Perhaps you might schedule Mommy playtime in the morning before work or school, and Daddy playtime in the evening as soon as he comes home from work, or every Saturday afternoon and Sunday morning. Children love this special time dedicated to playing together. They will look forward to it—and so will you.

And there is a huge variety of great activities you can do with your child—from a card game, board game, or puzzle to crafts or cooking to

Jack's Imaginary Friend

THREE-YEAR-OLD JACK loved the Wiggles, an Australian pop band for kids. He would listen to their CD in the car and at home, and he repeatedly watched his collection of Wiggles videos. Featured in Wiggles songs and performances were two life-size characters, Wag the Dog and Dorothy the Dinosaur. Jack was particularly fascinated by Dorothy. "Do you think Dorothy likes carrots?" he would ask me after we watched a Wiggles video together. "Does Dorothy have any brothers?" "Does she go to school?" Guessing the details of Dorothy's life proved endlessly interesting to Jack, and I noted that her likes and dislikes exactly paralleled Jack's.

One day, Jack's mother and I took him to see The Wiggles performing live in a huge arena in Sydney. It was like being at a rock concert for the under-fours. Delirious with joy, the children laughed and sang and screamed when they saw their favorites in person. When Dorothy came on stage, Jack's eyes widened with delight, and he cheered loudly.

The next day, Dorothy the Dinosaur came to live with us. I had no idea she had moved in until I came down to breakfast. "Don't sit there!" Jack shouted as I pulled out a chair. "That's where Dorothy is sitting." It took me a few minutes to get over my confusion and realize what was going on. From that moment on, Dorothy took part in just about everything we did. Jack's parents and I were amused by his imaginary friend, and we all went along with her presence, marveling at Jack's rich imagination.

Then one day, Dorothy was gone as quickly as she had arrived. Although she had lived with us only a few days, I missed her; I had gotten used to having her around. But the richly vivid imagination of a young child like Jack, which never ceases to surprise and amaze me, was already moving on to something else.

let's-pretend scenarios. When you play with your child, let him lead the way. Don't take over and begin to direct the game or try to control how your child expresses his creativity. When he draws a picture, the trees do not have to be green, and the sky does not have to be blue. His teddy bear can have magic powers, and his doll can have fifty brothers if he chooses. Children need to feel they can use their imaginations freely; this should be one area where there is no right or wrong way to do things.

Kids especially enjoy doing simple arts and crafts at home. If you are worried about the mess, place a plastic sheet on the floor and a full-length plastic painting apron on your child; that way, cleanup is not an issue. For kids over the age of two, stock an arts and crafts box with cards, paper, crayons, pencils, glitter, kids' scissors, stickers, tape, kids' glue, and magazines. Art ideas really do not need to be complicated. Your child will be so proud of his finished picture, and you will enjoy unleashing your creativity too. You'll find some suggestions on pages 238–39.

Reading with Your Child

Reading is especially important to a child's intellectual development, and

Books

Nanny Seal of Approval

(from simple to more complex)
- Dear Zoo by Rod Campbell (Lift-the-Flap Book)
- Spot Goes to the Farm by Eric Hill
- My First Animal Lift-the-Flap Board Book
- Are You My Mother? by P. D. Eastman
- Dinosaur Roar! by Paul Stickland
- We're Going on a Bear Hunt by Helen Oxenbury
- Thomas the Tank Engine by William Awdrey
- I Spy series by Jean Marzollo and Walter Wick
- Any book by Beatrix Potter
- Hairy Maclary from Donaldson's Dairy by Lynley Dodd
- Babar books by Jean de Brunhoff
- Madeline books by Ludwig Bemelmans
- Where the Wild Things Are by Maurice Sendak
- Magic Beach by Alison Lester
- Stellaluna by Janell Cannon
- The Classic Treasury of Hans Christian Anderson
- Where's Wally? series by Martin Handford
- Eyewitness Books series published by Dorling Kindersley

it is something a parent and child will enjoy doing together. It is a wonderful thing to introduce to a young child the delight of hearing a story unfold as he follows along with the illustrations. Try to read your child at least one book each day so you encourage his love of books and of reading, while also developing his language skills and intellectual growth.

You can read to babies starting at any age. They love simple, brightly colored books, and they love being read to and hearing the sound of your voice. By the age of one, kids enjoy flip-books and can recognize pictures, so ask them to point out the pig, car, or elephant in the illustration. And don't forget to ask them what noise the dog or chicken makes.

From eighteen months of age, children become fascinated with particular *things*—ducks perhaps, or shoes, or trucks. They enjoy reading stories featuring the things they are interested in. Two-year-old boys adore dinosaurs and four-year-old girls are overjoyed by princesses; they love to read books about these subjects.

As you read with your preschooler, ask questions about the story. "What did Joe do in the park?" you might ask, or "Why was Rebecca sad in the story?" These questions will help develop your child's understanding of story lines as well as his analytical skills. Books like those in the *Where's Wally?* or *I Spy* series also help develop observational and problem-solving skills.

And some things never go out of style. We love to read kids traditional fairy tales, nursery rhymes, and books with vivid or detailed illustrations, all of which fuel a child's rich imagination.

Nanny Seal of Approval

Board Games

- Candy Land by Milton Bradley
- Cariboo by Cranium
- Chutes and Ladders by Milton Bradley
- Hungry Hungry Hippos by Milton Bradley
- Pooh Memory Game by Hasbro

Nanny
Wisdom *Bringing Fun and Play to the Everyday*
Even the most mundane, everyday things can be turned into fun for kids.
Add play to getting your child dressed in the morning by reciting "This Little
Piggy Went to Market" or your own personalized version of "Dem Bones"; you know the
one: Hip bone connected to the thigh bone, thigh bone connected to the shin bone.
Transform a simple shopping trip into a guessing game: "Can you see a pineapple? Can you
find a banana?" Hide some children's toys in the garden before you go outside to work there,
and let your child play a game of treasure hunt as you do the weeding and deadheading. On
a rainy day, make castles or a pirate's lair from sheets and furniture, and stir your child's
imagination with some not-too-scary pirate tales. Your own imagination is your only limit
to turning the mundane into the magical and creating fun and play for your child.

Playing by Themselves

While kids love to play with adults, they also need opportunities for independent play. Yes, it's important to play with your kids, but if you entertain your child all day long, he won't learn to enjoy his own company or know how to entertain himself.

Even a baby can play by himself for a few minutes each day. Put your baby under a baby activity gym or in a baby bouncer with toys attached to it to amuse him. Supply older kids with toys that enable a range of activities—building blocks, books, or Playmobil, for example—and let them play on their own.

Of course, young children should always be supervised and safe when playing on their own.

Fun and Play Outside

Outside play is essential for children. Apart from the importance of kids getting fresh air and being under real skies, outside is where children can explore the larger world, learn to appreciate nature, have space to run and twirl or ride a bike, learn to play sports, or just enjoy whizzing down the slide in the park.

A backyard, if you have one, can be host to all sorts of play almost all year round, and it can become a temporary water park in summertime. Kids of all ages love small paddling pools, although of course you must never leave a child alone near water, and you must pay attention at all times. Toddlers in particular are fascinated by water play. One form of play we recommend is gathering plastic containers of different sizes, turning on the garden hose—very low or on the sprinkler setting—and letting your little one have fun filling the containers with water. As he does so, he will also be learning problem-solving skills, and he will be gaining an understanding of space and of shapes.

In any season except deepest winter, a small sandbox, with little spades, cranes, buckets, and kids' toys, is something children love to play with.

Adventures Away from Home

The *park* can be a world of adventure, and it's a good idea to take your child there regularly. It's a place for rolling down the hill, swinging and trying to touch the sky, playing hide-and-seek. Play ball games and tag with your child to encourage running and to develop endurance, coordination, and flexibility. Let your toddler push her doll's stroller around the park, or teach your preschooler to ride his bike on the pathways.

Parks offer more tranquil pleasures as well, which are equally rewarding. If your park has a duck pond, give your children stale bread to feed the ducks. Or help your kids collect rocks and sticks or look at birds, squirrels, and frogs in the pond, for ongoing lessons in nature and in observation and exploration skills.

If you live near the *beach*, you have access to endless possibilities for fun and play. You and your child can make sand castles, collect shells, and jump the waves together. On a rainy day, you can watch the waves come crashing down as the storm rumbles in. Or stimulate your child's curiosity by exploring in rock pools for interesting sea creatures.

The *library* is also a great place in which to spend a few hours with your kids. Let your child take his time choosing the books he is interested in. Most libraries also have stories on tape or CD, weekly story times, and children's videos you can borrow.

Take your child on *outings* to expose her to a range of different experiences: museums, art galleries, the aquarium, the zoo, and children's plays or concerts. Watch a child's delight at seeing the dinosaur skeletons in the museum, or huge colorful paintings and sculptures in art galleries, or elephants and lions at the zoo. Such outings open children's minds to new thoughts and possibilities.

But here's a tip to ensure that these outings are a hit and not a bore: don't try to do too much in one day. If your child's interest only lasts for an hour or two, don't push on to see the whole museum or zoo; save it for another day. Otherwise, the experience will be neither successful nor enjoyable for either one of you.

Similarly, don't force learning on kids by giving them every bit of information you know about a particular topic. Answer their questions on these outings with the kind of information that intrigues kids. It's more important for them to hear that "dolphins always sleep with one eye open" or that "kangaroos carry their babies in their front pouch" than for them to know the Latin names of these animals or where they live and how they breed. Overload children with too many details and they will tune out.

Encourage your preschooler to start a scrapbook of these special outings. Ticket stubs, postcards, and your child's drawings of things seen on the outing are perfect for gluing into their scrapbooks.

Playdates

Playdates are an integral part of the English nanny culture and community. They're an essential vehicle for us nannies: a way for us to support each other, to swap ideas and solutions, and to enhance our training and experience. "Have you tried this for Janey's tantrums?" a nanny might offer, or "Here's what I did when Michael got fussy." The same thing works for parents: playdates become a chance to chat with other parents who may be facing the same challenges or issues. So for all who care for children, playdates can represent a source of knowledge and information.

But of course, the real advantage of playdates is how much kids enjoy them and how much they can learn from them. Kids learn about friendship, communication, sharing, social behavior, other people's feelings and needs, and managing their own impatience and frustration. When children play together—when they build a house with Lincoln Logs, for example—they learn to cooperate, to work as a team. When they play "let's pretend"—a form

Create Your Own Playgroup

Maybe you're new to the area, or perhaps you're the first of your friends to have a baby. If so, a great way to get to know other parents is to create your own playgroup. Just put up a sign in a local children's shop or pediatrician's office, or strike up conversations in the park with other parents, or talk to other parents at your child's preschool or at any organized activities you take your child to. You can even check a community website such as http://urbanbaby.com/ to find other parents who might be interested. Say that you would like to start a playgroup either at your own house or on a rotating basis among the houses of those who join.

Even without a formal group, when you meet a parent you like, invite parent and child over to your house for a morning cup of coffee and play. They'll likely welcome the invitation and the extended hand of friendship.

of role-playing—they learn to be aware of another person's view of the world or another person's creative ideas. These are invaluable life skills, and while playing with adults is important, it is no substitute for this essential interaction with peers. So playdates fill an important need—even more so for only children.

Are babies too young for playdates? Not really. In a baby's first months of life, playdates are more for the parent than the baby. Of course, the adult interaction can be comforting and reassuring and is therefore valuable; in fact, as the months pass, these playdates provide a ready-built circle of support and friends for parents. But the statement that "babies don't play with each other, so why bother?" is not entirely true. Even at the age of four months, babies are interested in other people; by the age of seven months, babies are aware of other babies, even if they are only parallel playing. From the age of one year, even though babies may only be playing next to each other—with minimal interaction—they are still stimulated by the experience of another baby's presence. By the time they are eighteen months old, babies begin to play more with each other, and by the age of two years, they begin to really interact and play together.

But while playdates are invaluable, they can also sometimes be challenging for kids. Learning the ins and outs of social behavior is not easy. Inevitably, there will be hiccups; it is not at all uncommon to see kids refusing to share, hitting one another, even biting. The challenge for parents is to find ways to minimize playdate problems in order to maximize playdate value and fun.

In our view, the key to a successful playdate is keeping the length of time and the number of children in attendance appropriate to age. Too long a playdate, or one involving too many kids, can exacerbate the challenge of sharing toys, while the extra stimulation and noise can make it even harder for kids to interact calmly and patiently. So how long is too long, and how many kids are too many?

Playdates for kids eighteen months old or younger shouldn't exceed more than two hours, and need not involve more than two or three kids. Playdates for kids over two years of age can be longer, but we suggest that no more than four kids be included; more than four isn't a playdate, it's a party.

We also think that mornings, when kids are least tired, are the best time for playdates. Playdates at nap time just about guarantee fights and meltdowns.

As for your presence, it will most likely be required until your child is at least three or four years old. That's usually when you can drop her off at the home of a close friend for a short playdate—that is, if you and your child are comfortable with the idea.

Playdate Issues

The best way to avoid any problems on playdates is to keep things simple. For the most part, just let kids play with the toys or games they choose, although sometimes structuring a craft activity or a game can be useful and fun. We always offer a snack and a drink if hosting the playdate, or we let the kids share lunch. Kids typically eat better when a friend comes for lunch, and it introduces them to the pleasure of sharing meals with friends.

But inevitably, there will be issues during playdates. A child may be shy and clingy, not wanting to play. When that happens, it is advisable to let him settle in at his own pace. Don't force him to play with the other children if he doesn't want to. Instead, let him just watch for a bit, then try to interest him in a toy or game you know he likes. Or let him play on his own until he decides to approach the other children. It may take a few visits before a child feels comfortable enough to jump into play with others right off the bat. Sometimes, these children are more at ease when the playdate occurs at their own home.

Other common playdate problems are biting, hitting, and refusing to share—all quite normal as kids learn how to express themselves and their feelings. Always make it clear to the biter or hitter that the behavior is not acceptable. If age appropriate, issue a warning; then, if the behavior is repeated, either impose a time-out (see Chapter Six for more on time-outs) or just end the playdate as a way to get the message across.

Sometimes, of course, even the best of friends will not be in the mood to play with each other. Perhaps one child is overtired or grumpy or not feeling well. Whatever the cause, a playdate can go downhill within minutes. The solution is not to force the situation but simply to recognize that this particular playdate is not going to work, and that it's therefore time to say good-bye.

Organized Activities

The number and variety of interesting, educational, and enjoyable organized activities for kids just keep growing. In cities and suburbs, you can find everything from swim classes to gym, from dance and music to all kinds of sports. These organized activities can be a terrific experience for a child. They expose kids to new ideas. They offer kids practice in following instructions, understanding and listening, participating, and belonging to a group. Above all, they teach kids new skills and abilities, and as children find out what they're good at and what they like to do—as they master new skills—their confidence soars. In addition, proficiencies learned at a young age will be invaluable later on. Kids who have an interest in sports, for example, or who are passionate about dance or music seem to be more anchored as teenagers; they have something that is important to them besides just the opinions of their peers.

For the parents of young children, organized activities and classes are also a bonus because they provide a perfect opportunity to meet other parents and their kids. We nannies have made many good friends this way.

The obvious questions, however, as you begin to consider signing your child up for an organized activity are: What activity should you choose? How much should you spend? How do you know if the class is a good one for your child?

Of course, your choice of an organized activity will depend on what is available in your area. Cities seem to have endless options for kids, but you can certainly find sports, dance, and music activities on offer just about everywhere. You may want to base your choice of activity on your own interests or on what your child's friends are involved in. If yours is a musical family, a music class would be an obvious choice. If your best friend is starting her child in swimming class, it may be very pleasant—and certainly makes sense—for all of you to do it together.

Your budget will of course determine how much you spend. Some activities are very costly indeed: horseback riding lessons, for example, always a great favorite with little girls, can require expensive equipment. But the truth is you don't need to spend a lot to give your child the benefits of an organized activity experience. There are a lot of organized activities that cost only an entrance fee, if that.

Before committing to an activity, ask to observe a session of it or to let your child try it out; many activities do offer trial classes. Check to see if the teacher or instructor takes time to praise, motivate, and interest the kids, and whether he or she makes the children feel comfortable and encourages them to participate in what is going on. The class should be enjoyable; no young child should have to take part in a dull class or one that is rigorously strict. You want an environment in which learning is fostered through enjoyment, exploration, and experience. Keep in mind that some children do take a while to warm up when starting a new class; it can take four or five swimming lessons, for example, before a hesitant child is comfortable getting right into the water.

Finally, balance is essential. A few classes or organized activities can be wonderful, but too many can quickly become a chore for both kids and parents. Over-scheduled kids do not enjoy their activities, and kids who don't enjoy their activities quickly become overtired and unhappy. In addition, some kids like organized activities more than others, so try things out and don't be afraid to cancel a class if you feel you have taken on too much or if your child simply doesn't like it.

A New York Birthday Party

The first children's birthday party I ever went to in New York is one I will never forget. I was taking my two-year-old charge, Oliver, to his friend Peter's second birthday party. I was new to the United States and was excited about this chance to meet new people, especially other nannies.

We arrived at Peter's Upper West Side penthouse apartment and were ushered inside by a uniformed housekeeper. Through the floor-to-ceiling windows, I looked out over the stunning panorama of Central Park. Sculptures and other superb artworks were on display throughout the apartment, and every piece of furniture was pristine white.

Oliver hid behind my legs as we both took in the scene before us. The little boys were dressed in bow ties and smart jackets, and the little girls all had on their best party dresses with their shiniest shoes. Their parents were head to toe in Prada, Chanel, and Versace. Waiters dressed in black-and-white uniforms passed platters of hors d'oeuvres that included caviar and blini. Everyone sipped champagne from Baccarat flutes as if it were a completely normal activity for a child's birthday party.

But it was unlike any other children's birthday party I had ever been to. A life-size Barney soon came bouncing toward us, and I could see that the clowns were terrifying children in the other room. Oliver, along with a half dozen other kids, began to cry. I calmed him down and took him to the kitchen to get him something to eat, but I was surprised to find only bowls of pretzels and candy for the children to eat, even though it was lunchtime.

While the adults continued to sip champagne in the dining room, it quickly became clear that the entertainment, bought and paid for at what was no doubt a hefty price, was simply excessive. There was way too much going on at this party, which in my eyes wasn't a party a two-year-old child would ever enjoy. Faced with a hungry and uninterested Oliver, I decided it was time to head home. On the way out, we passed Peter, the birthday boy mid-shriek—at the height of a sugar-induced tantrum.

It had all been top-of-the-line, and while the parents may have enjoyed their caviar and bubbly, it wasn't much of a birthday party for children. I, however, had a New York kid's party story that would be a real hit back home.

The Birthday Party

The birthday party is a very special part of growing up—and a memory to cherish as an adult. The anticipation and excitement a child feels before a birthday party cannot be overestimated. It is the one day dedicated wholly to her, a moment in time when she is made to feel especially loved. The thrill of her favorite friends all in one place, the ceremony of the cake, the birthday games, and, of course, the gifts are all things to dream about in advance, to look forward to with excitement, and to look back on afterward with delight.

Such over-the-top, no-expense-spared events like the one in "A New York Birthday Party" simply aren't very much fun for kids. We firmly believe that the most successful birthday parties for young children are those that keep it simple, structured, and fun. Believe us, you don't need to spend a king's ransom, hire a performing clown, or blow up an inflatable castle for your child and his guests to have a wonderful birthday party. Friends, some games, a birthday cake, and presents are more than enough to make your child's wildest dreams for a happy birthday come true.

Planning the Party

Here's what you need to consider when planning your child's birthday party:
- the type of party
- the number of invitees
- the length of the party
- the menu
- the party bags and prizes
- the adult supervision
- the games

Type of party. First you need to decide where you're going to hold the event and whether or not it will have a theme.

Your child's age will be the most important consideration when planning the type of birthday party to have. A baby's first birthday party is of course more for adults than for the baby, so you can either invite four or five babies—at the most—and their parents to your home for an hour or two of unstructured play and some light fare, or you can plan an event that allows family and friends to celebrate your child's first birthday. One of the most memorable first birthdays I ever participated in was a Chinese banquet for a baby of Chinese descent. Her family and friends marked the milestone with an incredible meal and party, at which her grandparents announced to their community that their granddaughter was now one year old.

Nanny Wisdom

Keep Kids Together

For the duration of your child's birthday party, restrict the kids to just one area of the house—perhaps the playroom or the living room. You don't want half the kids going off and playing in your child's room while you are in the kitchen. For one thing, you will end up with a mess from one end of the house to the other. For another, over-excited kids can't help but get into trouble. Letting kids go off in different directions will virtually guarantee chaos.

For older kids, in many places it's now possible to "order" an organized event from commercial venues that do this as a business. So you can choose a sports party, a pizza party, a pottery party, or a video arcade party, among other options. The venue itself usually provides food and/or games for the children, but take note: these organized parties can be expensive.

It may be easier and more enjoyable—it will certainly be less costly— to have a party at home, if you have the space. So the question then becomes whether or not to give the party a theme.

Kids over the age of three love theme parties. Fairy and wizard, pirate and princess, and superhero parties are always huge hits. Whatever the theme, it can be the basis of your invitations, decorations, party favors, and games. For a fairy and wizard party, put some glitter or stars inside the invitation envelope; when the invited child opens it, she will be thrilled to see glitter or stars sprinkle out. A magical atmosphere can be created by giving each child a wand and a wishing stone on arrival—basically a pretty, colored stone. Games can also match your theme: a treasure hunt at a pirate party, where the treasures are candy,

Along Came a Spider

For DOUGLAS'S SIXTH BIRTHDAY, his uncle promised him a pet. The day before his birthday, a box arrived addressed to Douglas. He opened the box only to discover an empty glass tank and a note from his uncle that read: "You will need this for your new pet." We all assumed Douglas would be getting a fish.

The next day, a courier box arrived addressed to Douglas's mother. She opened it, let out a high-pitched scream, and jumped on top of the kitchen table. Still screaming, she pulled Douglas onto the table with her and pointed frantically to the far corner of the kitchen. My gaze followed in the direction of her pointed finger, and in an instant I leapt onto the table, too.

Hearing the commotion, Douglas's father came running into the room and saw what his wife was pointing at. "Oh," he said, "it's a spider."

"That's not a spider, that's a monster!" Douglas's mother protested.

"It looks like a tarantula," said Douglas's dad. "My brother must have sent it; it's probably Douglas's pet." He peered into the courier box. "Look, the plastic container it was in has broken. That's why it got out." He caught the spider using a dish and a magazine and put it into the waiting tank.

"Cool!" said Douglas as he climbed down to meet his new pet.

"A spider is not a pet!" said Douglas's mom, echoing my own thoughts on the matter. "Put a lid on that tank," she said to her husband, "and Douglas, you are not to touch it, ever!"

"Oh, honey," said Douglas's father, "I'm sure this spider is not poisonous."

They checked out the species of spider on the Internet, where Douglas's mother was shocked to discover it had an expected life span of fifteen years.

"Douglas will be away at college, and I will still be living at home with this spider," she said ruefully.

Douglas's fascination with the spider lasted exactly two weeks. It was good for impressing his friends at his birthday party, but after that he didn't think it was much fun at all. He certainly couldn't teach it to sit or do tricks, and he didn't much feel like snuggling with it while he watched TV.

For the record, the spider, named Harry, still lives with Douglas's parents.

or an obstacle course through the yard or around the house at a super-hero party.

Number of invitees. One of the most important pieces of wisdom we can give you is to keep the guest list short for your child's birthday. The traditional rule of thumb is your child's age plus one; if you have a two-year-old, that would mean three kids at the party. But we believe this rule can be expanded. For a three-year-old's party, four is too few, forty is far too many, and six to eight sounds about right. Too many guests can be overwhelming and confusing for kids, leading to chaos and major meltdowns. However, if you are inviting the majority of your child's preschool class, you probably should invite them all. To exclude a few children is unfair.

Party Seating

It is always best to seat all the kids when it's time for the food. Don't let them graze as they play; you want the meal itself to be an event. The seating plan will depend on the age of the children. For younger kids, eating at a table usually works best; it cuts down on distractions. For older kids, picnic-style seating with a food buffet is fun and easy. If you have a backyard and the weather is fair, consider feeding the children outside. It makes it easier to clean up the mess, and the inevitable drink spill won't create too much havoc—or be a permanent memento on your carpet.

Another thing to keep in mind is to invite kids the same age as your child. Six-year-olds can be out of place at a four-year-old's party. Veterans of birthday parties, older kids may try to dominate the party or refuse to join in the games. Older cousins, siblings, or close family friends, of course, should not be excluded for this reason.

Length of party. Successful kids' parties are short and sweet—two hours at the most for kids age two to five. After all, it's hard work for kids to share toys and try to be on their best behavior, and after a couple of hours of such effort, it may all begin to unravel. Specify the party hours on the invitation so people know what to expect.

Menu. Birthday parties are great opportunities to make festive, yummy foods that kids love. Check our recipes beginning on page 262.

Party bags and prizes. You don't need to go overboard with party bags and prizes. Small items like crayons, balls, novelty umbrellas, mini-paints, Play-Doh, toy cars, and plastic bracelets are always hits. For themed parties, include something that matches the theme—perhaps a small jar of bubbles for a girl's fairy party, or a plastic firefighter's hat for a boy's dress-up party.

Adult supervision. To make sure there is adequate supervision at the party, you may want to ask other family members and/or the guests' parents or nannies to help out. If your child is a preschooler, the preschool teacher can sometimes be invited to attend the birthday party; having this familiar figure of authority on hand can be extremely helpful.

Here's the ratio we recommend: one adult for every three toddlers, or one adult for every four preschoolers. We do not recommend swimming-pool parties for children under the age of six.

Games. While games provide a desirable structure that keeps birthday parties running smoothly, their real appeal is that kids love them; they make the party special. There does need to be a balance between too many games, which can be overwhelming, and too few, which can provide an opportunity to get into trouble. Be sure, also, that the games you stage are age appropriate.

Certainly there should be prizes for the game winners. If the party is for the under-five crowd, however, everyone should be a winner; otherwise, you run the risk of hurt feelings. For older kids, it's fine to give major prizes to the winners of individual games, but then think about staging a game like pass the parcel (see page 256), in which you might place a little something under each layer of wrapping—small packs of cards, toy cars, or small packages of candy. Then make sure each child has a turn at removing a layer of wrapping paper and receiving a prize.

Don't make the mistake, all too common, of letting the birthday child win all the prizes. He will receive plenty of presents, so let the guests win something. Another mistake is to offer prizes for such things as the "best dress-up outfit." Especially for kids under the age of two, who generally have no control over their outfit, such prizes are unfair and inappropriate.

THE NANNIES' CLASSIC PARTY GAMES

GAME	AGE	HOW TO PLAY
MAGICAL BUBBLES	All ages	Blow bubbles into the air; babies love this simple game. Let older kids blow the bubbles themselves. Use different sizes of bubble blowers to amaze young kids.
PASS THE PARCEL	2 years and up	First prepare the parcel before the party begins. Start by wrapping the big prize in a piece of newspaper or colored paper. Then place this parcel and a smaller prize in the center of another piece of paper and wrap very loosely. Repeat these steps until you have a parcel with as many layers—and prizes—as there are children coming to the party. To play the game, ask the children to sit in a circle. Give the birthday child the parcel to hold, put on some music, and have the children pass the parcel around the circle. When the music stops, the child holding the parcel gets to take off one layer of wrapping and wins the prize inside. Make sure everyone has a turn at receiving a prize.
RING-AROUND-THE-ROSY	Kids able to walk	You remember how it goes: "Ring around the rosy, a pocket full of posies, ashes, ashes, we all fall down." Hold hands, walk in a circle, fall down at the appropriate moment.
POLAROID PHOTO CARD	2 years and up	A good craft activity at a party, this requires a Polaroid camera. Take a photo of each child and then help the children paste their photos onto a piece of posterboard. Decorate with stickers (hearts, stars, etc.) and glitter glue. The kids can take their cards home with them.
MUSICAL CHAIRS/ CUSHIONS	3 years and up	Make a row or circle of chairs and/or cushions, one for each child. Have the children form a circle around the chairs or cushions. Put on some music; as the music plays, the children circle the chairs/cushions. When the music stops, the children must scramble to find a cushion or chair to sit on. Remove one chair or cushion from the row or circle. The next time the music stops, the child without a cushion/chair is out of the game. Repeat. Eventually only one child will be left sitting on the last chair/cushion—the winner.

GAME	AGE	HOW TO PLAY
TAG, HIDE-AND-SEEK, AND TREASURE HUNT	3 years and up	If you have a yard, get the kids outside to play these outside running games and burn off energy.
PIN THE TAIL ON THE DONKEY	3 years and up	You can draw a picture of a donkey or buy one from any party store. (Variations are "pin the wand on the fairy," "pin the eye patch on the pirate," and "pin the trunk on the elephant.") Blindfold the kids in turn, lead them to the picture, place the tail (or wand, eye patch, or trunk) in their hands. The kids will try to place the item where they think it belongs on the picture. The child who gets it closest wins.
PIÑATA	4 years and up	Buy a piñata—a hollow sculpture, usually of papier-mâché— and fill it with candy or small toys. Kids whack it with a stick to loosen the candy. Take care they don't hit each other with the stick. Help from an adult may be needed as piñatas can be hard to open.
MUSICAL STATUES	4 years and up	The kids dance to music; when the music stops, they have to "freeze" their position. Any child who moves is out of the game. The one remaining kid is the winner.
HOW MANY JELLY BEANS IN THE JAR?	5 years and up	Fill a clear jar with jelly beans; be sure to count them. Write the number down on a piece of paper and put in an envelope. Have the kids guess how many jelly beans are in the jar. Write down each child's name and guess, then open the envelope. The child whose guess is correct or closest is the winner.

Birthday Presents

It's been our experience that for children younger than four years of age, it is best to wait until everyone has gone home from the party before your child opens his presents. Kids younger than three may not understand why they aren't getting presents too, and are likely to assume that the gift they give to the birthday child is actually their own. In addition, the new gifts may cause some problems, especially if the birthday child would clearly prefer to play with his new toys than to join in the party games.

A Special Thomas the Tank Engine Cake

LIKE MANY TWO-YEAR-OLD BOYS, Matthew was obsessed with Thomas the Tank Engine. He played Thomas games all day long. In the car, his fingers became Thomas, chugging along his car seat. In the bath, shampoo lids became Thomas, chugging through tunnels made from bubbles. So for his birthday, I decided to make him a Thomas the Tank Engine cake.

The night before his birthday, all that remained to be done for the party was the cake. Matthew's mother and I had decided that we didn't need complicated instructions or a special cake tin; we were going to work this out ourselves. How hard could it be? we asked ourselves.

But we were off to a bad start when the cakes refused to rise; it was after ten at night before we had sponge cakes we could work with. We spent the next four hours mixing and dyeing icing, cutting candy, and sticking pieces of cake together at odd angles with toothpicks. It was in the early hours of the morning that we realized that our finished masterpiece was not going to fit in the refrigerator. We wrapped the cake in a tent of foil; we slept a few fitful hours dreaming about melted icing and collapsed cakes.

The next day, I carefully carried the cake to the birthday party. Matthew helped me remove the foil as gently as possible, and my tiredness disappeared when I heard his gasp of delight: "It's Thomas!" To this day, Matthew talks about his very own special Thomas the Tank Engine cake. That's what made it worth every bit of time and effort.

We like to write down who gave which gift, so the gift can be mentioned in the thank-you note. If your child receives many gifts for his birthday, you may want to do what a number of families we know do: sneak a few of the new toys away to bring out later in the year when your child's toys have grown too familiar to him.

Thank-you Notes

It is never too early to get your child into the good habit of sending thank-you notes. Doing so sends a message to your child that she should appreciate the effort, time, and money that someone expended to make her happy.

An easy and fun way to do thank-you notes is to make paint prints of your child's hand on paper. Then just write a brief message under the handprint: "Thank you for coming to my party and thanks for my lovely present"—or something similar. Or, take a drawing from the stock you keep of your child's artwork and write a short note on it. Relatives in particular will be delighted to have something personal from your child, and her little friends will be very excited to receive mail addressed to them.

Birthday Party Menus and Recipes

It's a party, after all, and we offer two festive menu plans for the over-two crowd here—one simple, one more elaborate. You don't need to go crazy with plates and plates of food; kids at a party are usually so excited they're not particularly interested in eating a great deal. Use paper or plastic cups and plates to minimize cleanup; for a theme party, try novelty items that work with the theme—pirate cups or Shrek plates, for example.

The Simple Party Menu

- finger foods—cheddar cheese cut into cubes, cherry tomatoes, guacamole, and corn chips
- small boxes of raisins
- fresh fruit chopped into small pieces: tangerines, berries, pineapple, melon
- finger sandwiches: Make sandwiches using fillings like cheese, ham, chicken salad, turkey, peanut butter, and egg salad. Cut off the crusts, and then cut the sandwiches into quarters to make triangles.

- hot dogs or mini-sausages: Cook store-bought hot dogs as directed, place in hot dog buns, flavor with ketchup. Cut in half for little hands to hold.
- Pita Pizzas: See recipe on page 182.
- Fairy Bread: Fairy Bread is standard at all children's birthday parties in Australia. Spread pieces of white bread with butter. Shake colored sprinkles over the bread. Cut into quarters.
- Easy Candy Birthday Cake: See recipe on page 263.
- Oreo Sundaes: Place one scoop of vanilla ice cream in a bowl, pour homemade or store-bought chocolate sauce over it, sprinkle with one crushed Oreo cookie and either one strawberry or a quarter of a sliced banana.
- Pink Fizz: Pour cranberry juice into the bottom quarter of a cup; add seltzer water. Stir and serve with a straw.

The More Elaborate Party Menu
- Fancy Sandwiches: Place fillings like sliced cheese, hummus, turkey, peanut butter, and ham on frozen sliced bread to make the sandwiches. (The bread will defrost slightly in the process.) Cut the sandwiches into different shapes with an array of medium-sized cookie cutters.
- Honey Chicken Drumsticks: Mix together 4 tablespoons honey, 1 cup soy sauce, and a splash of oil. Marinate 10 chicken drumsticks in the mixture for at least 15 minutes. Discard the marinade and place drumsticks on a baking tray and roast in a 450°F oven for 40 to 45 minutes until cooked through, browned and slightly crispy. Allow to cool a little before serving.
- Bite-size Turkey Burgers: See recipe on page 188; you can substitute ground beef for turkey if you like.
- carrot and cucumber sticks with hummus
- fruit salad: Mix berries and bite-size oranges, apples, and melon; serve in small bowls or cups.
- Pirate Jell-O Boats (makes twelve boats): Start by making the Jell-O as directed on the package, but omit a little of the suggested water, to make it more concentrated. Cut three firm oranges in half, and scoop out all the flesh, leaving only the skin and white pith. Pour the Jell-O

into the oranges. Repeat until all the Jell-O mixture is used. Refrigerate for five hours or overnight in a baking dish, so the liquid doesn't spill. When set, slice the oranges in half again with a very sharp knife. Place a small paper flag in the center of each to make the pirate-ship mast. You can find these flags at party stores, or make your own using a toothpick and paper.

• Happy Faces Cupcakes: See the recipe on page 264.
• fancy birthday cake: Kids love fancy birthday cakes in the shape of a train, racetrack, doll, or house. You can find recipes and directions for making these in cake decorating books, or you can buy the shaped cake tins from bakeware. If you plan to make one of these cakes, allow yourself plenty of time—it takes longer than you think—and always buy more ingredients than you anticipate needing, especially confectioners' sugar and candy.

Fun, Play, and Parties

★ Make sure your child has fun and play, every day.

★ A safe space, appropriate playthings, and time are the only requirements for fun and play.

★ Create opportunities for your child to have both structured and unstructured, both interactive and independent play.

★ A toy collection should combine the creative, the educational, and the sheer fun.

★ Birthday parties need not be lavish or costly; the best are simple, short, and structured.

Nanny Recipes

HOMEMADE PLAY-DOH

Kids love to play with Play-Doh, and you can easily make your own at home, then watch as your child creates shapes using plastic rolling pins, cookie cutters, and his hands.

> 2 cups flour
> ½ cup salt
> 4 teaspoons cream of tartar
> 2 cups water
> 2 teaspoons oil
> Food coloring

In a medium-sized bowl, mix flour, salt, and cream of tartar.

Make a well in the center of the bowl and slowly add water, stirring into dry mixture bit by bit until combined.

Pour in oil and mix; add food coloring until mixture is a vibrant color.

Place mixture in a medium-sized saucepan over medium-low heat and stir continuously. The mixture will begin to form small lumps. Keep mixing until it comes together into one big lump (this will take about 3–5 minutes). Remove from heat immediately.

Carefully remove from pan and place on a lightly floured surface; when just cool enough to touch, knead until elastic and smooth.

Soak pan immediately for easy clean-up.

Store in an airtight container. Play-Doh keeps for about one month; discard if it dries out.

Note: Do not allow children to eat Play-Doh.

EASY CANDY BIRTHDAY CAKE RECIPE

When you have neither the time nor the inclination to make a fancy birthday cake, this colorful cake will thrill your child just as much. The sight of candy is always exciting to children, so let loose: it's a birthday party, after all.

> 2 sticks softened butter
> 2½ cups confectioners' sugar
> 1 teaspoon vanilla extract
> 2 tablespoons milk
> Food coloring: pink, blue, or yellow
> 1 un-iced store-bought cake or homemade vanilla/chocolate cake
> Colorful candy: M&M's, Skittles, Reese's Pieces, gummy bears

In a bowl or electric mixer, combine the butter and the confectioners' sugar and vanilla until smooth. Slowly add the milk; mix well. The consistency of the icing should now be thick and smooth.

Add a few drops of food coloring and mix well; continue until the icing is the desired color.

Slice the cake in half horizontally; this is easily done with a large, long knife. Spread the middle of the cake with a quarter of the icing, and join cake halves together.

Spread the remaining icing generously over the cake. It is best to use a flat palate knife; ice the sides first, then the top.

Generously cover the top of the cake with the candy.

HAPPY FACES CUPCAKES

Makes 12 cupcakes

Cooking is a fun activity that kids love to do with adults. It teaches them a whole host of things: to listen and follow directions, to solve problems, even to understand something about math as they measure and pour ingredients. They experience the sensations of taste, smell, and touch. And most of all, they are very proud of the finished product. This is a recipe I have often made with kids. Once the cakes are cooled, ask your child (if he is two or older) to help you create faces to decorate them.

CUPCAKES
12 large cupcake papers
2 sticks butter (at room temperature)
1 cup superfine sugar
1 teaspoon vanilla
2 eggs, slightly beaten, at room temperature
1½ cups all-purpose flour, sifted
1 teaspoon baking powder
½ cup milk

ICING
2 cups confectioners' sugar
Warm water
Food coloring

Preheat oven to 350°F, and prepare the cupcake pan by placing cupcake papers into each space.

Place the butter, sugar, and vanilla in a bowl and cream until light and fluffy. Gradually add beaten eggs, mixing well after each addition.

Mix together the sifted flour and baking powder in a separate bowl.

Add the flour mixture and the milk alternately into the egg mixture, and mix well after each addition.

Spoon the cupcake batter into each cupcake paper halfway, then place in the oven for 25–35 minutes or until done.

To make the icing, place the confectioners' sugar in a bowl and add table-spoons of water, gradually stirring with a wooden spoon until a smooth, thick spreading consistency has been achieved. Add drops of food coloring and stir until the desired color has been achieved. Do not allow to sit long, as this icing is a glaze and will harden when it dries.

Check the cupcakes for doneness with a cake tester, skewer, or knife until it comes out clean and cupcakes are slightly golden. Cool the cakes on a wire rack; once cool, ice and decorate.

DECORATING: MAKING FACES
Decorate the cupcakes with faces before the glaze hardens; when it does, the glaze face will be set into place.

Use sprinkles or sanding sugar for hair, M&M's for eyes, and a small piece of licorice or Twizzlers for a smile.

Chapter Eight

Kids in Transit
Traveling with Young Children

The Ritz in Paris is one of the world's legendary hotels, but when I check in for a weeklong stay, instead of feeling excited, all I can think about is crawling into bed and falling into a deep, long sleep. The last twelve hours have felt like the day that would never end. I have flown from New York with six-month-old Fred, three-year-old Ashleigh, and ten-year-old Samantha. To begin with, our flight was delayed for more than three hours, leaving the kids bored, cranky, and tired before we even took off. Then, once we were actually airborne, Fred, who was teething, was so unsettled I had to spend most of the flight walking him up and down the aisles trying to soothe him to sleep. Ashleigh, who hated to sit still at the best of times, went stir-crazy on the plane. She antagonized her older sister for most of the trip, knocked over three drinks, and continually kicked the back of the chair in front of her, much to the annoyance of the elderly woman sitting there. Only Samantha took the journey in stride, happily watching the in-flight movies in between her younger sister's many interruptions.

When we finally arrive at the hotel, the desk clerk is just about to hand me the room key when a familiar voice calls to us from across the lobby. "My darlings! You made it!" It is Violet, the children's mother, who is running toward us. She has been working in Paris for the past two weeks, and we have traveled here to meet her. The children throw themselves into their mother's arms, and all four of them begin talking and laughing at once.

Moments later, we are on our way to our adjoining suites, followed by a procession of bellboys carrying our luggage. Violet notices my exhaustion and encourages me to settle in and unpack. I quickly agree, shut the door behind me, and sigh with relief.

The luxuries of my suite revive me somewhat. Outside my private balcony, Paris is at my feet, the Eiffel Tower rising proudly in the distance. In the bathroom, which is bigger than my home kitchen, there are a private sauna and a hot tub. A basket beside the bathroom sink overflows with every kind of fancy toiletry. Piles of huge, soft towels and perfumed French candles sit on the marble counters. Most enticing of all is the king-size, four-poster bed with its feather-filled covers and plump pillows, on which rests a chocolate truffle covered in gold paper. I sink down on the heavenly bed, close my eyes, and start to relax—when I feel a frantic tugging on my skirt.

I open my eyes to see a very unhappy three-year-old. "I can't find my teddy!" Ashleigh says in a wobbly voice. She begins to cry. "Did we leave him on the plane?" she asks between sobs. Before I have a chance to deal with this emergency, Samantha bursts into the room. "My ears are hurting," she wails. "They won't pop after the plane ride. Please make it stop!" Behind Samantha stands my boss, with baby Fred held out in front of her.

She hands him to me. "I'm really sorry," Violet says, "but I've been called to an emergency meeting. I'll be back in a couple of hours, and we can all have dinner together. Okay?"

Reality comes crashing into my fantasy world; it is now time for me to do my job.

During the next whirlwind week, neither the children nor I ever do get our body clocks readjusted to Paris time, and we never really manage to get to sleep at the right time. We have many adventures, wander all over the city, visit museums, take in the sights, and of course do plenty of shopping. But doing it all with three jet-lagged and often grumpy children is a test of all my nanny skills—a good reminder that traveling with young children can be quite challenging.

Whether they are at the Ritz, in a bed-and-breakfast, or camping in the wilderness, when children are away from the familiar surroundings of home and the familiar routine of their day, it can be unsettling. They may become irritable, clingy, or contrary. Mealtimes can be tricky when kids confront unfamiliar food; bedtimes can be disorienting because they're away from their own bedroom and off their usual schedule. On top of all this, both parents and kids may be dealing with jet lag and facing a busy vacation schedule.

These are the inevitable realities of travel, and while you probably can't avoid them, it is possible to minimize them and make them more manageable. That's what this chapter is about: making traveling with kids as easy and as stress free as possible. We tell you how to prepare for your trip, what to take with you, how to make the journey smoother, and how to enjoy your destination once you have arrived.

Pre-Trip Preparation

Back before you had kids, it was no problem to take off for a vacation at the last minute. If you forgot your swimsuit or had too little shampoo, it didn't matter; you could just pick up what you needed once you arrived—or do without it. But with kids, a teddy bear left behind or a forgotten fever reducer could mean a really bad start to your vacation. That's why getting well organized ahead of time is the key to enjoyable and successful travel with children. Consider three aspects of your trip when approaching pre-trip preparation: type of travel, accommodations, and packing.

Type of Travel

By plane. Different airlines have different policies regarding children. Some provide bassinets and car seats—some let you bring your own—and such services as bottle and baby food warming, and even escorts for single adults traveling with two children under eighteen months. So the first step if you're traveling by plane is to tell the airline your kids' ages and ask what services are offered.

If at all possible, reserve a night flight. That way, your child will be more likely to sleep for some or most of the trip. And be sure to request seat locations when you make the reservation. Book seats together; otherwise, you and your baby could end up in a seat at the front of the plane, your husband twenty rows back, and your eight-year-old somewhere in the middle. Don't rely on other passengers to move seats; people do not like to change their seat locations, especially if they've requested them ahead of time. Also, if you have a baby under six months of age, request a bulkhead seat; it generally has a bassinet that pulls down for a baby to sleep in.

As for meal preferences, make sure you request kids' meals. They won't be fabulous, but your children will be more likely to eat them than the adult meals.

By car. When planning a long-distance car trip, consider leaving in the evening after your children have had their dinner and driving through the night to your destination. This should guarantee that the kids will be asleep for most of the trip. Of course, this option only makes sense if you have someone to share the driving with, so one can sleep while the other drives.

Nanny Wisdom

Plane, Train, or Automobile?

Traveling by plane can be a hassle, especially with today's security procedures. Check-in lines can be long, and delays can be a nightmare—and once you're on a plane, there's no place to go. On a train, by contrast, you and your kids can walk around a little. In a car, you can make frequent stops to let your kids run around and let off steam, and they can be noisy without bothering other travelers. So where time and distance permit, think about train or automobile travel instead of plane travel.

If you are driving during the day, it's a good idea to plan stops at interesting sights along the way. Even if you must detour a bit to a park, a playground, or a petting zoo, it is well worth it to break up the long hours spent cooped up inside the car and to give the kids a good chance to run around before the next leg of the journey. These little stops keep everyone happy and make the trip much more pleasant.

Accommodations

Wherever you're planning to stay on your vacation, keep in mind that it needs to be equipped with certain kids' stuff—a crib, a high chair—that you'll either have to arrange for ahead of time or bring along with you. Hotels and rental properties may be equipped with some of this equipment, so make a list of what you'll need before you begin to investigate accommodations—and be sure to ask about it.

Hotel. There is nothing worse than staying in a place that is unwelcoming to families, a place where staff and guests sigh every time your child laughs out loud or skips through the lobby. So by all means telephone or

Relaxing Vacations with Kids

Start by having realistic expectations. A child who wakes up at six every morning at home is not going to sleep till nine just because you are on vacation. In fact, she may start waking up earlier than her usual time because the new surroundings or jet lag have unsettled her. So how can parents ensure that they won't come home from vacation more exhausted than when they left?

One suggestion is to plan for daytime downtime. We know one family that vacations annually on the coast of Mexico and schedules a picnic lunch on the beach every day; after lunch, the toddler naps in a hammock under a palm tree while his parents read books or nap.

Consider vacationing with your extended family or with friends who have kids the same age as yours. That way, you can take turns caring for each other's kids, and everyone will get some undisturbed time during the day—or a dinner out one night.

And of course, if you employ a nanny or babysitter, consider asking her to come on vacation with you to help out with the kids and ensure you get some downtime yourself.

check the web site to find out how child friendly a hotel is before you make a reservation. Some hotels claim to "tolerate" children—best find another hotel.

When you do find a child-friendly hotel, let the staff know you are bringing a young child and ask all the questions you need to. Staff should be able to suggest a room location that will give you more space and privacy. They will let you know if a crib is available—should you need one—and they should be able to tell you the brand and size of the available crib. If it's an old crib with wide bars or metal slats, it may be neither suitable nor safe, and you will want to bring your own portable crib along with you—a good option in any event, as your child will already be familiar with the crib and comfortable sleeping in it.

Ask the staff if the hotel offers babysitting services or children's camps and activities—if such services are of interest to you. And find out about the restaurant and room-service menu so you won't be surprised to discover they only offer raw fish or spicy food. Don't forget to ask if they have high chairs available, if your kids are at that age.

House/apartment rental. Our view as nannies is that the easiest and most enjoyable way to vacation with young children is to find accommodation in a rented house or apartment rather than in a hotel. Hotel rooms can be confining; a house or apartment affords more space for kids to play in and for you to relax. It also offers the freedom to cook and eat whenever and whatever you like; you won't have to rely on restaurant and room-service menus and times. What's more, staying in a house or apartment usually means access to laundry facilities—very handy when traveling with young children.

Of course, it's important to determine ahead of time that the accommodation is truly child friendly and baby safe. A vacation spent chasing your crawling baby away from a spiral staircase or keeping your toddler from smashing a delicate work of art is no vacation at all.

Packing

We advise checking the weather forecast for your destination online or in a newspaper several days ahead of time, so you'll know whether you'll need your child's warmest coat or just a good sweater. But don't rely solely on the weather forecast for your packing needs.

Well before the trip, make a packing list so nothing is left behind. Stick to basics, and be sure to pack the items that your child relies on for comfort, as well as those things that are indispensable for safety or in case of illness. We recommend that you begin collecting the things you want to pack a couple of days ahead of time so you don't have to rush—and so that you don't forget essentials. Bulky items like diapers or baby wipes can usually be purchased pretty much anywhere; pack enough for a day or two, then buy what you need when you arrive at your destination. Make a list of those items that will need to be "in use" until the last minute—a favorite teddy bear, a toothbrush, diaper cream—and pack them up just before departure.

Dogga's Adventure

Nanny Tales

DOGGA WAS EVELYN'S most beloved toy. A soft little toy in the shape of a dog, he had been given to Evelyn when she was just a few days old and had never left her side since. Each nap time and bedtime, three-year old Evelyn would cuddle Dogga and stroke his soft ears as she happily drifted off to sleep.

But on the way home from a trip to Spain, tired little Evelyn dropped Dogga on the airport floor—and we didn't realize it until we got home. That evening, poor Evelyn was distraught, and getting her to sleep without her faithful Dogga proved to be an ordeal.

In the morning, we received a call. A kind woman had found Dogga at the airport and promised to mail him back to Evelyn right away. How did she know where Dogga lived? Well, Dogga had his very own dog tag, a little plastic luggage tag with his home address and phone number, which he wore around his neck whenever we traveled. The next day, Evelyn was overjoyed to get Dogga back, although she told him sternly that he must not go adventuring on his own ever again.

The tale of Evelyn and Dogga proves that every valuable item of "luggage" needs its own identification tag.

Here are our suggested packing lists. We've broken them down into medical essentials, travel bag contents, and items you'll need when you get there—and we've included items you'll need if you're traveling with a baby. If your kids are older, you can of course disregard these latter items. Apart from that, we consider these articles the bare minimum, and when traveling with young children, we would never leave home without them.

The Nannies' Essential Medical Kit

It's important to take a functional medical kit with you when you travel. A pain reliever in checked luggage does you no good at all when your child feels sick one hour into a twelve-hour flight. And an antiseptic cream left at home is no comfort when your child cuts his hand in the hotel swimming pool. Here is our suggested list:

- thermometer
- fever reducer (Motrin or Tylenol, for example)
- Band-Aids
- teething gel (for babies)
- diaper-rash cream (for babies)
- antihistamine (Benadryl)
- antiseptic cream or tea-tree oil
- arnica cream for bumps and bruises
- tweezers for splinters, ticks, thorns (in checked luggage, if flying)
- acidophilus tablets or liquid for upset tummies
- motion sickness medicine, if your child is prone to need it
- calamine lotion
- hand sanitizer gel
- cotton swabs (Q-tips)
- any prescription medicines or remedies for illnesses to which your child is prone
- saline solution and dropper (for babies' colds)

Travel-Bag Contents

Whatever your mode of travel—car, plane, train, or boat— keep with you at all times a travel bag stocked with the items listed on the next page. If you are flying, add to the list basics you would need if your luggage were lost or delayed for two days—from baby formula to toothbrushes, from clean underwear to asthma medicine.

We recommend using a backpack or a bag with wheels and an extender handle as your travel bag. Fill it with the following:

- Diapers, diaper cream, changing mat or towel as needed.
- Baby wipes—even if you don't have a baby in diapers, baby wipes come in handy for cleaning little hands.
- Tissues.
- Spare clothing—in case of spills or other accidents.
- Sippy cups, baby utensils, bottles, formula as needed.
- Water, juice, snacks—plenty of fluids are particularly important if you're flying, as kids easily become dehydrated in the recirculated air. Don't rely on the airline to hand out food and drinks regularly; instead, bring them yourself.
- Pacifier as needed.

- Special blanket, teddy, pillow.
- Handy-sized and *quiet* toys, small storybooks, coloring books and crayons (no permanent markers), or puzzle/quiz books.
- Spare glasses if your child wears them.
- The Nannies' Essential Medical Kit.
- One day's worth of essentials—in case of lost luggage.

Optional:

- A cassette or CD player with a few favorite musical or story choices.
- A portable DVD player or laptop with headphones and a few favorite DVDs.

The Nannies' Essential Packing List

Here are our suggested essentials—the things you really don't want to leave behind when you're packing. You may need to adjust the list according to the age of your child.

- special blanket or teddy bear, plus a backup—maybe the second favorite bear—in case the favorite gets lost
- sufficient supply of diapers and baby wipes or washcloths to tide you over till you can buy more—or in case you can't
- pacifier, if used
- teething rings

- bibs as needed
- travel cups, baby bottles, one or two plastic bowls or plates, and two plastic spoons per baby
- Ziploc bags
- formula milk
- toiletry bag containing toothpaste, toothbrush, soap, shampoo, nail clippers, hairbrush, and comb

- clothes: underwear, socks, shoes, boots, T-shirts, sweaters, pants, pajamas, shorts, winter or summer hat, coat, jacket, gloves, scarf as needed
- sunblock (not for babies under six months old)
- suitable mosquito repellent (Avon's Skin So Soft)
- portable crib with sheet
- mosquito net (for travel to tropical locations)

- clip-on chair
- Baby Björn or sling
- car seat or booster seat if you're renting a car
- stroller
- alarm clock—helpful for adjusting to time changes
- good baby monitor—with an electricity adaptor if you're traveling to a foreign country
- few favorite toys
- few storybooks

The Trip

How can you make the journey easier and more enjoyable? Start by wearing comfortable clothes yourself and dressing your children for comfort. If you are traveling by air, keep in mind that planes can get quite cold, so even if you board the plane in sunny Arizona wearing T-shirts and summer sandals, bring along a sweater and socks so the kids can get cozy.

For long trips, whether by car, train, or plane, bring your child's pillow or a small blanket from his own bed. Kids feel comforted by these familiar items—even a baby can recognize the smell of his blanket—and will be more likely to sleep well.

For a car trip, bring a small tray for your child to lean on while playing games or drawing.

On any trip, kids preschool age and older may like to have a small bag they have helped pack with their own toys and books to keep them amused during the journey.

Tips from Frequent-Flyer Nannies

Flying with young children can be truly exhausting, but extra thought and preparation can help make things easier. Here are our frequent-flyer tips:

- Before you leave for the airport, call the airline to check that your flight is on time. It makes everything so much harder if you are on time but your flight is delayed, and keeping kids amused in an airport waiting lounge is no easy task.

- Feed your children a good meal before you leave for the airport or before you board the plane, in case the meal service is slow or the flight is delayed. Pasta is both simple and substantial, a good choice to tide kids over for a while.
- Ask to take your stroller to the gate, or use a baby backpack to carry your child so you have your hands free to carry bags and belongings.
- Takeoff and landing can be painful for little ears. If you're traveling with a baby, either nurse him or give him a bottle of milk or water at these times. Give your toddler a drink of water or juice, and offer an older child a sweet to suck on. These can all help ease the pressure.
- If you are traveling with another adult, alternate holding your baby or entertaining your toddler. That way, one of you can sleep for an hour while the other is on duty. Alternatively, if you have two children, each adult can take charge of one child for the duration of the flight so no one gets overwhelmed or overextended.
- Make sure your child has plenty of fluids to drink during the flight. If he isn't a big fluid drinker, offer fruit instead.

Nanny Wisdom   *Packing Tips*

- Put all leakable toiletries like baby bath oil, diaper cream, or shampoo into Ziploc bags. You really don't want to open your suitcase upon arrival to find sun cream coating your child's favorite storybook.
- Place shoes in plastic bags so they won't scuff the clean clothes.
- Take spare plastic bags to hold dirty clothes while you are away. When you return home, the plastic bags go straight to the laundry room, while the remaining clean clothes can go back into the drawer.
- Always put a tag with your name, address, and phone number on each bag—including carry-on luggage.

Travel Games and Activities

Nanny Seal of Approval

- **Are We There Yet?** by Alison Lester
- Car Valet by Alex
- Crayola Super Art Activity Desk by Binney & Smith
- Etch A Sketch by Ohio Art Company
- Old Maid by eeBoo
- Travel Bingo by eeBoo
- Travel Connect Four by Hasbro

- To make sure you don't leave something on board the plane, try sticking a Post-it on your wallet or passport noting the carry-on items you brought aboard. Check the list before you disembark to make sure you have every teddy bear, sippy cup, and coloring book you brought with you.
- For an older kid carrying his own possessions, write the number of items he has on his hand. If he needs to remember his skateboard, guitar, and backpack, just write "3" on his palm. That way, he is less likely to leave something behind and more likely to check under the seat, in the overhead locker, and in the seat pocket to find all three items.

"Are we there yet?": Keeping Boredom at Bay

It's the universal question: "Are we there yet?"—an expression of impatience from young children who are simply bored with what seems to them an endless trip. One way to help deal with the boredom is to talk to your children—at least, those over three years of age—before the trip starts. Tell them what to expect so they won't be surprised when the novelty wears off and the trip becomes tedious. Here are some other tips for keeping boredom at bay:

- Bring along your kids' favorite toys and books to keep them amused. It's also a good idea to get some new coloring books and pencils and even a new toy, but keep these new items in reserve until the time the kids get really restless.
- Travel games or a pack of cards work wonders. Old-fashioned games like "simon says" or "hangman" or "I spy" are great on the road, and if

Flying Lunch Boxes

MELANIE AND I MET one summer while working in the Hamptons on Long Island. In midsummer, Melanie and the kids were due to fly out in the family's private plane to visit the children's grandparents in California, where the children's parents would join them. Eager to have a look at the plane, I offered to drive Melanie and the four children to the airport.

But the five of them were taking so much luggage it was a struggle to fit everyone plus baggage into my car. There were several large bags, plenty of toys, a couple of surfboards, and even the family dog. I remember joking that it was just as well they had a private plane as they would never be allowed to take so much luggage on a commercial flight.

A quick tour of the plane left me impressed. It was large enough to seat twelve people very comfortably and had lots of gadgets and conveniences, including a television set for each passenger. The kids chose their seats, and four-year-old Ellie suddenly called out, "Melanie, what's in my flying lunch box today?"

"Something very yummy," Melanie replied, "but you will have to wait until we take off to find out." The "flying lunch boxes," Melanie explained, were lunch boxes she packed specially for the flight, one for each child. It struck me as a great idea: a wonderful way to add a little excitement to the tedium of travel—even travel by private jet.

It was time for the plane to take off and for me to leave. I quickly said my good-byes, gave one last, longing look around the plane, and waved farewell from the tarmac. Just as I was about to get into my car, I was distracted by something colorful in the backseat. It took only a second to realize that it was the kids' flying lunch boxes. My heart sank when I thought of how disappointed they would be to miss out on their special tradition.

Melanie told me later that once she realized what had happened, the pilot had very kindly radioed ahead to the next airport to order pizzas for the kids' lunch. The plane duly landed, picked up the pizzas, and headed off to California. But to this day, the kids still ask Melanie about the contents of the flying lunch boxes that were left behind, and every time they talk about it the lunch box contents become more imaginative and fantastical.

you're in your own car, you can have a sing-along to nursery rhymes or songs on the radio or CD player.

- If you have brought your portable DVD player or laptop along for a long plane ride, don't bring it out too soon. Movies buy time when kids are getting really bored, but make them your last resort. And don't forget to pack headphones and either an extra battery or an airplane charger so the movie doesn't fizzle in midstream.
- When traveling by car, books on tape or CD are a perfect way to keep kids amused and happy.
- Make use of the fact that a car's motion can lull kids to sleep, by encouraging kids to close their eyes for a minute or to play "the quiet game." With luck, they'll soon nod off.

Motion Sickness

Some children are more prone to motion sickness than others. If your child is susceptible to motion sickness, bring a small bucket or some sick bags, wet wipes, a small towel, and a change of clothing along on the trip. Have salted crackers or dry bread at the ready.

As to remedies, motion sickness wristbands work wonderfully for some kids and are definitely worth a try. It's important not to let your child read in the car. But looking out the window—sit your child in a booster seat if he is too small—and gazing at the horizon can help. If your child feels ill, try opening the windows for some fresh air. Salted crackers or dry bread can help settle the nausea, and a sip of water will help.

Healthy Snacks for the Road

To help your kids travel well, the food you bring must travel well, too. Things like crackers, rice cakes, cheese, dried fruit, carrot sticks, apples, tangerines, granola bars, and sandwiches are all perfect for traveling.

If you are traveling by car, it's advisable to stop and park while your child eats. The risk of kids choking is greater if they eat while a car is in motion, and you may not be able to assist them while you are driving. Most interstates and freeways are nicely equipped with roadside rest stops, many with picnic tables, where you can stop, rest, and have a snack or meal. Bring a cooler along to store drinks and to keep yogurt, cheese, and milk cool

Kids' Menus
Food like fries and chicken nuggets seem to dominate kids' menus all over the world. To add some variety to your child's diet when traveling, ask for a child's portion of an adult meal—maybe pasta, a sandwich, soup, or a simple dish like roast chicken and mashed potatoes. Alternatively, share your own meal with your child.

and fresh. Don't forget a small knife for cutting up food, some hand disinfectant for cleaning hands before preparing or eating food, and those all-purpose baby wipes for wiping sticky hands.

Arrival and Adjustment

Okay, you've arrived. The travel is over, the bags are unpacked. What's the first thing to do now that you're here? Give your children time to settle into their new surroundings and adjust to being on vacation.

If you have changed time zones, it's a good idea to take it easy for the first few days. Use this adjustment period to try getting the kids onto local time as soon as you can by keeping naps short during the day and keeping kids awake for their new bedtimes. Know when your child is overtired and let him take a nap even if he is past napping age. It's not a good idea to let jet-lagged kids nap past four in the afternoon, however, unless you are going out for a late evening. For older kids who don't want to nap during the day but are obviously tired or jet-lagged, encourage quiet time in the afternoons when the kids can watch a movie, read books, or do some coloring.

Kids will also probably not be hungry at local mealtimes for the first few days, so be prepared to give them a substantial snack like a banana or a small sandwich to get them through to the new mealtime.

Keep in mind that it is not uncommon for children to lose their appetite when traveling. Offer your child familiar food if he is unsettled and not eating well. Once he does settle down, however, encourage him to try the local cuisine, as discovering new foods is one of the enriching things about travel.

Be realistic when planning vacation sightseeing and activities. No young child, especially one who is jet-lagged, has the patience to spend the entire day at an art gallery. Instead, mix it up. Maybe spend an hour at the gallery, then head back to the hotel for a nap, then plan a visit to a park or the zoo or a ferry ride for the afternoon. Look for attractions suited for kids—a visit to an old fort or a ride on an old train—or plan a special outing for the whole family to enjoy. Most of all, have fun, relax, and enjoy your vacation with your kids.

Kids in Transit

★ Be organized; pre-trip prep can make all the difference.

★ Pack well, and be sure to keep your travel bag on hand, filled with essentials including first-aid items.

★ Keep boredom at bay: bring along amusing games, books, and toys.

★ Give your children time to adjust to their new environment.

★ Enjoy spending this time together on vacation.

Chapter Nine

It's Time for School

A New Chapter in Your Child's Life

I t is the first and only performance of the Busy Bee preschool's Christmas concert, starring—among others—my four-year-old charge, Harriet. The darkened hall is packed with parents, grandparents, family friends, and nannies, all eagerly awaiting the opening chords. I glance around the hall and notice that a few parents seem nervous; no doubt this is their first child's performance. As a longtime nanny, I am a seasoned veteran of such school performances, but I too feel butterflies in my stomach at the thought of Harriet's stage debut.

The pianist begins to play—a song I recognize at once because Harriet has been singing it every day for the past month—and then the curtain opens. Onstage, Miss Roberts, the preschool teacher, gives the cue, and the children begin to sing along with her. I scan the faces, looking for Harriet. There she is—the little girl with bright red hair, in an angel costume. I quickly point her out to her parents.

Harriet, intensely focused on Miss Roberts, is singing with all her might, even as she absentmindedly pats the feathers on her angel wings. I smile; I know how proud she is of her angel costume. She has been admiring it for weeks, impatient for the night when she will be able to wear it.

Suddenly, my mind flips back to Harriet's first day of school just a few months earlier. She had walked into the classroom hesitantly, tentatively, her eyes wide with fear of the unknown and her lip trembling as she tried her hardest not to cry. Now, she was at ease—serious, absorbed in her performance, but comfortable and confident.

On Harriet's right side is her good friend, Brad, who had strolled into school on the first day wearing a Superman costume, a smile, and an air of complete confidence. The only tears shed the day Brad entered school were by his mother, who had sobbed in the parking lot after dropping him off. She is wiping away a tear now, too, but is smiling as she does so.

And on Harriet's left side is Fred, another good friend. A moment ago, I was somewhat stunned to see Fred confidently singing a solo. This was the same Fred who had cried on arrival at school every day for two whole weeks; each morning Miss Roberts had to untangle Fred from his father's legs in order to get him into the classroom. Now, I look across at Fred's parents, who are sitting two rows over, and see them beaming with pride.

Hesitant, confident, frightened: however a child feels upon doing it, going to school is one of life's major rites of passage, and the school experience can bring significant changes. Going to school for the first time is a huge step in your child's development, the start of an important journey in his life. A whole new world is opening up for him, a world beyond his immediate family. It is a little scary and exciting at the same time, and for parents, it is often a little bittersweet.

It's important to start it off right. School, after all, will be your child's main activity for many years to come, so it's crucial to help her make a good beginning and build a solid foundation for a successful and enjoyable education. That's why when it's time for school, parents need to be ready: they need to have prepared their children for this milestone, and they need to have prepared themselves.

Keep in mind that different kids react in different ways to starting school. While some are proud and excited to be joining the world of the big kids, marching right in without a backward glance, others cry and cling to their parents, hiding behind them, unwilling or unready to leave their parent's side. It is an adjustment, and it can take a little time, which is why it is important to remember a couple of things:

First, the adjustment does eventually happen. As time goes by, the transition will get easier, and before you know it, your child will settle into school, and both of you will have adapted to this new beginning. Second, once settled, your child will blossom before your eyes, growing in confidence as she learns new skills of social interaction and as her mind is stretched and stimulated.

This chapter explains how to ease this rite of passage, how to get your child off on the right foot in school, and how to smooth the change in the household routine. On all these fronts, there will be challenges, and that's what we address here. And because school days change your days as well, we offer some recipes that are particularly relevant for families with school-age children: what to make for breakfast, for the lunch box, for the school bake sale, for sick days, and more.

Some Preschool Pre-Advice

Yes, there are preschools that put children and their parents through rigorous screening and interviewing, and through a formal admissions process. And there are parents who sign their kids up for such schools when the kids are just a few weeks old. But in most cases, fortunately, parents don't need to start thinking about preschool until a year or so in advance.

All these schools have their own personality, philosophy, style, and entrance guidelines, so your best bet is to call the schools that sound interesting, schedule visits, and settle on the one you like the most.

We offer just two bits of nanny wisdom about school. First, if your child *just* makes the cutoff age, think hard about keeping him home for an extra six months or a year. The youngest children in the class often have a harder time adjusting to school, find it more difficult to resist peer pressure as they get older, and can be at a disadvantage in physical and academic development. So it's a good idea to avoid sending your child to school too young.

Second, if you have a choice between morning and afternoon preschool, we advise you to choose the morning. This is because a child younger than four usually needs a nap, quiet time, or rest in the afternoon. When they attend afternoon school, they typically miss out on naps and quiet time, and this can lead to overtired, cranky children.

Prepare Your Child for School

Any change can be daunting. For little children, going to school is a *big* change—a complete overhaul of their familiar routine. So it is natural that some children experience a little nervousness, anxiety, and worry before starting school. How you approach this transition can make all the difference in the way your child makes the change—and how you all adjust.

Try to keep your home life smooth and calm during this transition. Avoid any other changes in your child's life at this time. For example, it's a bad time to move, so if you can, avoid or postpone so profound a change. Even having houseguests can be disruptive to your child. For those changes you cannot avoid, be sensitive to the timing of the start of school. If there's a new baby at home, consider holding off on sending your child to preschool. To a two-year-old who has a new sibling in the summer, being sent to preschool a few weeks later may feel like he's being sent away.

Prepare your child for the change by letting him know ahead of time that he will be going to school soon. You'll have to tread a fine line here: you don't want to spring such a big change on your child, but you also want to avoid making such a huge deal out of it that his imagination runs wild. What's probably best is to mention it every now and again—casually but positively—starting a month or so prior to the first day.

Books about Going to School

- I Love You All Day Long by Francesca Rusackas
- The Kissing Hand by Audrey Penn
- Miss Bindergarten Gets Ready for Kindergarten by Joseph Slate
- My Kindergarten by Rosemary Wells
- Spot Goes to School by Eric Hill

For kids over the age of three, it's a good idea to read books that contain stories about school—we've recommended our favorites by awarding them the Nanny Seal of Approval.

Visit the school with your child. Talk to him about what will happen during the school day and about the activities he can expect to do there. The idea is to make it a familiar place so it won't be unknown. We've noted how common it is for second children to have an easier time starting school, and we believe that's because they have seen their older siblings being dropped off at and picked up from school. So if your child is the oldest, you might try having him go along on a school run with a school-age friend or relative, just so he can see what it's like and how easily the friend or cousin does it.

Another way to generate that sense of familiarity is to find other kids who will be starting the same school as your child and get them together for playdates prior to the first day. That way, each child will see a familiar face when he looks around the classroom.

It is also important that everyone in the family show how happy and excited they are about your child's beginning school. Be positive about the school experience, about what it says to your child—"You're such a big boy now, you will be starting school soon"—and about what the experience will be like—"You will have so much fun in school. The teachers will read you stories, and you will do painting and play exciting games."

Tell everyone in your family to refrain from making negative comments. "I hated school" or "I had such a mean teacher in the second grade" are absolute no-no's. Take care not to put ideas into your child's head that he would not have dreamed up himself: "Don't worry, I'm sure you will make friends" or "Don't worry, I'm sure you'll get a nice teacher." Even such innocent comments as "I wish you didn't have to go to school; I hate that you're growing up so fast" are off-limits; a child may blow them out of proportion, so save conversations like this for friends or partners.

In addition to creating an environment of positive anticipation, there are some very practical and very important things you can do to prepare your child for school.

First, make sure your child spends some time without you. Let him stay at his grandmother's, with a relative, or at least with a babysitter for periods of time. A child who has never left his parents' side will have a big shock when he is left with his teachers for the first time at school, and will be more likely to feel separation anxiety. He needs to know that he will be okay and to feel comfortable when you are not with him.

 Nanny Wisdom

A Special School Item

A brand-new backpack, book bag, or lunch box can be a wonderful symbol of your child's new schoolkid status. Especially if it is branded with a favorite character—a Superman bag or a Cinderella lunch box—it may be just the thing to get your child excited about starting school. Or, take your child shopping to choose one or two special clothing items for school—a new hair clip, T-shirt, pair of shoes, or soccer jacket. This can become a tradition you do together at the start of every school year.

Second, give your child a head start by providing him with plenty of social interaction. Organize playdates and scheduled activities so he can learn such important social skills as sharing, and managing feelings like frustration and impatience.

Third, help your child learn the skills of independence. Teach him to put on and take off his shoes and socks, dress himself, and use the bathroom with minimal assistance. Ensure he has lots of practice following such simple instructions as "please get your coat" or "please bring your pencils and a piece of paper to me." Children who are able to listen and follow simple instructions will feel more confident than children who are confronted with such instructions for the first time.

Fourth, you can give your child a head start by teaching him simple "educational" skills like recognizing colors, counting, drawing circles, or coloring in coloring books. Make sure he is familiar with having stories read to him and with playing games. Give your child the experience of working on something by himself—drawing a picture, or making his own shapes out of Play-Doh. You needn't force your child to sit still for hours on end; even five or ten minutes of encouraged concentration provides good practice that will help your child deal with a similar situation at school.

Two Secrets of School Success

Our experience as nannies has convinced us that, before sending any child off to school, there are two main secrets for school success: plenty of sleep and a good breakfast. A child who goes to school tired or insufficiently nourished is behind before he even starts his day. He won't have the energy or the resources he needs for the challenges ahead of him. He will be less focused, less patient with his peers, and less capable of performing to the best of his ability. Kids under seven in school need to be tucked up in bed by seven or eight at night to ensure they get enough rest, and they need to be offered a nutritious breakfast each morning before school.

Children going to school must be up early, so if a child hasn't gone to bed till nine or nine-thirty, that early wake-up time will invariably mean that the child is tired and difficult to deal with. He is likely to be slow in get-

Nanny Wisdom

"Where do I live?"

It's imperative to teach your child his address and phone number as soon as he can understand and remember it. A child as young as three can memorize these important details, especially if you make up a little song or rhyme to help him. Should an emergency occur, your child's ability to give this information to emergency responders or to someone who can help could make all the difference.

"I don't want breakfast"

We know of three basic reasons for the often-heard refrain, "I don't want breakfast; I'm not hungry."

Reason One: Individual body clock/metabolism. Some children simply need a little time in the morning before they have an appetite for breakfast—anywhere from thirty minutes to an hour after wake-up.

Reason Two: Television. The child who spends his mornings in front of the TV doesn't want to leave it to eat breakfast.

Reason Three: Lateness. The child who gets up too late has no time to enjoy his breakfast; feeling rushed, he therefore rejects the meal.

If your child claims he's not hungry and doesn't want breakfast, we suggest getting the household up thirty minutes earlier every morning to encourage an appetite and to ensure enough time to share breakfast with your child without rushing. And leave the television off. Breakfast will soon become an important and enjoyable ritual in your house.

ting ready for school and to have a poor appetite for breakfast. We know: we've seen it.

Inadequate sleep and an inadequate breakfast can also lead to problems at school. Some kids get into fights, some have difficulty sitting still, and some can't really concentrate on a set task—all because of fatigue and lack of proper morning nutrition.

Your child's behavior and school performance will improve if he goes to bed early and eats a nutritious breakfast before school.

Bedtime Changes

If you will need to change your child's bedtime in order to ensure that he gets sufficient sleep and gets up early enough for a good breakfast, start making the change at least four weeks before school starts so he has time to get used to it. See page 109 for suggestions on how to move bedtime to an earlier hour.

The School-Day Breakfast

As for a good, nutritious breakfast, it is essential for the energy and concentration your child needs during the school day. What constitutes a good breakfast? Fresh, healthy foods. High-sugar cereals, Pop-Tarts, or breakfast bars will not do the job. Here are some good breakfast ideas for school-day mornings (and there's much more on the subject in Chapter Five):

- boiled, scrambled, or fried eggs with toast
- bacon sandwich
- grilled cheese sandwich, slices of tomato between pieces of hot buttered toast, or peanut butter spread on whole wheat bread
- bagel with cream cheese and fruit
- fruit, yogurt, muesli or oatmeal
- for rushed mornings: a quick fruit-and-yogurt smoothie; a healthy muffin with a glass of milk; cereals like muesli, granola, organic Weetabix, or other organic breakfast cereals (available in the organic section of the grocery store or at the health food store)
- for non-rushed mornings: pancakes served with fruit (the batter can stay in the fridge for up to three days), or baked eggs

The First Day of School

The big day has finally arrived, and the important thing to remember is that your child is looking to you for cues on how to act and feel. So even if you are nervous or anxious, do your best to put on a smile and appear at ease— for your child's sake.

Make sure you wake up with enough time for a relaxed and pleasant morning and breakfast together. If things are in a rush, your child will feel stressed, and that will only increase his fears. Offer lots of support and encouragement: praise your child's new book bag or special school lunch box, and tell him how smart he looks in his new school clothes.

Different schools have different procedures for opening day, and certainly things will also differ depending on whether your child is starting preschool or kindergarten. But here are some general guidelines to follow if you can:

When you arrive at school, show your child where to put his bag and coat. Remind him about what's in his bag—a sweater in case he gets cold, for example. Show him the bathroom, and ask him if he needs to use it

Nanny Wisdom *The Checklist*

The idea for a school checklist was born of necessity when I worked for a large family—four kids, each of whom had to remember to take different items to school on different days of the week. For example, on Mondays the girls needed to return their school library books; on Tuesdays the youngest had show-and-tell; on Wednesdays the girls had ballet lessons—they had to pack their ballet shoes—and the boys had soccer practice; on Thursdays there was more sports practice—different gear and shoes for everybody; and on Fridays the older boys had to wear ties to school. In addition, of course, all the kids had their own lunch boxes and homework. It soon became apparent to me that I needed a system that was organized to make sure nothing was forgotten.

I drew up a chart with the days of the week and each child's name. For each day I listed the clothing, gear, homework, and other items each child needed to remember. I taped a copy of the chart to the back of each child's bedroom door so we could all see it as we were leaving their rooms, and I taped another copy onto the front door so we could double-check everything as we left the house. When the children were young, the checklist was a reminder to me, and as they got older, it helped the kids themselves be more organized and independent. And throughout, the checklist was a simple and effective way to keep the house running smoothly and to eliminate those mad morning panics when you wonder what you've forgotten.

before you go into the classroom. Walk him into the classroom and take him over to the teacher to say hello. If this is kindergarten, chances are that you and your child will already have had an induction day, and your child will have met the teacher and become familiar with his classroom. The teacher will take over and tell you when it is time to go.

If this is preschool, the teacher will most likely get your child started on an activity or suggest that he choose a toy. Point out to your child any kids he already knows, or lead him over to a friend and get him involved in the activity the friend is doing. Or take your child to an activity you know he will like—a painting area, a story reading, or a dress-up box. Get your child absorbed in the activity; when he seems settled, you'll know it is time to go.

Certainly, many children do not settle right away. If your child is clinging to you and is very shy, you may need to stay longer to make sure he feels secure before you go. Do a few puzzles or activities with your child until he is more relaxed and comfortable before you decide to leave.

Some kids are particularly nervous and anxious; they need you to stay even longer while they adjust to the new environment. In such cases—and particularly if your child is upset—you will need to rely on the teacher to tell you when you should leave. Remember that the teacher is trained and experienced in helping make this transition easier, so you need to trust his or her judgment. Chances are the teacher will let you stay most of the morning the first day and will let you know the best time for you to leave. Distressing as it may be to leave while your child is upset, keep in mind that the teacher has done this many times before. In fact, you can bet that your child is not the most upset the teacher has ever seen. So when you're told it is time for you to go, do so—even if your child is clinging to you and sobbing. Over the course of a week or so, the teacher will surely recommend that you spend less and less time in the classroom before you leave. The day will soon come when your child runs into the classroom and hardly pauses to say good-bye.

Whenever it is time to go, use the Nannies' Short and Sweet Good-bye, an absolute essential to a successful start in school.

The Nannies' Short and Sweet Good-bye

It's simple, straightforward, and has only three steps:

1. Tell your child it is time for you to go now and that you will be waiting to pick him up when school is over. Do not sneak out without saying good-bye, as your child will become upset when he realizes you have disappeared.
2. Say good-bye calmly. Save your tears for when you are out of sight.
3. Kiss your child and leave. If he starts to cry and you have already started the Nannies' Short and Sweet Good-bye routine, follow it through; prolonging your departure will only make it worse and will ensure that your child will be even more upset when you do eventually go.

Your child will most likely stop crying once you are out of sight. Wait outside the classroom if you like, or call the school thirty minutes later to check on the situation—and to make yourself feel more comfortable.

If your child asks to stay home in the morning because he doesn't want to go to school, do not agree to this. If you do, it will lead to future problems, as your child will think school is an option, not a necessity. Of course, if your child is having a really hard time adjusting to school, talk to his teacher and work out a plan. That is what the teacher is there for.

In most cases, however, rest assured: your child will adjust, and in due course, he will grow to love going to school.

One more essential: always make sure you are on time to collect your child at the end of the school day. Be there when school lets out; it is very upsetting for a child to wonder when you are coming as he watches other children leave.

Nanny Wisdom

After-school Headaches

It is common for school-age kids to come home complaining of headaches. Our conclusion is that the main reason for the headaches is dehydration; without your supervision, your child may be going all day without drinking much at all. Offer her a big glass of water, a healthy snack, and some quiet time before you turn to medication as a solution.

After School

Starting school is a transition, and one place you may notice a change is in your child's after-school behavior. For the first few weeks or even months, be prepared for her to come home from school exhausted, hungry, grouchy, or with excess pent-up energy. She may revert back to her younger behavior—whining, sucking her thumb, or acting out to seek attention—or she may become overly clingy. You may need to be prepared for a rocky time as your child adjusts to the change.

Parents often ask us why their preschooler or kindergartner, who is so well behaved at school—they have the glowing reports to prove it—is uncooperative at home. The answer is simple: at school, your child has been working hard to follow instructions and to be on her best behavior. By the time she gets home she is worn out, but because she is at home she feels safe to be herself. During this transition, it's probably best at first to overlook behavior you would otherwise crack down on—to a certain extent, anyway—in favor of being supportive and comforting.

Too many structured after-school activities can also burden the transition. Your child will need some winding-down time after school—some space in which to play, relax, or run around to burn off pent-up energy. Playdates at home or in the park with children from school, reinforcing the new friendships, are a better idea than trooping your child around town to many organized activities. If the after-school exhaustion persists, think about an earlier bedtime or dinnertime—at least while your child is settling into the new routine of school.

New Challenges

The first day, the first week, even the first semester are behind you. Your child now rushes excitedly into school and is wise in the ways of being a school kid. But there are still challenges to face—hectic mornings, peer-pressure issues, behavioral changes, even homework—as you become parents of school-age children. Here are some tips on how to deal with the new way of life that starting school has launched.

The Morning Rush

It can be hectic. Getting everyone in the household up and ready, fed, and out the door on time without forgetting something is no easy task. Yet nothing can sour a day faster or more effectively than a chaotic, cranky morning, so here's how we nannies approach the morning rush.

First, we arrange for everyone to get up early enough for mornings to be calm and unhurried, with enough time to get ready.

Second, we have a very firm "no TV in the morning" rule that is iron-clad for every weekday morning. TV is simply too distracting. When we nannies or parents must compete with the TV for a child's attention, we are unlikely to win. Children lose interest in getting ready, eating a good breakfast, or leaving the house at all when the TV is on and calling to them.

Third, we like to get kids dressed before breakfast, so they have time during the meal to both chat and eat. Nothing is guaranteed to make a child eat more slowly than urging him to eat faster so you can get him dressed. Of course, it's a good idea to protect school clothes with napkins in case of spills.

Fourth, we always pack book bags the night before and always leave them in the same place so there is no last-minute stress when something important is missing.

This way, everyone gets out the door with everything they need and in good humor. And we get to have peaceful mornings and time for a nice cup of tea.

Peers and Friends

Five-year-old Bill couldn't stop talking about Sam Jones—"he's my best friend," Bill explained, "and he's six." At dinner, when I asked Bill if he'd like some butter on his peas, he replied, "Sam Jones hates peas."

When his father suggested that Bill tell me about dress-up day at school—he had just started kindergarten—he informed me that "I was a dinosaur, and Sam Jones was an astronaut. He has been to the moon in real life, hasn't he, Daddy?"

"Well, not quite," Bill's father answered gently.

"Yes he has, Daddy. He told me so."

"We feel as if Sam Jones has joined our family," Bill's father told me. "He is mentioned in every conversation we have." Then he whispered: "It's a serious case of big-boy awe."

As dinner went on, I learned about Sam Jones's opinions on the best color crayons, about his sneakers that lit up, about his aversions to girls and jackets, and about his great LEGO spaceship. By the time we got to dessert, Sam Jones seemed like an old friend I had known all my life.

The friends your child makes at school will become increasingly important in his life—and therefore in yours. You will hear all about Rebecca's favorite toy, John's new pencils, and Jane's cartwheels. Older children will become role models and heroes, and—as happened with Bill and Sam Jones—feats of extraordinary power and achievement may be ascribed to them.

It's important to listen well to these bits of information—even if the information may be inflated by hero worship. Showing your child you have an interest in his friends will establish a habit of open communication that can be invaluable when your child enters those tricky teen years, when his peers take on magnified importance in his life.

Some kids are shy about making friends; if that describes your child, let him get used to the social side of school slowly. Quiet encouragement works better on a naturally timid child than pushing him into situations and friendships he may be hesitant about. But if you can, organize play-dates with both girls and boys from the school, and encourage your child to have a number of friends.

The school environment will almost surely introduce your child to competition with peers—something he has not experienced before. Competition in sports and academics, performance comparisons, and the often-harsh critical judgments of older kids: your child undoubtedly has some or all of this in store. Some children will take it in stride; some don't seem to notice; but other kids become stressed out by competition. Make it clear to your child that all you really care about is that he try his best. Remember also that the teacher is there to help you—and that he or she has seen it all. Don't hesitate to e-mail, call, or set up a meeting to discuss your concerns.

There is another aspect to peer competitiveness, which occurs when your child begins to compare what he has and what he is allowed to do with what other kids have and are allowed to do. Why doesn't he have the latest video games that James has; why can't he go to McDonald's after school every day as Lisa does? These can be hard questions to deal with. They speak to different values and principles, and your child's questioning of them can make it difficult for you to enforce those principles. When you hear that Michelle and Megan from your son's class have seen the movie he is begging to see, the one you thought inappropriate for his age group, you may begin to wonder if you should just give in and let him watch it. Be aware that having kids in school means you will certainly be faced with such challenging decisions. All you can do is go with what you believe in and try not to fall into the trap of letting your child do something you don't agree with just because the other parents let their kids do it. These kinds of decisions will only become more frequent and more difficult as your child gets older, so you might as well start practicing on them now.

Sometimes compromise makes sense. Six-year-old John's family doesn't allow video games in the home. But when John comes home from a playdate at Nicole's house and bursts into tears, his mother learns it is because he was the only child at the playdate who didn't know how to play video games. His mother thinks about it long and hard and decides that the situation requires her to bend a bit. She decides to buy John a PlayStation for his birthday, but she insists that he limit his PlayStation time only to the weekends and only to an hour of play each day; what's more, there are to be no violent video games. It's a compromise that lets John's mother put limits on something she disapproves of while also letting her son feel included when he is with his friends.

"I don't feel well"

Another inevitable consequence of having a child in school is that he will likely catch every cold, flu, and sore throat that is going around. Of course, you should always consult your pediatrician if you are concerned about your child's health, but for common childhood illnesses, we also turn to a number of old-fashioned remedies that can soothe the discomfort of being ill.

A hot bath with a few drops of eucalyptus oil will clear a stuffy head; a damp washcloth on the forehead will soothe a headache; and a steam-vaporizing machine will work wonders for a tickly cough or a stuffy nose. At bedtime, a few drops of lavender oil on your child's pillow can comfort an achy head, and a little Vicks VapoRub rubbed into the soles of your child's feet can be warming and comforting.

Of course, children who are unwell need to get plenty of rest and drink lots of fluids, preferably soup, water, and fresh juice. For kids with sore throats, a bowl of soup, plain pasta, mashed potato, rice pudding, or yogurt—which are all soft going down—may prove persuasive. For children with upset stomachs, plain white rice, plain crackers, dry toast, or some applesauce can be easily digested.

Dehydration is a risk in young children who are suffering from vomiting or diarrhea. You need to give them plenty of fluids: water, electrolyte drinks, and flat lemonade are best. Closely monitor your child's fluid intake, and do not hesitate to call your doctor if you are concerned.

A perfect way to cheer up an unwell child is to make her a little bed on the sofa, read her some stories, and cozy up together to watch a movie. Big doses of care, love, and attention will certainly help your child to feel better and will have her back at school in no time at all.

Take care of yourself, too. Parents and siblings are likely to pick up what a child has, so dose up on vitamins, fresh fruit and vegetables, and lots of rest so you too can get through whatever is going around at school.

Behavior

School is enough of a change in a child's life to cause a change in behavior. Now that he has gained some independence, your child may want to again test his boundaries. Now that he has mastered language and is exploring his own assertiveness, he may start to talk back. Negotiation begins to play a huge role now. Before you know it, every request is followed by fifteen minutes of debate and bargaining; in your child's eyes, everything is negotiable. And now that your child is mixing with lots of other children, he may begin to copy the behavior of those other children—often in ways you don't like.

It is important to let your child know that his boundaries are still firmly in place when he begins to test them at this stage. It isn't easy in the face of constant attempts at negotiation. You give a simple instruction—"Please turn the TV off now; we are having dinner"—and you get "I don't want to. Can't I have dinner later?" You say: "We have to go home now," and your child comes back with: "Not now, in five minutes."

The way to deal with these attempts at negotiation is simply to be fair, firm, and consistent. Allowing one round of "five more minutes" is being fair, rejecting a request for a second round of "five more minutes" is being firm, and always rejecting that second request for "five more minutes" is being consistent. When you do this, your child will know what to expect.

Remember that it is okay to say no to your child, and when you do say no, you must mean it, and you must let your child know that you mean it. Be clear that negotiations will not turn a no into a yes. The Nannies' Terrific Timer may also be used to end negotiations. (See page 91 for more about the timer.)

Of course, one inevitable side effect of your child's school friendships is that you will see him copying the habits of his friends—not all of them good habits. You might see your kid imitating the way one friend uses "baby talk" to get attention, or the way another screams to get his own way. Kids are particularly susceptible to this kind of copycatting when they play with just one child to the exclusion of others, so it's a good idea to organize playdates with a range of other school peers.

It's also important to be very clear to your child about the kinds of behavior that are acceptable in your family and the kinds that are not. Rudeness, "attitude," and acting out: leave no doubt in your child's mind that new behavior like this is absolutely unacceptable. If you don't make it clear now, it can be the start of behavior patterns that go straight through into the teenage years, getting more intractable and more difficult to deal with as children get older. (See Chapter Six on how to deal with difficult behavior.)

The start of school, in fact, is the perfect time to introduce some responsibilities into your child's daily life: pulling up the covers on his bed each morning, or putting his dirty clothes in the hamper at bath time, or taking his plate to the sink after dinner. Simple as they sound, these tasks teach your child independence and responsibility—valuable life skills—and give him a way to contribute to family life. You will need to remind your child to carry out his daily tasks, but don't forget to also praise, encourage, and reward his efforts when he does so.

Homework: Starting Good Habits Early

There are now preschools that give kids homework. It is certainly not unusual for children to start getting homework in kindergarten, and by the second grade, just about every pupil is doing work at home. Regardless of when your child gets her first homework assignment or how much she is required to do, it is absolutely crucial to start off on the right foot with this important part of your child's education.

Across the range of families we've worked with, we've seen kids of all ages doing homework. Some love it, some just get on with it, and some really struggle with it. Yet struggle can be avoided if kids learn good homework habits early on. These good habits provide a deep well of skills your child can draw from later on when the workload gets heavier.

So here are the Nannies' Top Five Homework Hints. You'll see that they are aimed at creating an environment in which kids can concentrate and call on their own creativity—essentials for a successful school career. They embody the lessons we have learned that will carry you and your child from her first piece of homework all the way through high school. One more caution: if you don't make homework a priority, neither will your child. So we urge you to take the Top Five Homework Hints very seriously indeed.

The Nannies' Top Five Homework Hints

1. **Turn off the television.** TV is the main cause of homework misery. A child tempted by TV won't pay attention to her work, or will rush through it, or will simply not do it. We strongly recommend a limit on TV watching after school: either allow one show when the kids first get home, then turn it off, or allow one show after dinner. The best solution we have ever seen is the "no TV during the school week" policy, which totally eliminates all battles for more viewing time. In families where this policy is the rule, life in general is easier and calmer, and homework especially is hassle free. Take note: the very popular rule of "no TV until homework is done" is completely unsuccessful; it just gives kids a very enticing incentive to rush through their work.

2. **Snack first.** A child should have a healthy snack before sitting down to do homework—whether that homework is coloring a picture for preschool or advanced-placement calculus in high school. Avoid high-sugar snacks, however, as most young children have a hard time sitting still and concentrating with sugar pumping through their veins. Try a small sandwich, yogurt, or a banana instead; if your preschooler gets a taste for these healthy snacks before coloring, your high schooler will reach for them, too, before starting calculus.

3. **Balance homework, physical activity, and downtime.** Some children respond best to getting their homework done and out of the way straight after school so they have the rest of the afternoon and evening free. Others need wind-down time after the school day before they can settle down to concentrate. At some point, too, all children should have a run around to burn off pent-up energy and to get the exercise they need. You will need to experiment to find out how to balance these needs for physical activity, downtime, and homework in a way that suits your child best. As for weekend homework, here is our motto: get it out of the way on Saturday!

4. **Make room for homework.** Children need a special area in which to do their homework—a quiet place where they will be free from distrac-

tions so they can give the work their full attention. For small children, the best place is probably the kitchen table. Clear off a place, put away enticing toys, and, of course, turn off the TV. As the children do their work, you can help them while you prepare dinner. You can see what they are doing, but the focus is on them doing it themselves because you are involved in another task.

5. *Help—a little.* There is a fine line between assisting children with their homework and actually doing it for them. The latter does not benefit them; after all, it is they who must do the learning. Be interested, help out a little bit, and try to make learning seem exciting and fun, which it is.

Helping Your Child Succeed in School

The best thing you can do to help your child succeed in school is to be involved in his school life. Know his teachers, his school subjects, his friends, and the parents of his friends. The idea is to be always involved in his school and social life—from preschool through high school.

Educators emphasize that the learning shouldn't stop at the end-of-the-day bell, and it's up to parents to make learning a part of everyday life. Try to integrate what your child is learning at school into his life at home. For example, when your child is learning to read, point out words in the supermarket and on billboards, or ask him to recognize letters on license plates. Read, read, and read some more to your child.

Of course, it is important to encourage your child and to demonstrate how much you value her work and her entire school experience. Tell your child you are proud of her school achievements. Display her art and any awards she receives. Set high expectations for your child; let her know she must try to do her best.

Encourage her to be respectful of her teachers and others. Don't criticize the school or teacher in front of your child, but say positive things about school, as everything she hears you say will take on a magnified importance. Show respect for her school experience by attending such school events as an end-of-the-year recital, and certainly never miss a parent-teacher interview.

One final piece of school advice: if, over a period of time, you feel your child is not happy in school, it may be that it is the wrong school for her.

Each school has its own values, priorities, and culture, and it may be that they constitute an environment that simply doesn't suit your child's needs. A highly artistic child might not flourish in a rigorously competitive academic environment, for example, and while some kids thrive on informality, others do better in a more structured environment. If your child seems very unhappy in her school environment, talk to her teacher, consult with the administration, and above all, trust your instincts. If you really feel the school isn't right for your child, you may want to consider changing schools, but this should not be done hastily or often—it should be a last resort.

It's Time for School

★ Prepare for school. Talk to your child about starting school, be positive about it, and make any needed changes to your child's routine at least four weeks before the first day of school.

★ Remember that a healthy breakfast and an early bedtime are the secrets to school success.

★ Be aware that school days bring new challenges to both your child and you—behavioral issues, changes in routine, peer pressure.

★ Establish good homework habits now, and you will save yourself and your child many problems in the future.

★ Be involved through all your child's years at school. Know both his academic and his social life. Don't hesitate to speak to the teacher about your child's progress or about any issues or concerns you have.

Nanny Recipes

School-Day Recipes

HAPPY EGGS AND SOLDIER TOAST

1 serving

I had just returned from a month's vacation and was feeling recharged and happy to be back at work caring for two-and-a-half-year-old Evie. As we were getting Evie ready for preschool on my first morning back, I asked her what she would like for breakfast.

"A happy egg."

"Do you mean scrambled eggs?" I asked.

"No, a happy egg."

We worked our way through every type of egg dish I had ever cooked, with Evie supplying the same adamant reply to each suggestion.

"Susie makes happy eggs," Evie finally elaborated. Susie was the nanny who had filled in for me while I was away. A quick call to Susie established that a happy egg was a boiled egg with a happy face drawn on the eggshell. Before my vacation, eggs were invariably accompanied by "soldier toast," so named because Evie liked to dip strips of toast, the soldiers, into the yolk of a boiled egg. Now dubbed Happy Eggs and Soldier Toast, the dish was Evie's favorite breakfast all the way through her first year at preschool.

> *1 fresh egg, preferably organic*
> *1 piece of bread for toasting*

Place the egg in a small saucepan, cover with water, and boil for 6 minutes for a softer yolk or 8–10 minutes for hard-boiled eggs.

Meanwhile, toast and butter the bread.

Drain the water from the saucepan and run cold water over the egg to stop it from cooking and to make the egg cool enough to handle.

Place the egg in an eggcup; draw a happy face on the shell with a pen or marker; cut buttered toast into long strips. Cut the top of the egg off to serve.

THE LUNCH-BOX CHALLENGE

Filling a lunch box with nutritious and tasty meals day after day can be a challenge for many parents. Be guided by these three principles: balance, variety, and small portions. For example, try a sandwich, fruit, and a yogurt one day. The next day go for a little pasta salad, a chicken drumstick, and a box of raisins. Another day, try your child's favorite wrap, a piece of cheese, and an apple. Here are some more ideas for filling the lunch box:

Sandwiches/Wraps

Keep sandwiches simple; kids don't like too many ingredients. Use fresh bread for sandwiches or tortillas for wraps. Try these tasty fillings:

- a slice of turkey with mayonnaise and lettuce
- a slice of nitrate-free ham or turkey and a slice of muenster cheese and lettuce
- peanut butter and jelly
- egg salad
- tuna salad
- leftover roast chicken with mayonnaise and lettuce
- cheese and avocado
- hummus and sliced cheese

Sandwich Alternatives

If you make a lot of lunch boxes, it is easy to become bored with making sandwiches, so here are some alternatives:

- pasta salad—leftover pasta mixed with chicken, ham, or turkey, white beans, chickpeas, kidney beans, and salad vegetables, and an optional pesto or olive oil dressing
- potato salad
- cooked chicken drumsticks
- slice of quiche or frittata
- edamame, carrot sticks, cucumber sticks, cherry tomatoes
- hard-boiled eggs
- cheddar cheese with crackers

Fresh Fruit

A perfect lunch box always includes some fruit:

- a small apple or pear
- fresh fruit salad
- an orange cut into quarters
- a slice of pineapple
- a tangerine
- grapes
- strawberries

Something Special

Each morning, four-year-old Philip would ask me for "something special" in his lunch box. Philip had a sweet tooth, but fortunately, he considered strawberries and grapes to be really special. Every day I would give him fresh fruit, and once or twice a week I would also give him a cookie or a piece of cake. Here are some ideas for something special now and again in the lunch box:

- an oatmeal, chocolate chip, or shortbread cookie
- a small box of raisins or other dried fruit
- a slice of cake, a cupcake, or a mini-muffin
- Yogurt-covered raisins
- licorice

Drinks

Australian mothers send their kids off to school with a frozen drink in the lunch box every day; it not only keeps the lunch box contents cool throughout the hot morning, but by lunchtime the frozen drink melts and the liquid is pleasantly cold. If you want to try this idea, just keep bottles of water, boxes of juice, or a drink container filled with a combination of water and juice—cranberry, orange, apple, pineapple—in the freezer, ready to go straight into the lunch box in the morning.

AFTER-SCHOOL SNACKS

Kids are usually ravenous when they come home from school—a good occasion to give them a nutritious snack instead of candy or chips. Remember to make the snack small; otherwise they won't eat their dinner. Here are some tasty and popular ideas:

- popcorn
- fresh fruit
- banana
- half a sandwich—cheese, and peanut butter and jelly are kid-friendly fillings
- raisins
- cheese cubes and water crackers
- French bread (baguette) slices with grated cheddar cheese
- yogurt and fruit
- chips and salsa
- hummus, pita bread, and carrot sticks
- a smoothie

SCHOOL'S OUT BURRITOS

4 adult servings

With the families I have worked for I have always begun a tradition of throwing a small party for the kids and their friends on the last day of school. Friends are invited over for dinner and playtime or, for the older kids, to just hang out. Serve the chili filling with flour tortillas, avocado, salsa, salad, rice, and cheese, and let the kids make their own burritos.

> 2 tablespoons olive oil
> 1 onion, chopped finely
> 3 cloves garlic, crushed
> 1 teaspoon cumin
> 1 teaspoon chili powder
> 1 teaspoon turmeric
> 1 pound ground beef
> One 15-ounce can crushed tomatoes
> One 15-ounce can black beans, drained and rinsed
> 2 carrots, peeled and sliced very finely
> 1 zucchini, chopped finely
> Squeeze of fresh lime
> Optional: ¼ cup cilantro
> Salt and pepper to taste
> Flour tortillas

In a medium saucepan or frying pan, over medium-high heat, sauté the onion, garlic, and spices in the olive oil for 3–5 minutes, or until onion is soft.

Add ground beef and fry until browned, 5–8 minutes.

Add tomatoes, beans, and carrots. Stir and reduce heat to medium; allow to cook for 10–15 minutes.

Add zucchini and lime and cook for another 5 minutes, or until zucchini is cooked. Add cilantro if desired; season with salt and pepper to taste.

Heat the tortillas as directed on package.

Serve on a large platter with grated cheddar cheese, avocado or guacamole, fresh tomatoes or salsa, salad, and rice.

SICKNESS COMFORT: EASY CHICKEN NOODLE SOUP
4 adult servings

When a child is feeling poorly with the flu, a cold, or a sore throat, this simple homemade chicken noodle soup will be sure to comfort him and have him feeling better in no time. I sometimes add alphabet pasta shapes for fun.

> 1 tablespoon olive oil
> 2 cloves garlic, crushed
> ½ small onion, peeled and sliced very finely
> 1 stick of celery, sliced
> 7 cups chicken stock, fresh or canned
> 2 carrots, peeled and sliced finely
> Optional:
>> 1 large skinless chicken cutlet on the bone
>> ¼ cup chives or parsley
> ½ cup small pasta shapes, spaghetti, or alphabet pasta
> Salt and pepper to taste

Over medium-high heat in a medium saucepan, sauté the garlic, onion, and celery in the olive oil for 3–5 minutes.

Add chicken stock, carrots, and chicken, if desired. Add extra stock or water if needed. Cover the pot and bring to a simmer. Reduce heat and continue to simmer for 15 minutes; if you are not using chicken, go on to the next step. If you are using chicken, continue to simmer it for at least 30–40 minutes. When the chicken is cooked, remove it from the soup. Next, remove chicken meat from the bone, discard the bone, shred the chicken meat, and add back to the soup.

Add fresh herbs to soup, if using.

Meanwhile, cook pasta separately, as directed on package. Once cooked, add the pasta to the soup and remove from heat.

Season with salt and pepper to taste, and serve.

BAKE-SALE HIT: CHOCOLATE CHIP COOKIES

Makes 36 cookies

When your child starts school, you will begin to receive requests for home-made cakes or cookies to sell at school bake sales. We like to make classic treats like homemade chocolate chip cookies, cupcakes, or brownies for these occasions. These chocolate chip cookies are the real thing, made from scratch, very chocolaty, and a delicious treat. Kids really love to help make them, so make a fun activity of it, and let your child crack the eggs, stir the batter, and, of course, taste the finished product warm from the oven.

> 2 sticks of butter, softened not melted
> ¾ cup superfine sugar
> 1 cup brown sugar, firmly packed
> 2 eggs, at room temperature, lightly beaten
> 1 teaspoon vanilla extract
> 2 cups all-purpose flour, sifted
> A pinch of salt
> 1½ cups chocolate chips

Preheat oven to 375°F.

Beat butter and sugar until soft and creamy, using an electric mixer. Add eggs and vanilla; mix well.

Mix in sifted flour and salt. Mix in chocolate chips.

Place heaping teaspoons of cookie batter on an ungreased cookie sheet; flatten slightly with a fork, leaving room for cookies to spread.

Bake for 10–12 minutes, until slightly golden; take care not to overcook. Allow to cool slightly before removing to a wire rack.

Chapter Ten

Nannies and Babysitters

Finding Your Mary Poppins

" **I**t's Evie here," says the little voice over the phone, in her clipped British accent.

"Hello, my sweetheart!" I am always thrilled to get a call from Evie. I was her nanny for two years, from the time she was eighteen months till she turned three and a half. It has now been three years since I left, and I love that she still calls me on a regular basis.

"Mummy dialed your telephone number for me 'cause I have to ask you something very important," Evie continues in a serious tone.

"Okay," I say, trying to sound equally serious, "what is it?"

"You know my little rabbit, Alfie?"

"Of course." Alfie, a long-haired lop rabbit, was Evie's pride and joy. On visits back to London to see my former charge, I had spent many hours chasing him around the yard, desperately trying to usher him back into his hutch. Through time spent with Alfie and Evie, I had learned more about rabbits than I ever thought possible. I knew that Alfie was partial to yogurt drops, that he would go straight to sleep when Evie stroked his long ears, and that although he was quite happy to be wheeled around the house in a doll's baby carriage, he hated going back into his hutch.

"Well," Evie says now, "I have to go on a holiday to Spain with my Mummy and Daddy and they say Alfie has to stay at home. Mummy says Alfie doesn't like airplanes, and Daddy says he doesn't fancy chasing Alfie all over Spain. I was thinking you are my best person to come and look after my Alfie." She pauses. "He will be happy if he is with you."

The only problem, of course, is that I am in New York and Alfie is in London. I can't imagine my boss agreeing to give me time off to go to London to look after a rabbit for my favorite six-year-old. But it makes my heart melt to hear Evie describe me as her "best person," and to think that she has chosen me out of everyone to entrust her beloved Alfie to was very moving indeed.

We nannies can't help but form strong bonds with the children in our care. Evie and all the other girls and boys we have cared for—and their families—occupy a special place in our hearts. Each time we visit them, it is like going home. They remain in our lives, and in the case of many of these families, we continue to share such milestones as birthdays, graduations, weddings, and anniversaries.

The relationship between a nanny or babysitter and her charges and employer is absolutely unique, and it is one more and more families are discovering. Increasingly, as parents return to work or seek help with child rearing, they are turning to nannies for the one-on-one attention and the benefits of keeping a child at home that can only be delivered by a full-time caregiver.

That's exactly what a good nanny provides: her presence lets parents rest assured that their child is doing fine—in his own home—while parents are away. But that's only part of it. A nanny brings to your family her own child-care experience and knowledge. She comes equipped with realistic and practical advice. She provides your children a loving and structured environment. The best nannies, those with both a natural inclination for child care and experience in the field, know instinctively what children need. They work closely with parents and become an integral part of the family's support system.

In this chapter, we tell you how to make this unique relationship work well for everyone involved. We advise you on the best way to find a nanny, and we offer insight on how to keep your relationship a happy and communicative one. The aim, after all, is for both you and your kids to feel as Evie did—comfortable, secure, and content in the relationship with your nanny.

What Kind of Nanny?

Although nannies are nannies and babysitters are babysitters, there is a range of child-care options available, and it's important to understand the differences among them.

Professional nanny. For families that lead busy and hectic lives, a professional nanny—like us—may be the answer. A professional nanny is an experienced and knowledgeable child-care professional. Like a modern-day Mary Poppins, she should be able to come in and run the household while the parents are at work or traveling. In essence, the parents give her full responsibility for their children; she has sole charge of their care, which is why in Britain this type of nanny is typically called a sole-charge nanny. She will organize a child's day and will shepherd children to scheduled activities, playdates, and doctor appointments. Ideally, she will have extensive knowledge of child nutrition and development, will know how to get children to sleep, and will be capable of establishing a child's routine and putting it on a schedule.

Babysitter. A babysitter works more under a parent's direction rather than taking sole charge of a child's care. So a babysitter is usually not responsible for organizing playdates, social events, or doctor appointments; instead, she looks to the parents to tell her what the day's plan will be, then carries it out. She doesn't usually take on an advisory role regarding diet, sleep, or the child's routine and schedule. Some babysitters may work only in the evenings, when parents go out.

Mother's helper/part-time babysitter. A mother's helper works alongside a parent at home. And a part-time babysitter will come and play with the kids for just a few hours maybe a few times a week, giving Mom and Dad a chance to catch up on errands, work from home, or just have some time for themselves.

Au pair. An au pair is typically a young girl—usually from a foreign country— who comes to live with a family and to care for their children on a part-time basis in exchange for room, board, and a small wage. She is most likely not a child-care professional; in fact, her aim is often to improve her English-language skills. Think of her as something like a camp counselor: a playmate and supervising chaperone, but not a child-care pro. The au pair usually stays with a family for a year.

Nanny share. In a nanny-share situation, the nanny or babysitter takes care of two or more children from different families. This can work out quite well for some families in terms of finances, convenience, and benefit to the children. The families "sharing" the nanny also obviously share paying her fee, so the cost of the nanny is usually halved. If the sharing families know one another or live near one another, convenience is a bonus to the situation. And an added benefit is that the children the nanny cares for will be very well socialized, since they are interacting with other children on a regular basis. The nanny-share situation also works well if you only need to employ a nanny or babysitter on a part-time basis.

The Nanny-Child Bond

A nanny and her charge spend a great deal of time together, and they invariably develop a special bond. Some parents worry about this bond, fearing the nanny is replacing them in their child's affections. But don't worry; it just doesn't work that way. The fact is, a child always knows who his parents are. The nanny, instead, is something like an aunt and something like a friend. She occupies a unique role, and her bond with your child is a special one; it will last for years to come, but it will in no way compare to the parent-child bond.

So the very first thing to do when looking for a nanny is to think about which option will work best for your family. Do you want a professional nanny, or will a babysitter suit you better? If you decide on a nanny, figure out if you need a full-time, part-time, live-in, or live-out nanny. In other words, start with the fundamentals.

Nanny and You

Once you've established your child-care needs, think about this: the person you hire will not be just an employee but will be a part of your family—potentially a big part of your family. Especially if she lives in your home, she is going to see you at your most unvarnished and vulnerable—in your pajamas, with your hair a mess, and in times of stress. Your nanny will need to respect your privacy—and vice versa, of course. So it isn't enough for her to be knowledgeable and experienced; it's not even enough for her to be loving and kind with your children. She also needs to be someone you like, someone with whom you can communicate, and, ultimately, someone you can trust.

Each morning as you leave for work, you want to feel completely comfortable that your child is in the best possible hands. What you don't want is the anxiety that comes from worrying that your nanny is not quite the one for you. Certainly, it is normal for a new parent to feel anxious about going back to work; it isn't easy to leave a child in anybody else's care for the first time, especially a very young child. This is a transition that will take some time, but if it doesn't feel right because you're not sure you trust your nanny's instincts, then you've made the wrong choice. Yes, hiring a nanny is an employment transaction, but you're employing someone for an absolutely crucial role in your life and that of your family, so you've got to feel in your gut that your nanny is right for you.

That's why it's also important to remember that different nannies suit different families. A strict, starched nanny probably wouldn't be a good fit in a laid-back kind of family, and a more independent sole-charge nanny probably wouldn't do in a family in which the parents are home all the time and very hands-on about child care. Consider the kind of person you are looking for: do you want a young, lively nanny, someone more reserved, or an older grandmotherly type? Would you like your

The Nanny Hierarchy

I F YOU WANT TO SEE the British class system at work, just go any weekday morning to a certain park in a well-to-do area of London and check out the three park benches framing the playground for the under-fives.

On one bench sits a group of young women typically from Sweden, Russia, and Germany. These are au pairs. They're in London primarily to improve their English and to have fun—and they do: lots of friends, lots of outings, lots of parties. Cell phones seem to grow out of their hands as they constantly arrange their dates for later that night. While they love their charges and take good care of them, they are not child-care professionals.

On the bench directly opposite the au pairs sits a group of women who are very much child-care professionals, and they look it and act it. Matronly in their brown, starched, old-fashioned uniforms, these women are instantly recognizable to Londoners as Norland nannies—graduates of Norland College in Bath, England, which has been known for more than a century as the premier training institute for nannies. Renowned for their traditional views on child care, Norland nannies know only one way to do things, and that is the Norland way. You can spot Norland nannies at once—not only because of the uniform but because they are never seen without a cumbersome, old-fashioned black perambulator—the older the better.

The last bench is reserved for the predominantly English and Australian sole-charge nannies. These young women are often seen in the sandbox making castles for the kids or coming down a slide with a toddler on their laps. They are hands-on, no-nonsense women who find it easy to form friendships with each other and at-tachments to the children they care for. They also gossip a lot and are very

nanny to cook for your children, be fun, serious, quiet, organized, creative, sporty—or all of those things at once?

Think hard about what your family needs and about what kind of person would fit well into your family life. Then you'll be ready to try to find the nanny who will match those needs.

competitive about their bosses: "Oh, your family doesn't have a villa in Italy for the summer? What a shame!"

The hierarchy is clear to all, and the class lines are strictly maintained. Au pairs are at the bottom of the pack; they are not nannies, and should they dare use the word "nanny" to refer to themselves, there would be a quick rebuke from a real nanny. In the same way, if an English or Aussie sole-charge nanny were referred to as a babysitter or an au pair, she would huffily point out to the offender that an error had been made. The Norland nannies, of course, see themselves at the top of this hierarchy and barely need to speak at all. They do not associate with the Aussie and English sole-charge nannies, and they would not even glance in the direction of the au pairs.

So it was with interest that the whole park watched a Norland nanny summon a particular English sole-charge nanny over to the Norland bench one day. The two spoke a few words, and when the sole-charge nanny joined us again, we were all eager to hear about the exchange. "Cheeky cow!" said the nanny on her return to our bench. She explained: the Norlands had heard that the young nanny's boss was a friend of the pop star Robbie Williams and that he often dropped by to play soccer with the kids. Robbie Williams, it should be noted, is not just a pop star; he is the biggest male pop star in Europe and is the idol of women from Ireland to Italy. "The Norland asked me if she can start having playdates at my house so they can meet Williams," our fellow nanny told us, clearly astonished at the brazenness of the request. As if even Europe's hottest music star could ever dent the nanny hierarchy! In fact, after the Norland nanny's request was refused, the invitation to the Norland bench was never extended to any of us again. The hierarchy had recovered; in fact, it was more rigid than ever.

The Nannies' Nanny Criteria

What are the attributes of the ideal nanny? We've come up with eleven criteria that we believe describe the absolutely perfect nanny. Of course, chances are you won't find somebody who possesses every one of the eleven in full measure, so it's important to set priorities and to be prepared to compromise.

For example, you might find a very loving, responsible, intuitive nanny who doesn't know how to cook. You may decide you can work around this: prepare the kids' meals yourself so all Nanny has to do is heat them up, or give her some tips on your children's favorite meals, or even sign her up for a cooking class. Or maybe you are looking for a really creative nanny, but your favorite candidate freely admits she is not very tidy. Can you overlook her messiness because she involves your children in lots of artistic activities? It depends on your priorities, of course.

Here are our eleven essential nanny criteria:

The Essential Eleven: What to Look for in the Ideal Nanny

1. **Love of children.** This is surely the most important criterion—the one you shouldn't compromise on. You can find the most experienced and competent professional, but if she isn't loving toward your children, we don't see how she can be a good nanny.

   "Love of children" means, simply, that the happiness and well-being of the children in her care are the nanny's first priority at all times. Certainly it means that she never holds back kisses and hugs, that her instinct is to comfort a child who is hurt and upset, to remain at the side of a child who is sick, to encourage, praise, and support a child throughout his day. But above all, it means that she sees this loving attitude as the major responsibility of her job.

2. **Experience and/or training—including CPR or first aid.** Some nannies develop their skills through hands-on practical experience; some are formally trained at a nanny school—and there are lots of different kinds of nanny school. Experience should never be underestimated. If you need a nanny to care for your newborn, you will certainly want someone who is experienced in precisely that—care of newborns— whereas if you want someone to work mostly under your direction to care for your four-year-old, vast experience is not necessary.

   In fact, many kinds of child-care experience can work. Someone who has had few if any nanny jobs but has reared her own children is certainly experienced, as is someone who has cared for younger siblings. And sometimes, intuition and instinct around children make up for lack of experience.

One absolute essential for nannies and babysitters is CPR or first aid training so that you can be assured your nanny is prepared to deal with accidents and emergencies. CPR training requires recertification annually, and first aid courses need to be updated every three years. If you find a great nanny without this kind of training, consider subsidizing a course.

3. *Excellent references.* References tell you that your nanny candidate has experience with kids and let you know how she interacts with children and with the families she has worked with. We recommend asking for more than one job reference; if the candidate has worked only one job, however, ask for character references also.

Once you have the references, it is crucial to take the time to check them properly. After all, this person will be caring for your children, so no matter how impressed you may be with the nanny candidate and even if she comes highly recommended by a friend or acquaintance, check her out. The same goes for nannies referred by agencies; check those references, too, even if the agency claims to have done so already.

When you talk with a candidate's past employers, be thorough. You want to find out what she was like both as a nanny and as a person. Be sure to get complete answers to the following questions:

- How long did the nanny candidate work for you?
- Was she loving and kind with your children?
- Is she trustworthy and honest?
- Was she punctual?
- Did she take many sick days?
- What did you like best about her?
- What did your children like best about her?

Of course, references can't trump your instincts. One mother we know hired a nanny who looked good on paper, had the necessary experience, and said all the right things—even though the mother still had "a funny feeling" about the candidate. After a few weeks, the mother noticed the nanny was negative toward and critical of her children; she realized she hadn't once heard the nanny praise or encourage the children. She thought to herself, I should have gone with my original instincts. She was right—and the situation ended with her having to start the nanny search all over.

4. *Trustworthiness.* You're going to leave your children in the nanny's care. It's essential, therefore, that you trust her completely. You must feel assured that she will take the very best care of your kids—that she will strap them into their car seat, stroller, or high chair; be at the ready while they are learning to swim; hold their hands crossing the street. You need to know that she will stay in touch with you about the whereabouts and welfare of the children, and that she will assume responsibility for the job you have hired her for. A nanny who calls in sick fifteen minutes before you are due to leave for the airport, or who doesn't call you from the cell phone when she and the kids are stuck in traffic, or who doesn't fully supervise your child's play when she takes him to the park, is not sufficiently responsible—and not sufficiently trustworthy.

5. *Common sense. / 6. Intuition. / 7. Resourcefulness.* It all comes down to being able to adapt to changes in a situation and handle them well—that is, in a way that ensures your child's well-being and happiness. To do that, a nanny needs common sense, intuition, and resourcefulness. If your child develops a fever, Nanny needs the common sense to call you, give the appropriate medication, and call the doctor, if required. If your child is acting out and throwing tantrums every five minutes, Nanny needs to be intuitive enough to figure out why this is happening, and then act appropriately—take him home from the play-date perhaps, or put him down for a nap because she knows he is tired. If Nanny is driving the kids someplace and the car breaks down, or if she locks herself out of the house, she needs to be resourceful—not fall apart, not worry the kids, not come rushing to you this time and every time something goes awry.

8. *Good communication skills.* These are vital in a nanny or babysitter and are the key to a successful nanny-parent relationship. First and foremost, your nanny needs to be able to tell you about your child—whether he has been well behaved, is teething, or seems overtired. She needs to communicate issues as they arise—things like biting, not sharing, clinginess, or fussiness at mealtimes—so that together, you can address the issues.

Your nanny must also communicate her wants and needs; you need to hear from her if she is unhappy about something. It works the other way, too; you need to be able to tell her if you are unhappy with the way she is doing her job. Lack of communication can only lead to problems and will cause resentments that sour the relationship.

You also want your nanny to be able to communicate comfortably in social situations. It will typically be part of her job to find friends for your child, arrange activities, talk with teachers, and interact with other nannies and parents.

9. **Commitment.** Rotating nannies is not good for you or for your children. That's why it is common for parents to ask a nanny candidate for a commitment of one year or more. Of course, there are no guarantees, and either one of you may need to break the commitment. The nanny's personal life may undergo dramatic change, or you may decide to give up work, or your family may have to move to another city. Still, a commitment should be asked for on both sides—an indication that this is an important job.

10. **Flexibility.** Being a nanny is not a nine-to-five job. Employer-parents may have to work late, may be delayed arriving home, or may suddenly be called away, so flexibility on the nanny's part is essential.

But parents need to be cautious they don't expect too much flexibility too often. To begin with, if you know that your schedule is all over the place, make that part of the job description right from the start. Be practical: if you are a single parent, or if you are an emergency room doctor, or if you are often away for long stretches of time, it wouldn't make sense to employ a nanny who is married with four children, or a student who goes to college full-time. So it's important to assess up front how much flexibility you'll require.

It's also important to be fair to your nanny. She has a life too, and if you limit her ability to live it, she'll simply find another job. So be aware that nannies have doctor's appointments and birthdays and sick days and even wedding anniversaries—try and be flexible when needed. One important tip: it's a good idea to have a backup person in case your nanny cannot always accommodate your request for flexibility. Find someone you trust—a family member or close friend who can also help out when your nanny is sick or has a commitment or an emergency of her own. It is common in England for nannies to ask another nanny friend, particularly one who knows the children well, to serve as her backup person. The backup can either be paid for her time or will expect the nanny to return the favor at a later date.

11. *Sense of fun.* Your kids will thrive when they're in the care of someone who can turn any situation into a fun one, can find inventive play for a rainy day, can encourage singing and dancing and simple games kids love. She should bring a smile and a sense of humor into your children's lives. What you don't want is a nanny whose first and last solution for everything is to turn on the television.

"Nanny Wanted": How to Find a Nanny

Word of mouth is usually the best—and cheapest—way to find a nanny or babysitter. Strike up a conversation with nannies and other parents in the local park, join the neighborhood parenting group if one exists, or look on the bulletin boards of local children's stores. Is there a college, university, or nanny-training institute nearby? Check their placement offices or bulletin boards. Look in local newspapers, buy nanny magazines, or sign up with nanny agencies, which charge a percentage of the nanny's salary. If you need an occasional babysitter for an evening out, preschool teachers, summer-camp counselors, or friends of the family always work well.

And of course, advertise.

Include basic information and requirements in your advertisement. No need to say that you're desperate for help, your kids are great, and you'll pay a lot. Just something like the following will do:

Experienced Nanny Wanted

- Full-time live-out position
- Minneapolis location
- Sole charge of two boys, ages two and five
- Licensed driver; swimmer; nonsmoker
- Free gym membership/four weeks paid vacation
- English (or Spanish or French) language a necessity

Call 222-999-9999 after 9:00 A.M.: *Please leave message on voice mail*

After you have placed the ad, be prepared for hundreds of phone calls from applicants, some of whom will be completely unsuitable and inexperienced. One way to streamline your way through these calls is to create a voice mail message that asks for the caller's name and telephone number, and a brief description of her child-care experience. The messages you get should help you figure out whether your callers are genuine candidates or not. What's more, you will be able to pick and choose among candidates you like the sound of.

The Interview

The first step is to interview potential candidates over the phone. You can learn a lot over the phone and can often determine right away if you and this candidate won't suit each other. You can thus cut back on the number of interviews and save time and effort for both the candidate and yourself.

Keep a notebook handy and jot down the candidate's name, notes on her responses to your questions, and your impressions of her. If you do ask this candidate for a personal interview, you'll be glad to have the notes; they'll help you keep things straight. Ask the candidate about her experience with children, the ages of the children she has cared for, why she became a nanny, and where she lives. Be sure to jot down whether she has a résumé and job references. If you like the sound of her, you can then set up an appointment for a personal interview.

The personal interview needs to be kept on a personal level; this individual might very well end up working in your home, so keep things relaxed. Offer a cup of coffee or tea and a comfortable seat, then work your way through our suggested topics. Some parents prefer to have their kids with them when they interview a nanny, while others prefer to meet candidates when the kids are gone, or even to meet outside the home—perhaps at a café or coffee shop. It is not uncommon for parents to meet candidates alone for the first interview, then invite those who "pass" that interview to meet the children at yet another interview.

If your children are home with you while you are interviewing nanny or babysitter candidates, introduce the candidate to your children right off the bat, then have someone—spouse, relative, friend, or present nanny—take the children outside or to another room. This way you'll get a quick glimpse of how the candidate interacts with children, but the kids won't overpower the interview or distract the candidate from the interview process. In fact, kids who sense change and are feeling insecure about it may act out in front of the nanny—which could make your child feel even more insecure or could scare off the candidate.

If the interview goes well, let the nanny meet your children again before leaving. At this point, you should give her a chance to interact with them; let them play a game, or get your kids to show the nanny candidate their playroom or bedroom or favorite toys. These exchanges will let you see how the candidate and your children interact, but keep in mind that both nanny and child may understandably feel shy under this kind of pressure, so give it some time—and stay relaxed.

At the end of the interview, let the candidate know what you think. If you think she is not suitable for the position, be honest about it, and do tell her if you like her. It's both courteous and prudent to ask her if she is interested in the position; if she is really keen, you'll probably be able to tell. Thank her for coming to meet with you, let her know if there are other candidates you will be interviewing, and tell her when you will call her.

Here's that promised list of suggested topics to cover in the nanny interview. Of course, this list is not all-inclusive, and you will want to adapt it to your own family's needs. But in our experience, these are the basics you and your prospective nanny need to be clear about. What's more, hearing the candidate's answers and watching the way she conducts herself can tell you a great deal about the kind of person she is and the kind of nanny she'll be.

And remember: trust your instincts. Good luck.

The Nannies' Top Ten Suggested Topics for a Nanny Interview

1. **The basics.** Repeat the basics you asked for on the phone. This time you'll be face-to-face when you hear about her child-care knowledge, experience, and education. Look at her résumé and job references, and encourage her to talk about the children and the families she has worked with.

2. **Job description.** Be very clear about what is expected of her in the job; in fact, if you can, show her a prepared job description. The most common mistake parents make when interviewing a nanny is to be vague about

what they expect; nothing is more likely to cause problems and issues later on than lack of clarity—on one side or the other—about exactly what the nanny should and should not do. Explain the full duties, hours, and responsibilities of the job. If you expect cleaning, laundry, and ironing, say so now. Tell her if the job is sole-charge or if you want her to assist you. Let her know if you work from home—and if you do, be sure to tell her if your office is in the middle of the playroom, or at the end of the driveway, or in an isolated attic. Or let her know that you do not work at all. Tell her if you are married or single or if the other parent lives elsewhere—especially if your child must spend a portion of his time at the other parent's house. Do you keep a kosher home or follow a strict vegetarian diet? Let the interviewee know. We know of one nanny who accepted a nanny position only to discover on the first day that the family were nudists at home. This certainly took her by surprise. Now is the time to lay out all those sorts of things so there won't be any big surprises later on. Be clear about flexibility issues. Be up-front about overtime, late nights, and whether you will need the nanny to stay overnight or travel with you. Don't forget to tell her about the dog, spider, or tropical fish you may want her to walk or feed. In short, you're trying to give the candidate a clear picture of what the job will be like and what life in your family will be like. It's not only fair; it's the only thing that makes sense.

3. *Job package.* State clearly how much paid vacation the nanny will receive, how many paid sick days she is entitled to, what the rate of pay is for overtime, and whether you provide health care. If the position is a live-in one, show her the accommodations and tell her your policy on having friends and/or boyfriends visit or stay over. Talk about the use of the car. Discuss the use of common areas after work hours; for example, you may want the living room to yourself in the evenings. (If this is the case, it's a good idea to put a TV in your nanny's room. You also may want to put a small fridge in her room so she doesn't have to keep coming downstairs for snacks and drinks.)

4. *Personality and character.* Pose some questions that don't have simple yes or no answers: Why did you become a nanny? What is your family background? Do you have any siblings? What's your favorite children's age? What's your favorite children's book? Ask about her hobbies and

interests. These questions are a way to get to know the candidate, to learn more about her experience with children and her approach to them, and to get a feel for her personality and character.

5. *Discipline/behavior.* Ask about her views on discipline. How would she deal with hitting, for example, or rude behavior? Obviously, if she dismisses the question or says, "All kids hit, don't they?" or informs you that it's her practice to lock rude children in the cupboard, you will know she doesn't have a clue and is not suitable. Discuss your own views on discipline with the candidate; let her know your feelings about time-outs and your thoughts on consequences for bad behavior. This will let the candidate know whether she can work well with your family. Your aim here is simply to find out if you and the nanny candidate are on the same page when it comes to dealing with your children's behavior and approach to discipline.

6. *Emergency preparedness.* Ask her what she would do in an emergency situation—if your child had a high fever, for example, or choked on food or an object, or in the case of an accident. Her answers to these questions will let you know if she has basic knowledge about what to do in an emergency and if she has common sense.

7. *Structure/routine/schedule.* Ask her opinions on establishing a scheduled routine and on structuring rituals for sleep and diet. If you have completely different ideas on these subjects, this nanny-parent relationship may not work. If you are looking for someone who can help you change your children's diet, improve their sleep habits, or establish a regular routine and schedule, ask her about this at the interview. She may be able to suggest solutions that she would help you implement if she came to work for you. After all, you're looking for a child-care professional who can enhance your life and give you support and advice; you should be able to determine if this candidate is that person at the interview.

8. *Nutrition.* Find out if she cooks and try to get an idea of how knowledgeable she is about nutrition. Be very clear as to whether you want her to cook for your children or for the whole family, and let her know the kind of meal planning you are looking for. If she doesn't cook but you like everything else about her, find out if she would be willing to attend cooking classes or try to learn cooking on her own.

The Nanny Kitty

Nanny Wisdom

Do not forget to leave your nanny some petty cash each day. Incidental expenses are inevitable—a sudden need for a carton of milk or a package of diapers, spur-of-the-moment outings, last-minute lunches. It is perfectly reasonable to ask your nanny to keep receipts. In fact, many families have a petty cash book in which the nanny keeps track of expenses; this way parents can see how the money is being spent, and when the cash supply is running low, they can top it up.

9. **Activities.** Ask her about her ideas for daily activities, for socializing your kids with others, and for downtime. Find out how she feels about TV. Does she like to read to kids? And does she encourage listening to music, being creative, and engaging in educational play? Will she be willing to help your children with their homework—if that is something you need done?

10. **Commitment.** Let her know the start date of the job and the length of commitment you would like. Find out if either of these is a stumbling block for her. If you would like a two-year commitment, and she is only planning to stay for one year so she can then start college or travel around the world, it's best to find this out now.

Once the interview is over, if you like the candidate, ask her to come for a second interview. If you're leaning toward offering her the job, tell her you are very interested and you will call her once you have had time to think about it and check her references—and ask her to think about whether the position is right for her, too.

First Things First

Once you've hired someone, a breaking-in period is a good idea—either with your present nanny training your new nanny for up to a week, or with your new nanny spending a couple of days with you and your children before you go back to work. This lets the nanny see firsthand exactly how things run in your household at the same time that she is getting to know your children.

But such a breaking-in period isn't always possible, as we both know only too well, having sometimes been put into situations absolutely cold—without even having met the kids before. In such situations, a professional nanny's experience really pays off.

But whether your nanny has come in cold or has eased into the job, she needs detailed information about the children before they are left in her care. She needs to know your child's routine and schedule, bedtime rituals, diet, and scheduled activities. She also needs a complete who's who list. (See Essential Information table on pages 328–29.) At a minimum, this must include your cell phone number and work number, numbers for grandparents and/or close friends, the name and number of your doctor, and the location and number of the nearest hospital.

Also, be clear right from the start about your house rules and boundaries. Without knowing them, your nanny will be lost when faced with statements like "my mommy lets me have candy before dinner," or "I am allowed to go to bed whenever I want." Be clear and thorough when you give your new nanny information; too much is far better than too little.

Leaving Your Child in Someone Else's Care: How to Make It Easier
No matter how comfortable you are with your nanny, it can still be very hard to leave your child in someone else's care. Saying good-bye and stepping out the door for the whole day can seem like one of the most difficult things you have ever done. And if your child cries when he sees you leave, it can make you feel even worse. Don't worry, however: he should soon settle down, and he'll probably be playing happily by the time you have cleared the driveway.

But that's why good-byes need to be short and sweet. Lingering at the door will only encourage tears and drama, making it all the more difficult to leave. It's also why we suggest saying good-bye in a calm and straightforward manner; an overly emotional farewell will only make your child more upset. Tell him when you will be home, give him a kiss and a cuddle, and leave.

Telling your child you'll be home "after work" is pretty abstract, so it makes sense—and is reassuring to him—to hear that he will see you again at a recognizable milestone in his day: dinner or bath time, for example. "Sweetie, I am going to work now, but I will be home at dinnertime" is a promise that makes sense to a small child. Of course, you must make sure you follow through on your promise so your child will know he can rely on what you say. Certainly in the first days of leaving your child with the nanny, if you say you will be home after dinner, do in fact come home after dinner. Later on, if you get held up at work, your child will have become familiar with the whole idea of your going to work and coming home from work, so you can call and tell him you will be late and he will understand.

Nanny Wisdom

Be Involved

If you are out at work all day, it is even more important to be involved in your child's day. Make the time at day's end to chat about the day's events with your child and nanny. We also suggest giving the nanny a daily journal in which she can jot down what your child did during the day. Once your child is old enough, a journal is a fun activity for her to be involved in as well; she can draw pictures of the day's events and paste train and museum tickets into the book. But don't let a journal replace communication; we know one nanny who wrote "I quit!" in the nanny journal . . .

A good nanny or babysitter will really show her worth when you are leaving the house. That's the time she can bring to bear those nanny skills that let her take control of the situation and minimize the amount of distress your child experiences upon your departure. What are the skills we nannies use? We draw on a whole range of tricks to distract a tearful child: scooping him up in our arms for a cuddle, reading him his favorite book, giving him his special teddy bear or blanket, or grabbing his attention with a fun project like Play-Doh or painting. We might calm an older baby with music or show him his reflection in the mirror, pointing out his

ESSENTIAL INFORMATION
FOR NANNIES AND BABYSITTERS

HOME ADDRESS AND PHONE	
MOTHER'S WORK ADDRESS AND PHONE	
MOTHER'S CELL PHONE	
FATHER'S WORK ADDRESS AND PHONE	
FATHER'S CELL PHONE	
NANNY'S CELL PHONE	
FAMILY DOCTOR ADDRESS AND PHONE	
HOSPITAL ADDRESS AND PHONE	
ALLERGIES	
DENTIST ADDRESS AND PHONE	

eyes, nose, and mouth. And we might show a distraught toddler the family photo album; his crying will soon subside as he begins to look at photos of his family.

We know it can be hard to leave your child in someone else's care, even a professional nanny. But just think of all the nice things he and his nanny are doing when you leave, and you can rest assured he will be well cared for all day.

SCHOOL NAME ADDRESS AND PHONE	
TEACHER'S NAME	
SCHOOL HOURS	
GRANDPARENTS ADDRESS AND PHONE	
NEIGHBOR ADDRESS AND PHONE	
AUNT ADDRESS AND PHONE	
CAR SERVICE/TAXI ADDRESS AND PHONE	
EMERGENCY PLUMBER PHONE	
CHILD'S FRIENDS/ FRIENDS' PARENTS ADDRESS AND PHONE	

The Adjustment Period

Whether it's for the first time or the fifth, when your new nanny comes on board, give her some space to settle in and get to know your kids. It is, after all, an adjustment for everybody, and it's normal for adjustments to take time. The kids may respond with such out-of-character behavior as rudeness or clinginess, but parents and nannies also need a little while to get in the groove.

Use the first few weeks to iron out any mix-ups. Maybe you forget to tell your new nanny that your children are not allowed to drink juice during the day except at breakfast. Or, maybe, even though she originally agreed to use her own car to drive the kids, she now realizes how much extra she is spending on gas, and she would like you to reimburse her. These sorts of things happen all the time during the adjustment period; they're perfectly normal.

One trick for making the adjustment smoother is to give your new nanny and your child plenty of opportunities to be alone together. If you are around all the time, it will just take that much longer for your child to get to know her new nanny. So if you do not work, or if you work from home, make it a point to provide nanny and child with plenty of opportunities to get to know each other. Close the door to your office and discreetly disappear, or use the time to do all those things you never have time for—to see movies, go to museums, have lunch with friends. Otherwise, the adjustment period will take longer and it will be harder for your child and the new nanny to form that all-important bond.

Strengthening the Nanny-Parent Relationship

If we had to define the key to the nanny-parent relationship in one word, it would be communication. Letting your nanny know clearly and comfortably what you expect and how you think she's doing is essential, and keeping the lines of communication open so you get her feedback is equally important. Communication is also the best way to ensure that parents and nanny are working together and with consistency. And it is the basis of the support and trust that are so essential between parent and nanny.

A nanny-parent system works best when everybody is working together as a team; it's that kind of consistency that gives a child a sense of continuity, security, and love—and when a child feels all that, everyone is happy. Working at cross-purposes from your nanny on such issues as discipline, diet, sleep, manners, or mealtimes will only lead to problems and confusion. So you and your nanny need to be consistent in your approach, and that takes open, comfortable communication.

By the same token, you can't leave it to your nanny to be the only enforcer of rules and boundaries in your household. If you play "good cop" and make her "bad cop," it puts undue pressure on your nanny and frustrates her attempts at discipline. A responsible nanny may be much stricter with safety issues—after all, she is in charge of someone else's child—but that's no excuse for letting her be the sole disciplinarian.

Suppose Nanny tells your child that no, he may not have a piece of cake before dinner, and then you, for whatever reason, overrule Nanny and say he may have it. You're not only sending mixed messages to your child, you're also undermining Nanny's authority and pretty much telling your child he really doesn't have to listen to her. Double standards are nothing but trouble; your child will quickly see what is going on and will start playing you and Nanny off each other at every possible opportunity.

Crossover Time

Your child has behaved like a dream for her nanny all day long, but the minute you show up, she starts acting out or decides to throw a tantrum. It's crossover time, the transition from Nanny's sole charge to Mommy and Daddy being in charge again, when kids realize they have missed their parents, want to claim the parents back for themselves, and work hard trying to get their attention. Of course, this crossover time behavior can also be a matter of a child testing her boundaries and pushing everyone's buttons to see who will react first. In any event, the behavior is perfectly normal.

Our advice is simply to be aware of crossover time and spend it with your child. Give her your full attention for a few minutes before you begin to make dinner or return phone calls or get out of your business suit into your sweats. If crossover time continues to be tricky, shorten the time between your arrival home and your nanny's departure until this phase passes.

So it is essential that you support your nanny in her decisions. If you do disagree with something she is doing, discuss it with her away from little ears—and expect her to openly discuss any problems she may have, too. As you trust your nanny, you must also trust her judgment regarding your child's behavior. If you are not happy with the way she is handling things, you need to communicate that clearly to her—or perhaps end the relationship.

Different Nannies for Different Families

WHEN I FIRST ARRIVED IN LONDON, I began a job with the Cromwell family, who lived in Primrose Hill. Their home was a very old, very imposing townhouse. On my very first day, as I was being shown around the house, I noticed that the carpets covering the wooden floor were threadbare. The furniture was very old and looked in need of repair or replacement. I thought to myself that the family seemed to have fallen on hard times, and I began to wonder if they could really afford to pay me.

Imagine my shock when the housekeeper told me that the Cromwells were one of the wealthiest families in England. The carpets that I had found threadbare and the furniture I thought needed repair were in fact valuable and rare antiques. It was my first lesson in the trappings of English aristocracy, something I had never been exposed to before.

But I would soon become familiar with the many idiosyncrasies of this venerable, upper-class family, who expected me to wait on their son, Hamish, hand and foot—even to the point of ironing his socks and underwear daily.

"I do not need to put my toys away," he would tell me. "I am a master of a county, and one day I will be a lord just like my father."

"Well, Hamish," I would reply, trying to smile, "whether you are a master or a lord, you still need to pick up these toys. If you don't, we won't be going to the park today."

At teatime, Hamish's mother, Lady Cromwell, gave me a lecture about the cookies that accompanied the tea—biscuits, as they are called in England: "Nanny, these are the shortbread biscuits for the family. If you would like some biscuits, I will get you another variety. I hear the cheaper biscuits are actually quite good."

One weekend, Lady Cromwell announced that we would be going to a garden party where the Queen Mother would be in attendance. "Don't be nervous," Lady Cromwell said, "you won't need to speak unless spoken to."

After a few weeks of this, I duly gave my notice; this was not the job for me. The experience confirmed what I had known all along: different nannies suit different families.

The trust factor in the nanny-parent relationship also means that if you find yourself calling your nanny to check up on your child ten times a day, or if you frequently sneak home during the day to see what's what, then something isn't right. Either you need to consider why you don't trust your nanny, or you need a different nanny.

It is also unrealistic to expect your nanny and child to stay inside the house all day long, just so you can rest assured that you know where they are at all times. Both your child and your nanny will soon become very bored by such isolation, and for your nanny, being asked to remain cut off from other adults and the outside world is unreasonable. Playdates, socializing with nannies and parents, trips to the park, and scheduled outings make days together fun and interesting.

It is also important to be realistic in your expectations of your nanny or babysitter. Leaving long to-do lists to someone who is caring for three children under the age of five, for example, is simply unfair. The pressure to get everything done will place the nanny under unnecessary stress; she'll quickly burn out, and the last thing you want in charge of your kids is an exhausted nanny. Be sensible in your requirements. The most important thing at the end of the day is that your children are happy and well looked after, even if not everything on the to-do list has gotten done.

One last note about the parent-nanny relationship: a kind word at the end of a long day or week means a lot. Yes, you pay her, but your nanny also needs to know you value her, appreciate her, and understand the ins and outs of her day. Caring for children is a demanding job, and the occasional hour off or small gesture of kindness—a heartfelt thank-you, a movie ticket, chocolates, flowers—can speak volumes.

A Word from the Nannies to Your Nanny

If we could speak directly to your nanny, this is what we'd say:

Caring for children is a very important job. Your interactions with these children will have an impact on them now and in the future. Give them everything you have to offer, encourage them, teach them, nurture their strengths, and help them overcome their weaknesses. Be a professional, have high standards, and speak up when you need to.

Working from Home

If you work from home, consider establishing set times when you will enter the child's area. The reason is that when children see their parents coming and going all day long, it can be upsetting for them—and can make things harder for your nanny. For example, if you enter the kitchen where your child is happily eating lunch or dinner, he will want to stop eating and get out of his chair to see you, thus upsetting his meal. Better by far to wait until the meal is over before you enter the room. Better still to share lunch or dinner with your child; that will really prevent these problems.

Communication is the key to your relationship with your employer. Even before you start work, begin by being up-front about what you expect from your employers and by asking anything and everything you want to know. Find out as much as you can about the job before you take it; you don't want any big surprises when you start the job.

Once you're at work, do not be afraid to speak up. Talk to your employers about their children, and encourage the children to tell their parents what they did during the day. Work with parents to tackle any issues as they arise. Speak up if you are concerned about the children's behavior, happiness, or health. If you have noticed that a child is exhausted, or overwhelmed from too many scheduled activities, for example, discuss your concerns with your employers. They rely on you for information about their children and for your insight. In the same way, if you are not happy about the conditions in your job, get things out in the open right away. If you don't speak up, your employers will never know how you feel.

Cook fresh food for the children you care for, read to them, stimulate them with conversation, foster creativity and playfulness whenever you can. Encourage good manners and give the kids lots of love and care. Be responsible and resourceful, use your common sense, and you will be on the right path to being a great nanny.

When It's Time to Say Good-bye to Your Nanny

Sometimes a nanny grows out of her job, or a family outgrows a nanny. The young woman you hired may need to move on to study, to travel, to get married, or to have her own family. By the same token, a family's situation changes: kids grow up and go to school, or a parent may give up work to stay at home full-time. Whatever the reason, when a nanny leaves, the transition can be hard for everyone involved.

Try to make this change slowly. Prepare your children a few weeks before your nanny's departure. Talk about the change with your children—depending on their age, of course—and do encourage your nanny to call and visit in the future. We have both continued our special relationships with the kids we have cared for and with their families.

Nannies and Babysitters

★ Figure out what you want and need in a nanny; different nannies suit different families.

★ Take your time interviewing a potential nanny or babysitter.

★ Trust your instincts when deciding whom to hire.

★ Communication is the key to the parent-nanny relationship.

★ Let your nanny know you appreciate her.

Our Last Word

WE HOPE IT'S CLEAR BY NOW THAT KIDS AREN'T JUST OUR "JOB"; THEY'RE our passion. Whether we are feeding them, cooking for them, ensuring they're well rested, or playing with them, our whole hearts are with the children we care for. In fact, we see the nanny job as having two very clear goals—the happiness of the kids we take care of, and making sure they have the essential life skills they need.

We bring to the job a unique perspective, a point of view that sees daily how important a loving and supportive home is to a child, how such a home provides the comfort, stability, and confidence children need to get on in the world—both now and in the future.

We know parenting isn't easy, but we also know that the challenges are more easily met when you're loving, firm, and fun with your kids every day, when you enjoy their company, and when you give them the gift of yourself.

With our best wishes,

Justine   Kim

Afterword

I SUSPECT THAT EVERY PARENT CRAVES HAVING AN ENGLISH NANNY FOR themselves and their children. Who wouldn't love having someone right there to help them through the tough times, to put structure into their lives, to remind them to be healthy and to have fun—someone they can rely on?

My family's perfect English nanny is an Australian who came to us at a time of real need. I had recently relocated to New York; I faced a challenging career as a fashion photographer who needed to travel regularly; and I was the single mother of two young boys still struggling with their father's death, when I found Kim Nicholson, coauthor, with Justine Walsh, of this illuminating book.

I needed a full-time caregiver who would be responsible for getting the boys up and off to school, overseeing their homework, working with me to instill discipline, and providing them with meals. She needed to be smart, as well as sensitive in helping the boys deal with their ongoing sense of loss. And, of course, it was important that she fit into our family. It was a lot to ask of anyone, but Kim managed all of it with love, professionalism, knowledge, and a down-to-earth Aussie grace. She also proved to be the best cook we had ever known, and we have since found it terribly difficult to adjust to the fact that she no longer cooks for us every night.

For of course, in time Kim moved on. After seeing the boys through the difficult stages of adolescence, providing them invaluable support and advice, she was ready for a new challenge, and they were ready to be on their own. But none of us were ready to lose our nanny altogether, for she had become an integral part of our family, so today Kim is still in our lives, a friend and confidant to the boys and an ongoing source of help to me. She is someone I can turn to for caring advice, good sense, and savvy child-care knowledge.

It is wonderful that these two supernannies, Kim and Justine, have shared their special nanny wisdom with us in this book. They bring the great English nanny tradition right into our homes—and they bring it up-to-date. Everything they advise, all their tips and tales, is just filled with common sense. It's all so smart, so reassuring, and so comfortable. In fact, reading this book is the second-best thing to having the nannies here in person—and almost as good as eating their delicious meals.

Pamela Hanson
New York, January 2005

Acknowledgments

THERE ARE MANY, MANY PEOPLE WHO HAVE SUPPORTED US BOTH ON OUR journey as nannies and in our work on this book for the past four years. First, our profound thanks go to our incredible agent, Sarah Jane Freymann, who believed in us from the start and has guided us with her insight, professionalism, and grace every step of the way.

We would also like to give a huge heartfelt thank you to Carey Lowell, Richard Gere, and Pamela Hanson. We are both very lucky to have such inspirational people in our lives and we cannot thank them enough for their generosity in contributing to *Nanny Wisdom*.

We are grateful to the fabulous team at Stewart, Tabori and Chang—Steve Tager, Andrea Glickson, Ron Longe, Jessica Napp, Kate Norment, and Anna Christian—and especially to the wonderful Leslie Stoker for seeing the potential in the book and for her nurturing care throughout the process. We also give a huge thanks to our editor, Susanna Margolis, for her commitment, guidance, and hard work during the writing of our book.

Thanks to Dr. Jona Weiss, a truly committed and caring pediatrician, for her unique input and for giving *Nanny Wisdom* her stamp of approval.

Many other people contributed in myriad ways to the making of *Nanny Wisdom*—Simone Manwarring; Sam and Jake DeRiseis; Darrick Harris; Mei Tao and Dashiel Harris; Shawn Mattson; Chris Schmelke; Megan Huston; Joe Calcagno; Olga Liriano; Karen Klose; Ann Biderman; Jonathan Cott; David, Shanna, and Quinci Huston; Gabby Basora; and Piera Gelardi—and we are grateful to them all.

Finally, we would like to acknowledge and thank the amazing nannies we have met over the years. These dedicated women have passed the British nanny tradition on to us, and we in turn have passed it on to others, helping to keep this distinguished tradition alive. —*J. W. and K.N.*

I would especially like to thank Lucinda Chambers and Simon Crow, Debbie Deitering and Raven Metzner, and Richard Gere and Carey Lowell for their faith and guidance and for welcoming me into their wonderful families. I would like to acknowledge all the children I have cared for, in particular Max and Miles, Toby and Theo, Orion, Hannah, and Homer, as well as my younger siblings—my very special brothers Douglas, Matthew, Damien, and Luke and sister Evelyn—who inspired me to become a nanny in the first place.

I am extremely grateful to my friends James Brown, Julie Harte, Andrea Dinning, Alison McKenna, Manuel and Ligia Bolanos, Elisa Bluming, and Peggy Patterson for their support while I worked on this book.

For their love and encouragement, I would like to thank my family: Mum, Dad and Jan, Nan, Peg and Den, Dennis, Richard, Mason, Jeane, and Alan. And to my amazing sister Lisa, my niece Samantha, and my nephew Stevie, thanks for being my biggest support team and for always being there. Most of all, to my husband, Barak, thank you for your love, support, and encouragement each and every day. —J.W.

I am deeply grateful to Pamela Hanson, Skye Gyngell, Fiona Golfar, and Nicky Symonds for all they've shared with me and taught me. Thank you to all the children who have called me "Kimmy" and who have made me the nanny I am—especially David and Ashleigh, Max and Jack, Holly and Evie, and Nicky and Charlie.

A huge thank you to my friends, who have been such a support during the writing of this book: Sam and Tony Haigh, Sharni Cotter, Robbie Sellars, Wayne Gross, Emily Marshall, Jessica Williams, Jonathan Bricklin, Esperanza Reyes, and Dave Bronson.

I am forever grateful to my wonderful family for their encouragement and unwavering belief in me. Thank you to my Mum, Dad, David, and Ashleigh for teaching me the importance of family and for their unconditional love, and also to my sister Tracey for her loving presence and faith in me always. —K.N.

Index